ERNST BLOCH

Ernst Bloch is perhaps best known for his subtle and imaginative investigation of utopias and utopianism, but his work also provides a comprehensive and insightful analysis of western culture, politics and society. Yet, because he has not been one of the easiest of writers to read, his full contribution has not been widely acknowledged. Bloch developed a complex conceptual framework, and presented this in a prose style which many have found to verge on the impenetrable.

In this critical and accessible introduction to one of the most fascinating thinkers of the twentieth century, Vincent Geoghegan unravels much of the mystery of the man and his ideas. The book focuses on the major concepts and principal themes of Bloch's vast output. It begins with an account of Bloch's life, including his residence in the USA and East Germany, and his association with thinkers such as Benjamin, Weber, Lukács and Adorno. This is followed by a presentation of Bloch's main concepts. His extensive writings on culture are examined, in particular his ideas on cultural production, music, popular culture, expressionism, realism and the theatre. Bloch's life-long concern with religion is also explored through his controversial reading of the Bible, his analysis of heretical religious thinkers and his startling formulation of an atheistic Christianity. The final chapters deal with Bloch's stimulating analyses of Fascism and Marxism, and his approach to natural law, utopianism and nature.

Vincent Geoghegan is Reader in Politics at Queen's University, Belfast.

ERNST BLOCH

Vincent Geoghegan

London and New York

First published 1996
by Routledge
11 New Fetter Lane, London EC4P 4EE

Simultaneously published in the USA and Canada
by Routledge
29 West 35th Street, New York, NY 10001

© 1996 Vincent Geoghegan

Phototypeset in Palatino by Intype, London
Printed and bound in Great Britain by TJ Press (Padstow) Ltd,
Padstow, Cornwall

British Library Cataloguing in Publication Data
A catalogue record for this book is available from the British Library

Library of Congress Cataloguing in Publication Data
A catalogue record for this book has been requested

ISBN 0–415–04903–2 (hbk)
ISBN 0–415–04904–0 (pbk)

For David

For David

CONTENTS

ACKNOWLEDGEMENTS

I would like to thank Chris Rojek of Routledge for asking me to write this study, and for patiently waiting through the many delays. Colin Harper has provided invaluable help, sharing with me his great bibliographical knowledge of Bloch, and bringing to bear his deep understanding of Bloch's philosophy on my many inadequate drafts. Yves le Juen's unstinting reading of various versions of the text has greatly improved the final draft. Larry Wilde and David Officer kindly read the work in its entirety and made valuable suggestions. I would also like to thank a number of colleagues in Belfast, notably Bob Eccleshall, Jim Martin and Iain MacKenzie, for their comments on the text, and also a former colleague, Mike Kenny, for his remarks. The book was also improved by the criticisms of two anonymous referees. Some of the initial work was completed during a sabbatical Visiting Fellowship at Wolfson College, Cambridge. I would like to thank the President and Fellows for providing me with that opportunity.

INTRODUCTION

Ernst Bloch is an exhilarating thinker. There is an intellectual excitement in his work which is to be found in relatively few other twentieth-century philosophers or social theorists. This is partly due to the range of Bloch's concerns. He ignores traditional scholarly divisions of labour, and instead chooses to roam across specialist disciplines and to investigate whatever is of relevance to his central concerns, wherever they might arise. Within one single text, biblical exegesis and theological speculation may rub shoulders with literary criticism, modern physics, historical analysis, philosophical clarification and political polemic. With a breathtaking élan Bloch can combine fairy-tales with sophisticated conceptual development, utopian hopes with modern theoretical physics. This imparts a richness of content to his work. He constantly draws out connections between disparate phenomena, establishing, for example, links between ancient Greek myths and contemporary detective stories, and between endurance dancing competitions and the Third Reich. Throughout, one is aware of the innovatory nature of his enterprise: he seeks to subvert the given, and totally reconstruct conceptions of reality. To this end, he develops his own systematic metaphysics and ontology, which in turn feeds into distinctive analyses of culture, religion, society and the like. The effect is to usher us into a world made new, in which many of the old familiar landmarks are gone; a unique Blochian world with its own topography, systems and processes. There is also the great imaginative sweep of his work. As befits the strong utopian impulse in all of his endeavours, there is a sustained visionary dimension in his writing, and a highly nuanced one. He is both a scholar and a practitioner of utopia. His work is

1

undoubtedly insightful, and on occasions achieves genuine profundity. This study is therefore motivated by a belief that Bloch *is* indeed worth reading: not simply as an historical curio nor a mere arcane footnote in the history of Marxism, but as an important writer and thinker, who combines an ingenious, subtle and imaginative investigation of utopias and utopianism with a comprehensive and often penetrating analysis of western culture, politics and society.

There are, however, obstacles to be overcome in an appreciation of his work. Bloch is a theorist who is known about rather than known. The three intimidating volumes of *The Principle of Hope* are recognised, but tend to remain on the library shelf. He has an undoubted following, and a growing one; but his work has yet to attract the readership it merits. Bloch's writing is forbidding; structural complexity and formal eclecticism are combined with a writing style studded with opaque metaphor, untranslatable puns, obscure neologisms and overblown rhetoric. Readers of the original German may have compensations not available to those who only know Bloch in translation. A number of commentators have pointed to a level of artistry in the original German; for example, in George Steiner's estimation,

> Bloch's earlier prose has its own abrupt lyric insistence. In Bloch's mature style, there are pages we can set aside Hölderlin and Nietzsche for their subtle brightness. Like few other masters of German, he has broken the generally ponderous, clotted norms of German syntax.[1]

Even sympathetic ears have to admit, however, that even in the German, all is very far from plain sailing. J. K. Dickinson speaks of the 'idiosyncrasies' of Bloch's German style thus:

> aphoristic simplicity interlaced with a sometimes baroque and completely unabashed complexity; prose poetry of considerable beauty combined with what at times seems a turgid verbosity, and all delivered with a self-assurance which, too easily felt as dogmatic self-righteousness, can repel or intimidate a reader.[2]

Confronted with this in English translation, the response of Ronald Aronson, *vis-à-vis* the translation of *The Principle of Hope*, is not untypical: 'much of the book's second and third volumes is not only a torture to read, it is impossible to follow.'[3] Furthermore, many of the texts display a deeply unattractive Marxism-Leninism, in which glowing tributes to the Soviet Union sit side by side with quotations from Lenin and Stalin. Finally, in these 'post-modern' times where 'grand narratives' are roundly condemned, Bloch's vast system will strike many as positively antediluvian. His attempt to encompass the whole of reality, from the atom to the cosmos, harks back to the mighty enterprises of Hegel, Aquinas and Aristotle, and, in comparison, makes the ambitions of most twentieth-century Marxism seem modest. David Kaufmann, although himself convinced of the strengths of Bloch's work, articulates this sense of anachronism, in a comparison with Walter Benjamin:

> Contemporaries and rather uncomfortable friends, Walter Benjamin and Ernst Bloch seem to come to us from different epochs. Bloch died quite recently (in 1977) yet his philosophy, especially in *The Principle of Hope*, appears to be fired by the peculiar intellectual passions of the first decades of this century and presents itself as a somewhat antiquarian curiosity.[4]

Not surprisingly, therefore, people have approached Bloch as they would a piece of stark and challenging monumental sculpture – they can appreciate its epic nature, but have no use for it themselves.

This study seeks to provide an introduction to Ernst Bloch's thought; a hazardous task, for it is easy to get sucked into the systematic and linguistic world of Bloch, to start mirroring his conceptual framework and to end up speaking with his voice. The intention, therefore, is to make the study clear and sympathetic, but also sufficiently detached. It is neither an intellectual biography of Bloch nor a detailed account of the chronological evolution of the Blochian system, but rather an examination of the major concepts and themes in his work.

Any competent dismantling of the massive edifice of Bloch's thought must also reveal the stresses, strains and fault-lines of the whole structure. In this study, the first chapter begins with a brief account of Bloch's long life (1885–1977). We will see the development of an early mystical vision, alongside a leftist perception of the potentialities and constraints of society. In time, a distinctive, Marxist reworking of these ingredients

creates a historical materialist eschatology, set against a willingness, under certain circumstances, to suppress or stifle doubts
about so-called 'objective' revolutionary forces. For many decades of his life, the practical outcome was a juxtaposing of
profound utopian speculation with a seemingly naive adherence
to the fortunes of the Soviet Union. After the Second World
War, on moving to East Germany, the tensions in this combination became unbearable and he was forced to face both the
grim reality of actually living under Stalinism and the costs of
Marxist-Leninist discipline. Traduced by the party/state, and
deeply hurt by his treatment, he was to spend his final years in
West Germany. His Stalinism, though it often demonstrated both
ignorance and stupidity, was to a great degree sustained by a
belief that future perfection comes neither easily nor cheaply.
For the sake of the future he made a Faustian pact with a
duplicitous present. More specifically this part of the chapter
will follow his early years, education, intellectual contacts and
first works; his theoretical and geographical wanderings in the
1920s and 1930s; the period of exile in the United States after
Hitler's rise to power; his troubled post-war period in the GDR,
and his final years in West Germany.

The second section of the chapter attempts to explain a particular range of Blochian concepts. Bloch is an energetic creator
of new concepts, a self-conscious conceptual innovator, coiner
of numerous hyphenated neologisms such as the 'not-yet-conscious', and intriguingly named concepts such as *Novum*, *Front*
and Extra-territoriality. Here again, the tension between the
desirable and the possible will be evident, as Bloch attempts to
create a dynamic and open-ended metaphysics. He develops a
whole armoury of concepts to encompass the utopian moment
of fulfilment – *Ultimum*, *Totum*, the Upright Gait; but he also
provides qualifying utopian concepts, through which, for
example, the 'objectively-real' possible has to be distinguished
from the merely 'formally' possible. Likewise, the blockages and
resistances to the future have themselves to be identified. The
problems and dilemmas arising from this basic tension are themselves registered in his distinction between revolutionary
'enthusiasm' and 'sobriety', and between the 'warm' and 'cold'
streams of Marxism.

Chapter 2 examines one of the major interests of Bloch's life
– culture – and discusses his ideas on cultural production, music,

4

popular culture, Expressionism, literature and realism, and theatre. In his cultural writing Bloch was concerned to identify the utopian moment in a variety of cultural forms, and also to isolate the conservative and reactionary aspects of modern culture. As a cultural analyst his work is frequently sensitive and insightful. His work on popular culture is particularly stimulating: he has an eye for the utopian gleam in phenomena as varied as the circus and the fair, the popular novel and the fashion accessory. Bloch is also very much at home in European high culture, especially in music and literature, and he is capable of producing strikingly original readings of the artistic creation of this culture. Throughout, one can detect the implicit deployment of a notion of 'authentic' culture, which draws on both classical and modernist aesthetics, and whose canon includes both Beethoven's *Fidelio* and the montage techniques of Expressionism. Also evident are a fierce anti-Americanism and a fawning defence of the cultural life of the Soviet Union. His obvious (and emphatically stated) distaste for much modern American culture – jazz, Hollywood films, etc. – derives in part from his exclusive definition of cultural authenticity, and partly from his political sympathies. In the case of the USSR his *political* adherence causes him undoubted difficulties in the *cultural* sphere: committed to the USSR, yet hostile to socialist realism and enthusiastic for an Expressionism condemned by Soviet critics, he is reduced to rather limp appreciations of Soviet folk dance and the Bolshoi Ballet. Constrained by his belief that the Soviet Union has to be defended at all costs, his cultural theory becomes contaminated by vulgar apologetics.

Chapter 3 concentrates on another of Bloch's perennial concerns – religion – and considers his reading of the Bible, his use of the post-biblical thinkers, Joachim of Fiore and Thomas Münzer, his examination of the relationship between humanity and nature as expressed in religious thinking and his startling proposal of an atheistic Christianity. Bloch's religious thought is of a very high order indeed, and has been recognised as such by a number of prominent modern theologians. His delineation of a radical 'underground' dimension in the Bible is a bravura performance, an undoubted *tour de force*, in which the figures of Adam, the Serpent, Job and Jesus are fundamentally reinterpreted. He also brings to bear a highly developed sense of the mystical, of the awesome, which enables him to engage with religious traditions. We sense in these writings some of the depth and sublimity of Bloch's own conception of the utopian moment. In this transcendent mode, Bloch seems so far away from practical concerns that some critics have argued that he collapses his Marxism into religion; others have argued, however, that he has merely grafted elements of religion on to an inadequate Marxism.

Chapter 4 addresses Bloch's analysis of Fascism, and the nature of his Marxism. His analysis of Fascism deserves to be far better known. He recognised that the Nazis had been able to tap into the fantasy world of a variety of social classes, while the Left had largely abandoned these hopes and fears as mere irrationality. People could be physical contemporaries and yet carry within themselves various 'non-contemporaneous' elements, some of which held rich utopian contents. This exploration of the dreamscape of Weimar Germany is fruitful and illuminating. Less so is the rather rigid Marxist-Leninist sociology and politics in which it is often encased; Bloch employs highly orthodox categories of class – for example, with an idealised proletariat, and an insufficiently critical approach to the German Communist Party (KPD). Looking at Bloch's Marxism we will see that the influence of the early Marx is obvious. This, in turn, is grounded in his broader process philosophy with its dynamic universe. While at the political level, his ideas would change over time, in the 1930s, 1940s and 1950s the malign influence of Stalinism was evident.

Finally, Chapter 5 examines Bloch's stance on natural law, utopianism and nature. Bloch's interest in the natural law tradition was a long-standing one, and he spent many years on a manuscript dealing with his theme. Bloch at once distinguishes the concern of natural law with human dignity from the concern of social utopianism with human happiness, and looks forward to a fruitful combination of both traditions. In the 1960s he used discussion of natural law to help develop a critique first of Stalinism and then, to some extent, of Marx himself. It is difficult not to see the effect of personal experience in his denunciation of Stalinist violations of human dignity; though whether he fully appreciated the cost of his previous adherence to the cause of the Soviet Union is open to question. Bloch came to concede that although Marx had much to say on the nature of *exploitation*, his contributions on the theme of *degradation* were significantly fewer.

The second section of the chapter is concerned with utopianism. In a sense, all of Bloch's work is concerned with this; but it is worth looking specifically at his attempts to map the various forms of the utopian. In what many would consider to be his masterpiece, the three-volume *Das Prinzip Hoffnung* (*The Principle of Hope*), Bloch uses his expanded definition of the utopian in an encyclopaedic survey of the phenomenon. Maintaining that the utopian is so much more than the utopian fantasy pioneered by Thomas More, he delineates medical utopias, technological utopias, geographical utopias and indeed others, in addition to the more familiar social utopia, and discusses examples as varied as the visions of the mentally ill and the Gothic cathedrals of medieval Europe. Political order is introduced into this diversity in his distinction between 'abstract' and 'concrete' utopia – where only the latter actually carries the future into the present. At its worst Bloch's distinction leads to a narrow definition of the progressive, and to an authoritarian style in politics. In a number of statements which Bloch made during his residence in East Germany, the future seemed to be reduced to the party line.

The final section of this chapter deals with Bloch's startling speculations about nature. He follows through what he takes to be the implications of his radical materialism – that nature, having produced humanity, has not exhausted its creative potential. In a grand utopian conception, he plays with the idea of a future natural subject, where humanity and nature engage in 'co-productivity' – an impressive ecological vision reaching back, via nature philosophy, to ancient animist thought. Not surprisingly, some critics have argued that at this point the utopian element in Bloch's thought has completely parted company with any sense of the possible.

Whereas it is necessary to know the historical, intellectual and biographical context of Bloch's work, and to appreciate the tensions within his ideas and, indeed, their principal inadequacies, the reader needs to obtain more than this for a deeper motivation to turn directly to Bloch's writings. Bloch himself argued that significant artists and writers produce a cultural surplus – a body of work which, while rooted in a particular time, none the less transcends that time. This study claims that

7

Bloch produced just such a surplus. There is an originality and an imaginative intelligence in Bloch which give his writings an enduring value. To use an image he himself often deployed in his own investigations of various cultural and social forms, there is real gold to be found in his work – though there is also hard rock to shift in the process.

1

LIFE AND CONCEPTS

LIFE

It is worth reflecting on Bloch's sheer longevity. He died in 1977 aged 92. His death locates him in the contemporary world (he died, after all, only six years before Michel Foucault), yet his birth occurred in the distant world of late nineteenth-century Imperial Germany. He was well into his sixties before the bulk of the work for which he is best known was published, and much of that appeared in his seventies and eighties. A lifetime's experience of the turbulence of the century was already behind him. He was in his thirties at the time of the Bolshevik Revolution, in his late forties when Hitler came to power and in his sixties when he ended his period of American exile and embarked on his first academic post in East Germany. Still to come was the decision in his seventies, precipitated by the building of the Berlin Wall, to make his home in West Germany. He encountered all of this as a left-wing, Central-European Jew; politics, geography and culture conspiring to place him at the storm-centre of the modern era. There was much involuntary wandering – flight from the war fever of First World War Germany, flight from the terror of the Nazis and flight from the tyranny of the GDR. Hard political decisions had to be made, particularly over the question of support for the Soviet Union. Bloch nailed his colours to the new Soviet experiment, a decision that was to have momentous consequences for both his life and thought. Throughout, his monumental theoretical system was developing. There is an enduring visionary and messianic dimension in his work – an almost visceral yearning for the utopian and the eschatological. Alongside this, however, is

9

the desire to be hard-headed in the ways of the world, not to succumb to sentimental fancies or naive strategies and tactics. His own life testifies to the strains of this tension.

Ernst Simon Bloch was born on 8 July 1885 in Ludwigshafen, Germany.[1] His father, Markus Bloch, was a railway official, married to Barbara (née Feitel), and the household could be broadly described as assimilated Jewish. Bloch recollected to his third wife, Karola, an unhappy childhood with uncultured, unsympathetic parents and an academically undistinguished school career.[2] In his writings childhood misery and elementary utopian longings are undoubtedly connected. In *Spuren* he says that 'boys experience a curious intoxication when their school reports keep on getting worse and misery has really taken wing', and that 'the small sparkling ecstasy in unhappiness presents the enjoyment of a defiance ... which makes us strangely free. ... There a piece of that which has not yet come lies hidden'; while in *The Principle of Hope* one senses a strong autobiographical element in his depictions of youthful daydreams:

> parents and teachers can be relied upon to put a damper on things. Suffering at school can be nastier than any other later form of suffering, except that of the prisoner. Hence the wish to break out, shared by the prisoner; because outside is still indistinct, it becomes a place of wonder.[3]

Only school friendships (themselves only obtained with time) helped mitigate matters. In an interview in 1967 he describes his youthful self: a boy 'hungry' for something that could not be obtained from parents or teachers, reliant on friends, oppositional sentiments developing early.[4] In these years he also began his life-long love affair with the adventure stories of Karl May, which both stimulated and helped to feed the utopian hunger of the young Bloch. He placed May in exalted company: 'there is only Karl May and Hegel, anything in between is an impure mixture.'[5] May's mythic Wild West frontier world of 'Old Shatterhand' and 'Winnetou' was to become a permanent feature in Bloch's mental landscape.

Ludwigshafen is separated by the Rhine from the city of Mannheim, and when writing, or questioned, about his early life, Bloch portrayed this juxtaposition as a microcosm of the contradictions of the modern world: 'Seldom did one have the realities and the ideals of the industrial age so close together.'[6] Ludwigshafen was, in Bloch's words, 'a workers' city',[7] home of I. G. Farben ('moved here so that the smoke and proletariat did not drift over Mannheim'),[8] and the location of his early encounters with capitalist industrialisation, the working class, the Social Democratic Party and Marxism. Mannheim, by contrast, was a sophisticated, elegant, cultured and thoroughly bourgeois city where, ensconced in the castle library, the young Bloch (forbidden to read philosophy at home as it took time away from 'proper' homework) immersed himself in the German philosophical tradition, particularly the writings of Hegel. The contrast between the two cities is, on occasions, simplified into a metaphor: Ludwigshafen and Mannheim as home and away; the world of work and the world of the mind; politics and culture; the new and the old; Marx and Hegel; elements in tension, in need of reconciliation.[9]

Bloch's studies between 1905 and 1914 can be briefly summarised. He studied philosophy and psychology with Theodor Lipps in Munich, and with Oswald Külpe in Würzburg; subsidiary studies were in German studies, music and physics; he graduated with a critical dissertation on Rickert's epistemology. This was succeeded by less formal study, first as a member of Georg Simmel's private colloquium in Berlin, and then in association with Max Weber's circle in Heidelberg.

Bloch's relationship with Weber was not a smooth one. Paul Honigsheim, a fellow member of the circle, recalled Weber's dislike of what he saw as Bloch's relative indifference to the question of empirical verification: 'the man', Weber protested, 'cannot be taken seriously in scientific matters.' On the other hand, Weber was to cite Bloch in his own work, and later, as a journal editor, published an article by Bloch. Weber also disliked the prophetic manner he believed Bloch had adopted, and which so annoyed some members of the circle that they stopped attending the regular Sunday meetings. An exasperated Weber is reported to have said: 'I would like to send a porter to his house to pack his trunks and take them to the railroad station, so that Bloch would go away.'[10] One catches a whiff of what probably got up Weber's nose in the memories of Margaret Susman, who knew Bloch from the time they were both in Simmel's colloquium in Berlin. She describes Bloch as 'a man for whom the future burned like a great light on his forehead', who 'self-consciously sought to break through the conventional

11

life forms, and expected the same from every human being that he recognized as kindred'.[11]

Bloch and Lukács began their important relationship in this period. Despite an initial meeting arranged by Simmel, where Bloch was unimpressed by Lukács, a close intellectual bond was to develop between the two men. In Bloch's very first letter to Lukács he writes: 'your manuscript [from *Soul and Form*] made quite an extraordinary impression on me',[12] while Lukács refers to Bloch in a letter to Leo Popper as an 'inspiring intellectual . . . a real philosopher in the Hegelian mold'.[13] 'We quickly discovered', Bloch was later to say, 'that we had the same opinion on everything.'[14] Both were always to acknowledge the intellectual debts they owed to one another. Bloch taught Lukács the value of traditional philosophy, from Aristotle to, above all, Hegel;[15] and it was through Lukács that Bloch gained a familiarity with Dostoyevsky, Kierkegaard and the German mystic Meister Eckhart. In Heidelberg, in fact, the two men were deemed to be highly unorthodox, mystical and religious thinkers; Marianne Weber in the biography of her husband Max, without referring to Bloch by name, recalled:

> A new Jewish philosopher happened to be there – a young man with an enormous crown of black hair and an equally enormous self-assurance. He evidently regarded himself as the precursor of a new Messiah and wanted to be recognized as such. From the height of his apocalyptic speculations he directed all sorts of questions to Naumann, who was very amiable but obviously had the impression that he was dealing with someone a bit cracked.[16]

She also referred to 'the young philosophers' (only Lukács is named, but the reference is to Bloch also) who 'were moved by eschatological hopes of a new emissary of the transcendent God' and who 'saw the basis of salvation in a socialist social order created by brotherhood';[17] in Helmut Plessner's recollection, 'they were rumoured to be gnostics. . . . "Who are the four evangelists?" the question was frequently posed. "Mark, Matthew, Lukács and Bloch," the answer ran.'[18] In later reminiscences Bloch asserted that both Lukács and himself stressed the need for order in politics. Bloch related to Michael Landmann that at the beginning of their friendship, 'Lukács and I put order above freedom, put Marx above Bakunin for the same reason, admired the Catholic hierarchy and transferred this too to the political sphere.'[19] Karl Jaspers remembered the pompous aspects of this relationship: 'after a lecture by Lukácz [sic] Bloch stated ceremoniously: the world spirit [Weltgeist] has just gone through this room ... and he let a pause ensue before he continued.'[20] Lukács' Hungarian friends were alarmed by the religious and utopian direction of his current thinking and blamed Bloch; the philosopher Emma Ritoók wrote to Lukács, 'this way of thinking, the theological wording of ideas and concepts, I heard the first time from Bloch – and I believe, it is unworthy of the high quality of your thinking';[21] the poet Béla Balázs confided to his diary that Lukács 'is really a rational thinker and this utopian trait does not suit him well at all. I cannot stand this tendency of Bloch at all that he has to proclaim a new religion whenever he is lighting up a new cigar.'[22] Balázs did however acknowledge that there might be more to Bloch than was immediately apparent, as in this more rounded description:

> There is no minute and thought in his day when he does not speak philosophy. If he puts a cube of sugar in his tea, he asks himself what is the metaphysical significance of the fact that one body dissolves to become the taste of another. He has a hypnotic influence on Gyuri [Lukács] which is unsettling. It is also true, however, that he has set in motion a creative period for Gyuri which surprises all of us, including Gyuri himself. ... He is a spiritual *condottieri* who is redeemed only by the fact that he is at the same time a child and a Don Quixote. Perhaps he is only an empty dreamer, but it is also possible that he will be a great man one day.[23]

This period of near unanimity between Bloch and Lukács began to break down for three reasons: growing theoretical disputes on philosophical and aesthetic matters; Lukács' decision to become a combatant in the First World War, which deeply offended Bloch's pacifism (Bloch ended his friendship with Simmel for the same reason);[24] and Bloch's reaction to what he saw as the narrowing of Lukács' intellectual horizons when the latter became a communist. Yet Bloch could still say in 1974 that 'there are parts and ideas in *History and Class Consciousness* which are expressions of a common point of view and which really came from me, just as parts of *Geist der Utopie* and aspects of its contents originated in conversations with Lukács.'[25] At the personal level, Lukács' family and a number of his friends saw Bloch as a malign influence, who exploited Lukács' wealth and connections; one friend, Edith Hajós, in a letter to Lukács, echoed Weber's desire: 'If I were you, I would buy Bloch a one-way railway ticket and then tell him, in the name of sacred friendship, to go to hell.'[26] Jaspers, however, paints a more benign picture of Bloch in Heidelberg as 'rather a down-to-earth quite open fellow who by his warmth and outgoing manner . . . aroused some sympathy'.[27]

In the period of the First World War Bloch's political beliefs could be broadly described as pacifist and leftist. It was not really until the early 1920s that Bloch began to develop a self-consciously Marxist position. His pacifism did not make him neutral *vis-à-vis* the belligerent powers. 1917 found him in Switzerland, very hostile to the policies of Imperial Germany. It is possible that his contacts with the anarchist Hugo Ball in Switzerland helped to attenuate his previous hankerings for 'order', for a pronounced critique of autocracy is to be found in his contemporary writings. In a 1918 pamphlet, *Would Military Defeat Help or Hurt Germany?*, he argued that 'Germany must first freely undergo the destruction and defeat of its military autocracy in an "unhappy" outcome of the war'[28] if a genuine transformation was to occur in that country. Unlike the 'revolutionary defeatism' of Lenin, with its notion of 'a plague on all your houses', Bloch hoped for the triumph of the 'democratic' entente powers. His dislike of autocracy led him to make some highly critical remarks on Lenin and the Bolsheviks with the onset of the Russian Revolution. He welcomed the revolution but feared the consequences of the dictatorship of the 'red czar'. His attitude was also influenced by literary and mystical notions of Holy Mother Russia which helped generate a primitivist fantasy of 'eastern' spiritual renewal. Underpinning both reactions was an awareness of Russia's political and economic underdevelopment. The Bolshevik understanding of these events, which he was later to publicly defend, is not to be found in his responses of the period. He appears to have been both enthusiastic and anxious.

Geist der Utopie (*Spirit of Utopia*), Bloch's first major work, was begun in Garmisch in 1915, 'with much Beethoven as well as Hegel in the head, and not without a touch of Expressionism';[29]

14

completed in 1917 in Grünwald, it was published in Munich in 1918. The foundation of this work, indeed of all his subsequent work, was his 'discovery' in 1907, at the age of 22, of the category 'Not-Yet' (*Noch-Nicht*) (it was this achievement which later persuaded an initially reluctant Simmel to invite Bloch to become a member of his prestigious colloquium[30]). This complex category, which he was to use in different ways, he called 'the origin (*der Ursprung*) of my philosophy'.[31] *Spirit of Utopia*, in its articulation and defence of utopianism, encapsulates a whole range of Bloch's early interests. Almost one-third of the text is taken up with the theory and history of music. Bloch claimed that in musical matters Lukács deferred to him entirely; and Otto Klemperer, who in 1916 received a manuscript version from Georg Simmel, read the musical chapters and later declared them 'the work of a man of genius';[32] it was only his publisher's commercial fears that dissuaded Bloch from entitling the entire work *Musik und Apokalypse*.[33] Other concerns in *Spirit of Utopia* include the philosophy and history of art, traditional and modern philosophy, esoteric, heterodox and mystical religion and Marxism; Expressionism is to be found in the style and aesthetics of the work. The same creative wave produced his 1921 study of the radical reformation visionary, *Thomas Münzer als Theologe der Revolution* (*Thomas Münzer as Theologian of Revolution*). Bloch published a heavily revised version of *Spirit of Utopia* in 1923.

It was *Spirit of Utopia* which signalled to German intellectual circles that an important new voice was to be heard. Adorno read the work in his last year at school, and in later reminiscences recalled his fascination with the book:

> The dark brown book, four hundred pages long, printed on heavy paper, promised something of what one had hoped for from medieval books and of what I sensed as a child in the pigskin-bound *Heldenschatz*, a late work on magic from the eighteenth century. . . . It was a philosophy which could stand shoulder to shoulder with the most advanced literature, which had not been schooled into the despicable resignation of method. Ideas like 'the inward journey' . . . which lay on the narrow boundary between a magic formula and a theoretical proposition, were evidence of this.[34]

Another member of the Frankfurt School, Herbert Marcuse, at a conference in the 1960s attended by Bloch, was equally fulsome in his assessment of *Spirit of Utopia*:

> I am . . . happy and honoured to talk to you in the presence of Ernst Bloch today, whose work 'Geist der Utopie' published more than forty years ago, has influenced at least my generation, and has shown how realistic utopian concepts can be, how close to action, how close to practice.[35]

There was also a good deal of negative response to the work. Reviewers and readers complained about oddity of style, impenetrable prose, slipshod scholarship and fantastic and mystical ideas (even a fellow utopian, Gustav Landauer, found the book 'occult');[36] the first airing, in other words, of the charges that were to dog Bloch throughout his life. None the less, he had made his first major mark.

The 1920s and 1930s were decades of marked changes for Bloch. There was geographical change. Between 1919 (when he returned from a period in Switzerland) and 1933 he lived in Germany, Italy, France and Austria. During this last year, in the wake of Hitler's rise to power, he narrowly escaped Nazi efforts to apprehend him, and became part of the diaspora of leftist Jewish intellectuals, and lived in Zurich, Vienna, Paris and Prague, before emigrating to the USA in 1938. There was personal change: his first wife Else von Stritzky, whom he married in 1913, and whom he credited with awakening his religious sense, died in 1921, which plunged him into depression; in 1922 he married a painter, Linda Oppenheimer – a relationship which effectively lasted less than a year, although a formal divorce only occurred in 1928; 1928 also saw the birth of his daughter Mirjam to a former lover Frida Abeles; in 1934 he married his third wife, Karola Piotrkowska, a Polish architect, a marriage which lasted until his death; their son, Jan Robert, was born in 1937. There were important new friendships, which stand out in Bloch's reminiscences: Siegfried Kracauer, Walter Benjamin, Theodor Adorno, Otto Klemperer, Kurt Weill and Bertolt Brecht. There was continual experimentation with form, with the essay as the principal focus; even his major books of the period, *Spuren* (*Traces*) (1930) and *Erbschaft dieser Zeit* (*Heritage of Our Times*) (1935), are mosaic-like in their construction out of the small scale; a delight in the episodic and the particular is evident.

Bloch also enlarges his conceptual armoury in this period, fashioning ever more rigorous conceptual tools in the development of his utopian social theory. Finally, one should note Bloch's evolution into an explicit Marxist, and his public endorsement of the Soviet Union and Stalinist Bolshevism (he publicly defended the Moscow Show Trials,[37] and was quite prepared to believe that Trotsky was a Gestapo agent![38]); as he stated in a letter of 1937, 'the truth lies in the Moscow version, no matter how paradoxical.'[39] Leon Feuchtwanger had recourse to Bloch in his own defence of the Moscow trials: 'Were I asked for the quintessence of my opinion, I could perhaps only follow the example of that modest essayist Ernst Bloch, and quote Socrates, who, when questioned regarding certain obscurities in Heraclitus, replied: "What I have understood is excellent. From which I conclude that the rest which I have not understood is also excellent." '[40] His wife, Karola, was an active member of the Communist Party; party instructions to her accounted for the Blochs' movement in 1936 from the relative safety and pleasant ambience of Paris to the potentially more dangerous and relatively alien city of Prague. Such commitment did not exempt Bloch from criticism from within the Communist movement. Lukács in 1935 in a review of *Heritage of Our Times* saw a contradiction between Bloch's pro-Soviet political views and his philosophical approach. He hoped that Bloch's 'honest and brave participation in the fight against fascism will help him to overcome the blatant contradictions present today between his clear political posture against fascism and his philosophical concessions to idealistic and reactionary trends.'[41] Fragments of this time remain in letters and reminiscences. He is to be sighted in the intellectual, political, cultural and bohemian circles of the time. There are his quirky contacts with Benjamin: on Capri together; experimenting with hashish; Bloch's recollection that 'we experienced a true symbiosis in Paris in 1926 that lasted half a year', but also that 'we had a bit too much of one another due to this enforced proximity';[42] Benjamin's belief that Bloch is plagiarizing his work, 'burglarizing my property', but although 'the relationship can never evolve to the complete satisfaction of both parties, I will nevertheless most definitely accept responsibility for preserving the association';[43] Benjamin's dislike of what he saw as a priori theoretical dogmatism in Bloch: 'What I deplore very much is that Bloch, who has no less need of being set straight by competent friends than anyone else, charts his wide-ranging excursions without taking his friends into account and is satisfied to have the company of his papers.'[44] There are the Berlin days spent with the radical writers of 'Gruppe 1925', or at the artistic haunt the 'Romanische Café', or at the Kroll Opera.[45] He can be found having tea with Thomas Mann in Switzerland;[46] meeting Brecht in 1935 at 'The First Writers' Congress for the Defence of Culture' in Paris;[47] and the surreal sighting of him at a party in Berlin in 1928, dancing a minuet with Igor Stravinsky![48]

Between 1938 and 1949, Bloch lived in the USA – in New York until 1940, in Marlborough, New Hampshire until 1941, and in Cambridge, Massachusetts until his return to Germany. We gain an insight into Bloch's hopes and fears at the beginning of this period from a lecture he delivered to a gathering of German émigré writers in 1939. He posed the question of how people like themselves could survive in the strange new environment of America, yet continue to develop as both writers and opponents of Fascism. In particular he focused on the problem of existing in an alien linguistic culture: 'How can we, as German writers, do our duty in a country with a different language? How can we make our living?'[49] His appraisal of American society was never again to be as positive. Although there is a Marxist critique of the excesses of American capitalism and references to the Ku Klux Klan and vigilantes, the tone is predominantly upbeat; glowing references to the country's 'very democratic . . . very humanistic ideology', its excellent educational traditions, and the 'great and healthy American will – the will to live and to believe in the continuation of a better life'.[50] A much more jaundiced view would in time replace this assessment. In the lecture he outlined three possible ways in which German writers could respond to their new home; there are those who repudiate their German past and language, and seek to become completely absorbed in American life – a form of self-hatred, according to Bloch; there are those who take the completely opposite approach and act as if nothing had happened, seeking 'to create a German island of culture here' – a recipe for stagnation; finally there is the 'correct attitude', where German language and culture is retained, but draws sustenance from the new conditions: 'the German refugee writer brings his roots with him: a mature language, an old culture. He brings these values to America. And he remains faithful to them not by making museum-pieces out of them, but by testing and quickening his powers on the new stuff of life.'[51] Ironically, Bloch's actual life in America conformed more to the second model than it did to the ideal. He kept to German circles, failed to learn English, and his 'engagement' with American ways increasingly took the form of a highly critical distance.

Bloch had high hopes of gaining a position at the Institute for Social Research, then based at Columbia University, but he was gravely disappointed when Horkheimer quite openly rejected him on the ground that his political views were 'too communist'.[52] Attitudes to the USSR caused deep divisions within the Institute, and Bloch was associated with the pro-Soviet wing. Leo Lowenthal, a member of the Institute, recalled:

> In the 1930s the basic conflict involved the Soviet Union and the trials. There was quite a split about that, and it frequently resulted in heated conversations and unpleasant scenes. The defenders of the Soviet Union were Wittfogel, Grossman, and Bloch – although the latter was not strictly a member of our group. It went so far that one of these three called us the 'swine on 117th Street' (that was where our Columbia house was located).[53]

This is confirmed in a letter of 1942 where, in a discussion of 'the hatred against Stalin', Bloch makes a clearly disparaging reference to 'Horkheimerism' ('Horkheimerismus').[54] There were also theoretical differences. In 1937 Adorno and Horkheimer dreamed up a scheme whereby they would publish in their journal an extract from Bloch's manuscript on materialism in return for a mention of their own work in Bloch's published text. Unfortunately, on reading Bloch's text, Adorno found a 'certain irresponsible philosophical improvisation', and, according to the most recent historian of the Frankfurt School, Wiggerhaus, it was this rather than the utopianism and communism which sunk the project in Adorno's mind.[55] Employment in American institutions was precluded by Bloch's inability to acquire any proficiency in English (Karola Bloch says that he was a poor linguist). When pressed by friends to study English, he replied that the very first person from whom he had asked directions to Times Square had turned out to be a former cigarette seller from Munich who had answered him in German![56]

It was not just a matter of language: he felt that he was ill-equipped to be anything other than a philosopher, and he resented the American ethos that if one was unable to make a living out of philosophy one should seek more lucrative work – 'Should I have become a dishwasher?'[57] (His reiteration of this theme misled Adorno at the time; Adorno, in a published appeal for Bloch, claimed that the latter actually had been reduced to washing dishes for a living!) Therefore while Bloch studied and wrote, Karola Bloch, who had trained as an architect, obtained a job in an architect's office and became the bread-winner for the family – a fact Bloch was always gratefully to acknowledge.

Bloch's circle of friends was also drawn from the German exile community, and included the composer Hanns Eisler, the theologian Paul Tillich, the theatre director Erwin Piscator, Adorno and Klemperer. With America's entry into the war Bloch's nationality not only made him an enemy-alien, but his left-wing past was deemed to make him a 'premature anti-fascist'![58] Officialdom's suspicion of him was such that it took him two years longer than it took his wife to become an American citizen, even though she had been an actual and active member of the German Communist Party (KPD), whereas he had never held membership. Bloch used this period of exile to start work on a number of texts: a study of the natural rights tradition entitled *Naturrecht und Sozialismus* (*Natural Law and Socialism*); a work on religion, *Religion des Exodus und des Reiches* (*Religion of the Exodus and the Kingdom*); *Subjekt–Objekt*, his book on Hegel; and his masterpiece *Das Prinzip Hoffnung* (*The Principle of Hope*). Only bits and pieces of this productive period emerged in print at this time. A Spanish version of the Hegel book was published in Mexico in 1949. Friends tried to use their influence to obtain a publisher for the burgeoning manuscript of *The Principle of Hope*; the writer Hermann Broch wrote to the Bollingen Foundation: 'Bloch's work to date has already ensured him a place among the foremost philosophers of our age; his writings are the output of an intellect as profound as it is original, a mind of encyclopaedic knowledge'[59] – to no effect; the book was also rejected by Oxford University Press as 'too cryptic';[60] and a mere part of it was published as *Freiheit und Ordnung, Abriss der Sozialutopien* (*Freedom and Order, A Digest of Social Utopias*) in New York in 1946.

In 1948 Bloch was offered, and accepted, a chair in philosophy at the University of Leipzig. Unbeknown to him, this was a source of great controversy in Leipzig. His appointment could be seen as the triumph of the political over the academic.. Bloch had some partisan support at the university, but the Faculty of Philosophy at Leipzig had grave reservations about him: he was considered to be a writer and cultural critic, with, in the opinion of some, distinctly odd ideas, but not a 'real' philosopher, fit to succeed Gadamer. The appointment was, however, pushed through by the Party/State which was of the opinion that Bloch was politically sound.[61] It is also possible that the support of Lukács, who had gained a respectable Marxist-Leninist pedigree during his years in exile, may have helped Bloch secure the position; certainly it was Lukács' belief that 'it was partly due to me that he was appointed to a chair at Leipzig University'.[62] Karola Bloch was very reluctant to return, given that the Nazis had murdered her parents and brother, but 'Ernst's willingness to accept such a professorship and the hope of helping build a socialist Germany were decisive'.[63] This was his very first academic appointment, at an age (in his mid-sixties) when most would be thinking of retirement; it was also his first regular salary – his previous income had mainly come from family, friends and wives. He was clearly delighted (it was not as if he had been inundated with offers!), and spread the good news in letters to his regular correspondents and to his old friend Georg Lukács, then Professor of Philosophy in Budapest: 'So we are now in a sense colleagues.'[64] In contrast to the luminaries of the younger generation, Marcuse (who had been approached about, but was not interested in, a post in Leipzig),[65] Adorno, Horkheimer, who based themselves in the West, the old-timers Bloch and Lukács continued their commitment to the 'socialism' of the East. Bloch's move to East Germany in 1949 had therefore both career and ideological motivations. In an interview he gave in August 1949 to the party organ *Neues Deutschland* he makes his sympathies abundantly clear: 'I have left a rotten world. I come so to speak to the land of Metternich and the Holy Alliance. Formerly that was called the "New World". But now the New World is here with us.'[66] Karola Bloch, who stayed in the USA a few months before joining Bloch, recalled that his early letters from Leipzig 'were wonderfully optimistic and full of joyous expectations'.[67] Between 1949 and 1955 Bloch published a number of works: a German edition of his Hegel book

Subjekt–Objekt. Erläuterungen zu Hegel (Subject–Object. Comment-aries on Hegel); two texts based around historical thinkers, *Avicenna und die Aristotelische Linke (Avicenna and the Aristotelian Left)* and *Christian Thomasius. Ein deutscher Gelehrter ohne Misere (Christian Thomasius. A German Scholar without Misery)*; and most importantly, the first two volumes of *The Principle of Hope*. Rudolf Bahro illustrates Bloch's prestige in Leipzig when, as an aspirant undergraduate in the early 1950s, Bahro sought to study philosophy, and encountered a very intimidating secretary: 'When I timidly enquired whether I could study there, she solemnly rose to her feet and boomed out that this was Leipzig, and that the professor of philosophy was no less a person than Ernst Bloch. That was the end of Leipzig for me.'[68] Bloch lectured in the largest lecture room in the Karl Marx University to packed audiences, and not only gained an enthusiastic student following but also had some impact on party ideologists, notably Kurt Hager, the Central Committee Secretary.[69] He also appears to have been highly influential on a whole generation of young GDR writers, most of whom were either studying at the University in Leipzig or at the Johannes R. Becher Institute (set up to encourage socialist writing) in the city. One such writer, Gerhard Zwerenz, recalled the impact Bloch made on him:

and then I saw the man. He was short with a stocky body. His hair fell in his face. Wearing thick glasses, he ran down the hall and almost knocked me over. Only in the last moment could I avoid a collision.... At that instant, I realized that I had to study philosophy.[70]

Ehrhard Bahr, writing in the late 1970s, made a very big claim for Bloch: 'the emergence of the literature of the German Democratic Republic and its advance to international prominence and reputation during the last twenty years can be traced back to Ernst Bloch and the impact of his philosophy.'[71] The later recollections of his students are not, however, entirely uncritical. Ruth Römer, who considered her time with Bloch to be the highlight of her academic career, also noted that in sexual matters he was very conventional, and 'made spiteful remarks about [a colleague's] homosexuality' and had a 'chauvinist' attitude towards women.[72] In this period Bloch's work was reaching a new generation in West Germany. Habermas recalled his student days in the 1950s: 'Thanks to the writings of Bloch and Adorno we discovered, to our astonishment, that Marx was not over and done with, that the Marxist tradition was of more than historical and philological interest, and could be of relevance to systematic inquiry.'[73] Bloch is ambiguous in his recollections as to the nature of his lectures in Leipzig. In one account he claims that his lectures contained very little of his own theory, and this is explained in terms of psychology and his distinctive method of composition:

> When ideas came to me while talking, I kept them to myself and wrote them down later.... It was probably a subtle mixture of modesty and arrogance... I lectured pedantically in the style of the 19th century handbooks.... There ensued six typewritten compendia of about 800 pages each, in which not one idea is my own. Any new ideas came only implicitly in my analyses... I was comfortable in this *incognito*.[74]

Elsewhere, however, he claimed that his lectures were full of his own ideas, and that the element of concealment was purely tactical: 'In Leipzig I apparently taught only history of philosophy. But, I took the occasion to bring in everything else, even if only allusively.... I seemed to conceal myself but this was only a trick.'[75] Both accounts bring out the cautious, dissimulating aspects of Bloch's personality; the latter recollection, however, points to darker features of Bloch's life in East Germany.

Relationships between the East German state and Bloch altered in response to a series of political crises. Bloch's philosophical stance was always light-years away from official Marxist-Leninist orthodoxy but his heterodoxy was *publicly* tolerated when the state felt secure. Even in the good times, however, his independence, *privately*, was far from sacrosanct. Research by Jürgen Jahn in the archives of Bloch's East German publisher (*Aufbau-Verlag*)[76] reveals persistent pressure on Bloch to adhere more closely to orthodoxy, including the acknowledgement of Stalin's status as a theoretician. Bloch had to negotiate his proofs through to publication. The relationship between Bloch and his publisher consequently became increasingly irritable, and after 1957 was thoroughly poisoned. The Slansky trial in Czechoslovakia (1952) created the sort of insecurity which encouraged public attacks on Bloch's 'idealistic' reading of Hegel. He survived this and, in the wake of a period of liberalisation, received a great deal of official recognition (including the National Prize and full membership of the German Academy of Sciences). All this came to an end with the crisis in the Communist bloc generated by Khrushchev's denunciation of Stalin at the Twentieth Congress of the Communist Party of the USSR. Bloch's own response to the revelations is not clear. It is the view of his son, Jan Robert, that Bloch responded to the revelations of the Twentieth Congress with a degree of detachment which suggested no great re-evaluation of his political past. He cites Bloch's remark in May 1956, 'How simply getting rid of something can enrich us', and argues that it is as if a 'relieved, observing cavalier was speaking and not a philosophical protagonist of precisely that which had been "gotten rid of" '.[77] He also notes Bloch's fears that 'a few reactionary rats would creep out of their holes with the liberals, too'.[78] Karola Bloch, on the other hand, argues that Bloch was more actively opposed to Stalinism in this period, was sympathetic to the opposition in Poland and Hungary, and 'in October 1956 ... sided with the anti-Stalinist Gomulka'.[79] Be this as it may, the state considered Bloch to be a threat – particularly on account of his influence on past and present 'oppositional' students. A period of intense persecution began for Bloch. He was deemed to be the spiritual leader of the democratic socialist group associated with Wolfgang Harich. Members of the group were arrested, imprisoned or went into exile; Hager now demanded that Bloch 'state his position ... about the anti-state activities of his students';[80] Karola was expelled from the party after twenty-five years' membership; Bloch was banned from the university and vilified in the press; in a typical piece of Stalinist historical re-creation, the 1956 volume of the *Deutsche Zeitschrift für Philosophie*, the journal Bloch had previously edited, ignored all references to works by him in its index;[81] books were published and conferences held branding him anti-Marxist, revisionist and even 'imperialistic'; the party leader Ulbricht, who had long smarted over a slighting remark Bloch had made about him, denounced him as a 'seducer of youth'. Karola and Bloch only narrowly escaped arrest. 'Still we did not flee', Karola recalled, 'that would generally have been regarded as a betrayal of socialism.'[82] It hurt. Bloch was to have bitter memories: 'After loyal, intensive teaching, after the publication of works which surely did not disgrace our republic and our cause, I was treated in an incomprehensible, almost unparalleled ugly and crude way.'[83] Rudolf Bahro confirms that Leipzig and Bloch were singled out for special treatment: 'the Stalinist opposition to Bloch . . . [was] far more unpleasant than anything we experienced in Berlin.'[84] It was only in 1959, after 'two unpleasant years',[85] that Bloch began to emerge from this nightmare. He was even allowed to publish the third volume of *The Principle of Hope* without any of the changes the party had long demanded (Rühle speculates that with a West German edition imminent the party realised it was wasting its time[86]). This event elicited curmudgeonly reviews from party philosophers such as Manfred Buhr who asserted that Bloch had succumbed 'to ideologically anti-socialist forces'.[87] Bloch-baiting still went on: Karola recalled that in 1961 their son Jan Robert, in his final examination, was asked 'Name a revisionist. . . . The examiner wanted Jan to name his father. When he remained silent, he got "unsatisfactory" which was later changed to satisfactory.'[88] It was the building of the Berlin Wall which finally precipitated Bloch's move from the East. He and Karola were visiting West Germany when the wall went up, and they decided to stay. Karola argued that they did this because they feared that in this new climate they might never get out of the East again, and Bloch might be prevented from publishing in the West.

From 1961 until his death in 1977, Bloch was based at Tübingen. At first Bloch seemed to have merely added to his public notoriety. In the East he was denounced as a 'deserter, renegade, traitor, conman [and] dangerous criminal', while the West German press made pointed references to his Stalinist past, and expressed scepticism about what it interpreted as his current 'conversion' to Western values (the absurdity of a 'communist Saul' suddenly becoming a 'humanist Paul', as one paper put it).[89] With time, however, the clamour subsided, and Bloch was able to begin his Tübingen life. Throughout, Bloch retained his optimism. In his inaugural lecture at Tübingen in 1961, the 76-year-old Bloch asked the question 'can hope be disappointed?'. His affirmative answer was not a disillusioned account of political and personal disappointment, but rather an explanation of the open-ended nature of the historical process, and the continuing need for educated hope. This was harvest time for a whole crop of books, notably: *Naturrecht und menschliche Würde* (*Natural*

Right and Human Dignity); *Tübinger Einleitung in die Philosophie* (*Tübingen Introduction to Philosophy*); *Atheismus im Christentum* (*Atheism in Christianity*); *Das Materialismusproblem* (*The Problem of Materialism*); and *Experimentum Mundi*; he also took an active role in the revision and publication of the seventeen volumes of his collected works, and lived to see all but the last in print. This was also the period in which young radical theologians such as Jürgen Moltmann and Johannes Metz sought to use Bloch's philosophy of hope in their own reformulation of theology. Through them, Bloch became an important author for Christians seeking a 'dialogue' with Marxism. Moltmann also became a personal friend in Tübingen, and spoke of Bloch's 'original thought' and, more surprisingly, 'childlike nature'. His further description – 'the old man with the raised fist'[90] – rightly suggests that Bloch's political passion had not left him; he expressed himself loudly and clearly in print and on platform, for example, denouncing both the Americans in Vietnam and the Soviets in Czechoslovakia. Other struggles he backed included those against anti-Semitism, the right-wing press, nuclear weapons and the political control of civil service appointments (*Berufsverbot*). Nor had he lost his zest for life. Michael Landmann gives a snapshot of Bloch aged 83 at a conference in Yugoslavia in 1968:

> Even in the most difficult times I have never seen Bloch ill-tempered or despondent, but now he seems more cheerful than ever, free of the burdens that have sometimes weighed down on him.... At this congress Bloch is as indefatigable as ever. He attends meetings for long hours each day. After dinner, when I recline paralyzed with exhaustion, the irrepressible Bloch is jovially telling anecdotes over his cup of coffee.[91]

This period saw his elevation to the pantheon of 'Western Marxism'. Since he now condemned both superpower blocs, his differences with, and different trajectory to, figures such as Marcuse and Adorno were not so apparent. Furthermore, his habit of heavily revising earlier texts before republishing also assisted this process. He spent these final years (beset by blindness) writing, teaching and lecturing. As at Leipzig, he inspired loyalty and affection in his students, and on his 80th birthday they held a torchlight procession in his honour. He received many honours and awards, from various national prizes to honorary doctorates from Zagreb and the Sorbonne. The end was also linked with the beginning when he was given the freedom of Ludwigshafen. He died of heart failure on 4 August 1977 aged 92. His last words: *'Ich kann nicht mehr'*.[92]

CONCEPTS

Bloch created major difficulties for anyone attempting to provide an introduction to his concepts. He was a conceptual innovator. Throughout his long life he was constantly creating new concepts or refining old ones to register what he took to be his growing insight into the basic categories of the universe. Any comprehensive mapping of Bloch's basic concepts would involve plotting his complex shifts in conceptual usage over time – an enterprise far beyond the scope of this introductory study. The problems would be immense because, for instance, Bloch's early concepts variously disappear, reappear under different designations or endure, but with succeeding layers of meaning. Bloch may use the same word or words within a single text to convey a range of different meanings, sometimes because the texts themselves may have evolved over long periods of time, sometimes because Bloch employs one concept to do a variety of tasks. Furthermore, Bloch constantly returns to similar sorts of problems and concerns over time, each time trying to develop more cogent and trenchant modes of attack. A degree of conceptual proliferation inevitably occurs: new concepts may overlay or overlap older ones, with different concepts covering similar material, and it is for this reason that it is never easy to ascertain just how much work a particular concept is doing in a given piece of text. Insofar as this is acknowledged by Bloch himself, it is justified in terms of the experimental, open and unfixed nature of reality, which requires a flexible conceptual reflection.

There is also a great deal of material in Bloch's work which, for want of a better phrase, one could term non-conceptual. The great philosophical systems of the past are but one of the sources of Bloch's approach. He delights in the use of the esoteric and the literary, which are deemed to be necessary modes for expressing some of the complexities of the world. Thus it is that side by side with the challenging vocabulary of his philosophical analysis, we find expressionistic utterance, elliptical metaphor, quasi-mystical effusion and a liberal drawing on the artistic and occult traditions of past millennia. This latter material, though central to his work, is difficult to transpose into the language of conceptual discourse.

It is no easy matter to establish the various influences on Bloch's philosophy with any precision. One senses the emergence, at an early age, of a highly distinctive personal vision, which then thickens its texture through the appropriation of a host of external ideas, concepts and systems of thought. In the process, material is often ripped out of context and re-formed in a Blochian cast. In these instances it could almost be said that we are dealing more with Bloch's influence on other thinkers than the converse! None the less, Bloch's vision did not emerge in an intellectual vacuum, nor was it immune to significant structuring by a range of important influences. One would have to say that the figures of Hegel, Schelling and Marx are of especial importance. Hegel was an early and lasting influence. He found in Hegel a dynamic, encyclopaedic account of universal history, encompassing humanity and nature. Bloch was particularly attracted to 'process' philosophers,[93] thinkers who rejected static models of the real in favour of conceptions which stress movement, change and dynamism. Although critical of elements in Hegel, particularly the lack of open-ended novelty in the system, Bloch found the sheer sweep and comprehensiveness of Hegel's vision endlessly fascinating. Schelling, another early influence, offered a corrective to the logical aridity of Hegel, but did so in the context still of a dynamic, process theory. For Bloch, Schelling demonstrated the inadequacy of Hegel's world process as the cyclical and logical movement of perfection, via imperfection, to perfection. Schelling offered instead a conception which stressed a *real* historical movement from imperfection to perfection – in which history was a process driven by absence, or lack. Schelling's perspective was still, however, idealist in nature; there was no grounding in the actual material process of life, merely a conception of religious movement.[94] In Marx, Bloch was to find the basis for a dynamic materialism in which the interaction between the human and the natural, grounded in want, propelled the historical process forward. Bloch moved beyond Marx, however, in his desire for a system of Hegelian proportions, where not simply the social held centre stage, but the entire universe, including nature's further potentialities, was to be comprehended.

Bloch was also drawn to, and influenced by, the various philosophical antecedents of these dynamic, process thinkers. He is clearly excited by what he terms 'left-wing Aristotelianism', the development by medieval Arab writers (Avicenna and Averroes) of Aristotle's conception of matter (particularly Aristotle's notion of the realisation or 'entelechy' of matter). His exploration of their belief in a dynamic creative matter provided an important element in his attempt to create a philosophical grounding for a radical materialism. Also of abiding interest is the qualitative materialism of the Renaissance sages, Paracelsus, Böhme and Bruno, their quasi-occult notions of the vitality of nature – the spirits of the material. Likewise Leibniz who is, in a sense, the linchpin of the ancient and modern sources of process philosophy. It was Leibniz who, in Bloch's estimation, 'for the first time since Aristotle . . . opened up with genuine ideas of process the concept of *possibility* again', and 'definitely stands in the landscape of process entered by Paracelsus and Böhme';[95] while in a recollection of his youthful philosophical reading in the library at Mannheim, Bloch referred to his immersion in the 'great philosophical rainbow from Leibniz to Hegel'.[96]

It is more difficult to determine the influence of more recent writers. Bloch himself acknowledged the influence of the 'Transcendental Realist' von Hartmann, and in an interview he linked together 'Schelling, Hegel, Leibniz and Eduard von Hartmann'; while Wayne Hudson surprised Bloch in a late interview when he suggested the influence of the process philosophy of Jakob Froschammer: 'How do you know that?', Bloch responded. 'In the whole world only you and I know that.'[97] Hudson, in fact, has unearthed a considerable range of likely contemporary philosophical influences on the young Bloch, from the theorist of 'intentionality', Brentano and his disciple Meinong, through the neo-Kantians, Rickert, Cohen and Simmel, to the phenomenologists Husserl and Scheler.[98] Bloch was thoroughly immersed in the German philosophical literature of his day.

Bloch's philosophical ambitions were always to be lofty – nothing less than the elaboration of a new metaphysics, a mighty system in which all the forms of being would be comprehended. From the time of his youthful discovery of the category 'not-yet' to the final major work of his late eighties, *Experimentum*

Mundi, he strove unceasingly to deepen his understanding of the fundamental categories of the universe. In a century whose dominant philosophical temper has been anti-metaphysical, he embarked, with a defiant contrariness, on the creation of a system intended to surpass the great metaphysical systems of the past. This metaphysics was to be both modern and open-ended. Alongside highly technical, quasi-scholastic categorical distinctions, Bloch introduces what for him was the aesthetic cutting edge of modernity, Expressionism – in the form of an oblique, staccato prose style. This was also deemed to befit a metaphysics which had broken with the static systems of the past. The universe was unfinished; it was in need of completion, it was 'not-yet', and its future was decisively in the hands of an active humanity, and aesthetic radicalism was on the front line. It was inevitable that the age-old tension between the desirable and the possible intruded. Bloch developed concepts to express both the highest expectations and to register the inevitable drag of reality. He also coined various concepts to express this very tension, distinguishing between the exuberant enthusiasm for the infinite and the cool-headed appreciation of the constraints of the finite. The resulting philosophy thus threw down a gauntlet to the positivism and empiricism of the time. Fredric Jameson, in a reflection on the marginality of Bloch's work, expresses his sense of the compelling nature of this philosophy:

> Mainly, however, the neglect of Bloch is due to the fact that his system, a doctrine of hope and ontological anticipation, is itself an anticipation, and stands as a solution to problems of a universal culture and a universal hermeneutic which have not yet come into being. It thus lies before us, enigmatic and enormous, like an aerolite fallen from space, covered with mysterious hieroglyphs that radiate a peculiar warmth and power, spells and the keys to spells, themselves patiently waiting for their own ultimate moment of decipherment.[99]

The objective of this section is both modest and impertinent: modest because there is no attempt to reconstruct the complex evolution of the Blochian oeuvre; and impertinent because it will present a *system* of concepts which, at any particular point in his life, Bloch himself would undoubtedly have repudiated.

This system will assemble concepts from different periods of his life, and will unpick only a few of their possible meanings. Certain concepts are included because they were clearly central to Bloch's own project and occur repeatedly throughout his works, albeit with shifts in meaning. These are interpreted to bring out the overarching, predominant or distinctive meanings – so far as this is possible. Other concepts are included because of their value in providing a way into Bloch's deepest concerns, even if they were not perennial concepts in his work. Yet other concepts are discussed because, in addition to helping to reveal the nature of Bloch's work, they are intrinsically interesting themselves.

Bloch is unusual in the Marxist tradition in his self-conscious use of metaphysics. He shares the concerns of the classical metaphysicians in his search for the fundamental categories of the universe: essence, being and the like. However, he distinguishes the *static* metaphysics of the past from his own *open* metaphysics; whereas the former merely registers the fixed categories of a closed system, the latter is the fluid and experimental approach to a changing, open-ended process.

Bloch is at pains to stress the materialist basis of his philosophy. Building on a conception he credits to the 'Aristotelian Left' (notably Avicenna and Averroes), he maintains that *matter*, the substance of the universe, is to be understood as an active category. Matter is not inert, but rather, in nature and humanity, is capable of movement and development:

> Matter ... is not the mechanical lump.... [it] is Being which has not yet been delivered; it is the soil and the substance in which our future, which is also its future, is delivered.[100]

Bloch's belief in a dynamic matter distanced him from the predominant trend in twentieth-century 'Western Marxism' which sought to prioritise the social over the natural; and this belief even encouraged him to attempt a reformulation of something which was anathema in such circles – a dialectics of nature.

The subject matter of an open metaphysics is an open world: a world redeemed from stasis and passivity by *possibility*, defined by Bloch as 'partial conditionality'.[101] In other words, the universe is not predetermined, there is a fundamental element of indeterminacy which allows for development, novelty, intervention and alternative outcomes: 'We live surrounded by possibility, not merely by presence. In the prison of mere presence we could not even move nor even breathe.'[102] This is Bloch's ontology of *Not-Yet-Being*.

Bloch registers his belief in the openness of the world by his use of the concept *process*. When describing phenomena as processes, Bloch is seeking to convey qualities such as mutability, provisionality, activity, motion and development; that the thing, in short, is not in a condition of solid completedness; the overarching conception is of a dynamic universe in which both natural and social processes can be identified. From a human perspective the open-endedness of processes is both an opportunity and a limitation; the possibility of choice coexists with the hazards of uncertainty. Thus humanity is necessarily experimental: 'world history itself is an experiment – a real experiment conducted in the world and aimed towards a possible just and proper world.'[103]

There are different forms of possibility in an open world. Individuals can conceptualise possibilities which are merely nonsense or which link together things that are factually impossible; or they may envisage possibilities on the basis of faulty or only partial factual beliefs. Openness should give no licence to ultra-subjectivity, nor to hyper-voluntarism. People are born into a pre-existing world in which there are distinctive limitations and tendencies, which circumscribe what is actually possible. This form of possibility Bloch terms the *objectively-real possible*. It is the possibility grounded in past development, but which also contains the seeds of future development: 'it is a future-laden definiteness in the real itself.'[104] It therefore combines aspiration with a non-positivist empiricism – 'process-empiricism'.[105]

Bloch, following Hegel and Marx, describes the movement of reality in dialectical terms. These terms are deemed to denote actual categories of reality, for movement in reality is itself dialectical. Matter is in tension, the actual with the potential; it manifests 'the dialectical principle, S is not yet P'.[106] (In fact when challenged to sum up his entire philosophy in one sentence, Bloch replied 'S is not yet P'.[107]) Two categories he frequently uses are *tendency* and *latency*. Tendency is the accumulating pressure of the objectively-real possible as it is blocked by the existing. An historical example would be the pressure of the bourgeoisie in the feudal mode of production.

Latency is the possible content of the future, lying latent in the present. The categories interconnect past with present and future: 'material capable of ripening makes itself evident as still continuing tendency, still dawning latency.'[108] Again, he wishes to distance himself from any closed teleological usage of these categories which, on the analogy of the acorn and the oak, would envisage humanity in terms of a fixed future inevitably growing out of inexorable historical trends. The element of subjectivity interacts with objective development and drives the dialectical process onwards into the uncharted waters of the future. Bloch maintains that the development of the proletariat as a potentially revolutionary force is a demonstration of this process:

> the subjective factor – against all abstractness and the corresponding boundless spontaneity of consciousness – has mediated itself with the objective factor of the social tendency, of the Real–Possible. . . . Both factors, the subjective and the objective, must rather be understood in their constant dialectical interaction, one which cannot be divided or isolated.[109]

In the human world the most basic dynamic is generated by the presence of need – the *Not*. Absence, initially of food, drives the individual on to more and more sophisticated forms of interaction with nature and society. The Not becomes more sophisticated but remains unsatisfied:

> all that lives must tend towards something, or must move and be on its way towards something; and that in its restlessness the void satisfies beyond itself the need that comes from itself. . . . But satisfaction is always transitory; need makes itself felt again.[110]

Humans are thus *Not-Yet*, they are unfinished, the completion of their being lies in the future: 'I am. But without possessing myself.'[111] Bloch frequently calls humanity *homo absconditus* (hidden man)[112] – 'the man who has never seen himself face to face'.[113] History's dynamic dialectical character is grounded in this ever-striving need, this hunger for oneself, which necessarily is social in nature:

> if unfulfilled need is the *motive* and *motor* of the dialectical–

material motion, then – on the basis of the same, not yet present content – the totality of the not present All is its cohering goal.[114]

If *Not* is the negative aspect of this process, *Hope* is the positive. Bloch distinguishes *subjective* hope from *objective* hope. Subjective hope involves the perpetual and ubiquitous representation of that which is deemed to be absent. Bloch's massive *The Principle of Hope* is an encyclopaedic account of the many manifestations of hope in history and contemporary life, from simple daydreams to complex visions of perfection. Objective hope is the concrete possibility generated by each successive age, which enables subjective hope actively to develop the world. Together, they constitute the 'subjective and objective hope-contents of the world'.[115]

Bloch wishes to put the conscious in its place. Consciousness is a very narrow, patchy band, or field. It is patchy because there is more material present than is actually or fully conscious, in, for example, impressions not experienced, pain unfelt. Of the two boundaries of the band, the lower one is to be found at the point where consciousness fades: the area where consciousness turns into forgetting. This is the boundary between the conscious and the *No-Longer-Conscious*. The No-Longer-Conscious is oriented to the past: it is the realm of evening, of the night-dream – the forgotten and the repressed. This is the area that has been explored by Freud. The upper boundary is where the new dawns: where material not previously conscious enters consciousness. This is the boundary between the conscious and the *Not-Yet-Conscious*. The Not-Yet-Conscious is oriented towards the future: it is the realm of morning, of the daydream – 'the preconscious of what is to come, the psychological birthplace of the New'.[116] This is an area as yet unexplored, the area Bloch wishes to map.

As the images of 'morning', 'dawning' and 'the New' might suggest, Bloch notes a strong relationship between the Not-Yet-Conscious and youth. The Not-Yet-Conscious is deemed to be present in the excitement, the sense of endless possibility, and the strong but dimly understood desires of the young. Bloch also applies the category of youth to historical analysis: certain historical periods can be called youthful in that new objective possibility is breaking through, as in the Renaissance. In such times the Not-Yet-Conscious is evident in the revolutionary transformation occurring in all aspects of life. A potent fusion of the personal and the social, the subjective and the objective, can occur when youth harnesses its energy to times of change, exemplified for Bloch by the revolutionary youth of Tsarist Russia.

Bloch isolates three stages in the process whereby the Not-Yet-Conscious becomes a creative force in the world: incubation, inspiration and explication. Incubation is the period of active fermentation where the new material is developing, much of it beneath the surface of consciousness, until a point is reached when it bursts into the conscious world. This is the moment of inspiration, a sudden, lucid moment of illumination, whose sheer euphoric power led people to believe that it was of magical or divine origin. Once again, Bloch is at pains not to isolate these individual processes from their social and historical context; the newness, which he terms the *Novum*, emerges with the confluence of subjective and objective conditions. The historical timetable generates the material which is incubated in the individual, and the inspiration is as much historical as individual. A Marxist sense of history informs this interpretation; rising, progressive classes are the fundamental fact in the emergence of the Novum:

> without the capitalist mandate, the subjective mandate towards cogito ergo sum would never have found its inspiration; without an incipient proletarian mandate, the discovery of the materialist dialectic would have been impossible or would have remained merely a brewing aperçu. [117]

The wishes and aspirations of humanity, its possibilities, can only be actualised if there is the objective ground of intellectual, social and economic development. This is not to say that the Novum emerges initially throughout specific classes. Bloch believes that the initial entry occurs through immensely gifted individuals, geniuses. The young Marx's work is considered to be an example of this. The realisation of inspiration requires the third stage in the process – explication. This is the immensely difficult task of adequately representing and articulating the newness of the Not-Yet-Conscious, such that it re-enters the historical timetable as immanent potentiality – the *Not-Yet-Become*.

In this process the New has also to deal with the resistances of the existing world to novelty. Bloch calls the site at which present and future meet the *Front*. As in the military use of this word, it is meant to suggest an advancing, though not necessarily straight, line into as yet unconquered territory. The Front is where humanity and the world are moving into newness.

Throughout his life Bloch constantly tries to refine his analysis of what is, for him, the marvellous moment where the new emerges in the individual. He is looking for concepts that convey the paradoxical nature of an event which seems to unify antinomies. Thus there is both absence and presence, for the new is both not-yet and here-and-now; there is also both clarity and obscurity, the inspirational intensity of the new combined with the uncertainty of strange novelty. A recurring attempt to encapsulate this process is to be found in his image of the *darkness of the lived moment*. Part of this is, for Bloch, a physiological/psychological truth – namely that immediacy, close proximity cannot be experienced: 'all nearness makes matters difficult, and if it is too close, then one is blinded'.[118] When asked in an interview, 'What is the basic idea in your philosophy?', he replied, 'that I cannot see anything at very close quarters, anything that presents itself in front of my eyes. There has to be distance. . . . Proverbs express it very simply. . . . "At the foot of the lighthouse there is no light." '[119] Bloch uses the term 'darkness' to convey, using the analogy of the eye's blind spot, the inability of the mind to grasp the present, rather than the past or future, and therefore to suggest the pull of the not yet present ('no person is really here yet'[120]). There is also, in line with the open-endedness of reality, the darkness of the void which can be filled with either the joy of creation or the coldness of eternal night – action/inaction, success/failure. It is a 'lived moment' because, in an almost mystical fashion, the mind can experience the not-yet of the future:

> the darkness of the lived moment . . . coincides in its total depth with the essential, but not here-existing mode of existence of the goal-content itself . . . and which . . . is in fact the goal-content, that does not yet exist here, has not yet been brought out, of existing itself.[121]

Also, as in the mystical tradition, this moment links the individual with the supra-individual, because in the darkness of the lived moment there is the possibility of encountering the objective possibility of the world – an anticipation of concrete utopia: 'the knot of the riddle of existence is to be found in this nearest.'[122]

Another concept attempting to grasp the phenomenon of the future experienced in the present is *Vor-Schein*. A number of English translations of this term have been offered, attempting to capture its complex resonances – 'ontological anticipation', 'pre-appearance', 'anticipatory illumination'.[123] It expresses Bloch's belief that it is somehow possible to experience a kind of foreglow of future possibilities. He also wants to suggest that this anticipation is both objective *and* open; it is not mere phantasising, but neither is it an advanced copy of a pre-ordained and fixed future. Great works of art display *Vor-Schein*; they communicate a rich otherness which is both attractive and rooted in real possibilities in the world; and great images of religion have the same capacity. Only free human praxis can determine whether, to what extent and in what form *Vor-Schein* will actually become concretised.

Bloch considers the role of memory in consciousness. He perceives a conservative function in many forms of memory, and uses the Greek word *anamnesis* (recollection) to designate this phenomenon. In *anamnesis* there is no novelty, merely the re-experiencing of the old. Its classical formulation is in the Platonic definition of knowledge:

> The doctrine of *anamnesis* claims that we have knowledge only because we formerly knew. But then there could be no fundamentally new knowledge.... *Anamnesis* provides the reassuring evidence of complete similarity.... *Anamnesis* has an element of attenuation about it, it makes everything a gigantic *déjà vu*.[124]

Freud's system is similarly pervaded by *anamnesis*. Bloch does not, however, dismiss memory as inevitably conservative and backward-looking. *Anamnesis* (recollection) is distinguished from *anagnorisis* (recognition). In *anagnorisis* memory traces are reactivated in the present, but there is never simple correspondence between past and present. Recognition is a creative shock, where an element from the past jolts consciousness out of joint and thereby helps in the creation of novelty. Here the power of the past resides in its complicated relationship of similarity/

dissimilarity to the present: 'anagnorisis ... is linked with reality by only a thin thread; it is therefore alarming. ... In anagnorisis there must always be a distance between the former and present reality otherwise it would not be so difficult and astonishing.'[125] Anamnesis is not simply an epistemological concept for Bloch, it is also ontological. Ontological anamnesis occurs in systems of thought which predicate an entire creation ·at the beginning of reality, where subsequent movement is, at best, mere emanation from this prior, eternal core. The production of authentic newness is thus precluded. Hegel's system is deemed to contain this flaw. Although there is a rich and momentous dialectical dimension in Hegel, this is hamstrung in Hegel's own system by, among other things, the closure imposed by the pre-existing universal spirit at the commencement of the drama. Nothing occurs in the Hegelian system which was not already there at the beginning. Bloch considered his own open system to be following Marx in rejecting ontological anamnesis. The fullness of creation lies in the future, not the past: 'The totality of dialectical matter does not lie at the horizon of the past, as is the case with the remembrance mind of Hegel ... but at the horizon of the future.'[126]

Bloch unashamedly celebrates the role of utopianism in the development of the Not-Yet-Conscious. The emergence of the utopian is the process in which the Not-Yet-Conscious becomes conscious and known. Bloch distinguishes between abstract utopia and concrete utopia. Bloch uses the concept of abstract utopia in both a historical and critical sense. It can refer to utopias created prior to the emergence of the revolutionary proletariat, which are consequently too early; or it can refer to subsequent utopianising which is either detached from the progressive proletarian movement or antithetical to it – utopias which are ungrounded. Concrete utopia, in contrast, is rooted in objective possibility; it is grounded in the ascending forces of the age, and is the most pregnant form of the utopian function. Concrete utopia is Bloch's reformulation and further development of Marx's concept of praxis, the unity of theory and practice; it is both goal and the actual creation of that goal. At the level of consciousness the best elements of historical abstract utopia need to be refined, and the dross of contemporary abstraction removed, to produce docta spes (educated hope) which, in turn, becomes an intellectual and material force in the production of concrete utopia:

> Thus the only seemingly paradoxical concept of a concrete utopia would be appropriate here, that is, of an anticipatory kind which by no means coincides with abstract utopian dreaminess, nor is directed by the immaturity of merely abstract utopian socialism.[127]

This requires both the *warm stream* of passion and imagination, and the *cold stream* of rigorous analysis: 'enthusiasm assists sobriety'.[128]

An aspect of Bloch's conception of history as an open-ended and fluid process is his conviction that individuals and groups may be contemporaries in a physical sense without necessarily being so in terms of forms of life and consciousness. He deploys the term *non-contemporaneity* (sometimes translated as *non-synchronicity*) to designate the experience of belonging to a time earlier than the present, yet inhabiting the present:

> Not all people exist in the same Now. They do so only externally, through the fact that they can be seen today. But they are thereby not yet living at the same time with the others.[129]

An example he gave in the 1930s was the peasantry whose old forms of production, ancient customs, attitudes to nature and so forth, pre-dated the urban culture surrounding them. They were thus in contradiction to the present: a *subjectively non-contemporaneous contradiction* of anger and rage against the present, and an *objectively non-contemporaneous contradiction* of a way of life not finished off by capitalist industrialisation. Marxism had been blind to the subversive and utopian elements in non-contemporaneity, and had thereby left these strata to be co-opted and distorted by Fascist ideology. The cutting edge of revolutionary action is to be found in the *subjectively contemporaneous contradiction* of proletarian activity, and the *objectively contemporaneous contradiction* of the socialism with which capitalism is pregnant. Contemporaneous contradictions would be strengthened by the mobilisation of non-contemporaneous ones. He therefore looked to a proletarian-led triple alliance of proletariat, peasantry and (another class with important levels of non-contemporaneity) the impoverished middle class, where the

'gold-bearing rubble' of the latter two classes would be transformed into revolutionary treasure.

When it comes to talking about the future – and better –
society, Bloch has to reconcile utopianism, and its connotations
of a completed goal, with his commitment to open-endedness,
where goals can only ever be provisional. He shares the Marxist
fear that utopias might foreclose the future, but the existence of
utopian dreams is at the very heart of his theory. Following
Marx, he talks in terms of negativities and generalities – future
society will not be certain things, while its positive dimensions,
insofar as they can be talked about at all, can be broadly extrapo-
lated from historical tendencies. However, it has to be said that
he goes beyond Marx in allowing his rich imagination to flesh
out so-called 'objective' potentialities. He delights in extracting
what he takes to be the futuristic kernel of truth in a vast range
of historical visions. Once again he creates an extensive and
overlapping conceptual vocabulary to aid him in this enterprise.
One can only give a flavour of these concepts and some of their
variable meanings. Concrete utopia we have already encountered. The term *Totum* conveys the all-embracing, integrative
totality of the goal, as well as the idea of the fulfilment of the
whole of the historical process. *All* suggests the plenitude of
being in the new society, while *Ultimum* evokes the idea of the
simultaneous culmination and transformation of time – the last
of class-ridden prehistory, and therefore the beginning of true
history in socialism (for the Ultimum is itself a Novum).

An image Bloch uses to suggest the transformed nature of
humanity in future society is the *Upright Gait* (*aufrechter Gang*,
sometimes translated as the *Upright Carriage*). Uprightness is
both a goal and a means to the goal. On the one hand, there
is the implied contrast with the bent-low gait of humanity in
class society, unable to fully extend themselves. Uprightness is
'the proper stature he has not yet achieved'.[130] On the other
hand, movement towards that goal requires people to abandon
their prone position: 'the first real trickle of life-force comes
from that principle within us which makes us stand up
straight',[131] clearly manifested, for example, in historical acts of
rebellion:

> The claim to the upright gait was within all rebellions;
> otherwise there would not be uprisings. The very word

uprising means that one makes one's way out of one's horizontal, dejected, or kneeling position into an upright one.[132]

He criticises Marxism for privileging exploitation over degradation, and thereby neglecting the demand for the upright gait. The classical natural law tradition, in contrast, has far better credentials in this respect: 'the wish of natural law was and is *uprightness as a right*.'[133]

Bloch also deploys that very evocative word in German culture, *Home* (*Heimat*). Since absence characterises humanity in class society, individuals are, in a sense, constantly in search of themselves. They are homeless. The not yet glimpsed by people is therefore a glimpse of coming home, but to a home that they have never yet occupied. Bloch concludes *The Principle of Hope* on this note:

> Once he has grasped himself and established what is his, without expropriation and alienation, in real democracy, there arises in the world something which shines into the childhood of all and in which no one has yet been: homeland (*Heimat*).[134]

The term is also meant to evoke the emotions and connotations of being at home, at ease, in comfort and of having a sense of belonging; of familiarity, freedom and so forth. Coming home is not meant to suggest finality or closure; home is the arena in which humanity will flourish: 'True genesis is not at the beginning but at the end.'[135]

Bloch also speculates about the possibility of a *natural subject*. He is hostile to crude anthropocentric conceptions of nature which reduce it 'to the level of an unconscious preamble, an unoriginal ante-room to man. Nature is not just chaff, or at best, raw material for the house of man.'[136] Given that matter is active and dynamic, and that consciousness in the shape of humanity has emerged out of it, is it not possible to conceive of further creative development in the realm of nature?

> Wouldn't it be really absurd to maintain that the vast moving universe and its motion, wholly unmediated with us in the multitude of its stars, has its 'continuation' *pure and simple* in the *existing* history of mankind, and has achieved its substantial goal in existing cultures?[137]

41

Furthermore, since the human cannot be radically separated from the natural, Bloch conceives of a creative interaction of the two in the home of the future:

> The more a technology of alliance... were to become possible... a technology of alliance mediated with the co-productivity of nature, the more certainly the creative forces of a frozen nature will be released again.[138]

Nature too has its not-yet, its totum and ultimum.

The complexity of such a universe, Bloch argues, requires that we abandon classical conceptions of space and time. Instead, models are required which articulate the variability and plurality of space and time. Bloch is attracted to the non-Euclidian conception of space developed by Riemann in which space is altered by local variables such as to make a traditional universal geometry inapplicable. He proposes, by analogy, 'a *kind of "Riemannian" time*'[139] where time is not deemed to be universal and unilinear, but rather contains a plurality of differing time scales corresponding to differing local contexts. Translated into the terms of his active universe, these differing times arise as a result of the variable dynamics of the material world. Time in music; work time, historical time and geological time are thus not reducible to an underlying common time but are rather intrinsic to the specific movement of each of these spheres. Consequently, temporal movement towards the not-yet will necessarily be variable:

> progress itself does not advance as a homogeneous succession of events in time; it moves forward on different levels of time that are below and above one another.[140]

However, he speculates, the interaction between humanity and nature in the future may involve the convergence of times, a temporal togetherness:

> The really common uniform time of the process of history and, indeed, of the world process, springs and is springing forth universally only as a temporal form of emergent identity: that is, of non-estrangement between men, and of non-alienation between men and Nature.[141]

All of this not-yet is, for Bloch, 'extra-territorial'. *Extra-territoriality* is meant to denote the element of otherness in possible futures. Since the not-yet by definition does not actually exist in the present it must be deemed to lie outside the present, to be extra-territorial to it. On the other hand, given that 'S is not yet P', extra-territoriality is inherent in the present, it is an aspect of the straining definition of the existent. Bloch therefore speaks of the 'core of the Earth as real extra-territoriality'.[142] It is the dimension of immortality in Bloch's system, since death cannot destroy that which has not yet come into being. The extra-territorial is beyond the ravages of the territorial.

Thus are we brought to the utopian heights of Bloch's metaphysics. It is important to grasp the systematic nature of Bloch's thought. Although specific aspects of Bloch's work will be investigated in the subsequent chapters of this study – culture, religion, Marxism and Fascism, natural law, utopianism and nature – from Bloch's perspective they are but elements in a whole. Bloch does not conceive of himself as a literary critic or a historian of utopias. These specific investigations are simply necessary components in the establishment of his new metaphysics – his new open-ended ontology of all being. None the less, one can reject Bloch's metatheory and still benefit from the specific investigations. There is a richness to the analyses which can survive scepticism of the general cast of the metaphysical system.

A good deal of criticism has been directed against the manner in which Bloch presents his ideas; clarity, it has been argued, has all too often been a victim of Bloch's philosophical approach and style. Some have argued that Bloch's stylistic radicalism has, at times, resulted in a slide into obscurity and opacity. Thus Jack Zipes speaks of the translation by Frank Mecklenburg and himself of Bloch's 'elliptical and metaphorical style', where, at times, Bloch's 'syntax and formulations were confusing and baffling', and concludes: 'it is sometimes impossible to understand Bloch, even when one has a firm command of German'.[143] Others argue that Bloch's system has to a greater or lesser extent become divorced from reality. J. K. Dickinson who, like Zipes, is sympathetic to Bloch, none the less calls Bloch a 'logocrat', which he defines as 'one who enjoys an illusion of being in control via mastery, as their creator, of words and/or abstract systems'.[144] From this perspective, Bloch creates a linguistic universe of a complexity unwarranted by the underlying reality:

'in dealing with reality Bloch created a world of words, connected at various points to reality, but in such a way that his mastery of words could substitute for a mastery of reality.'[145] Ronald Aronson gives this type of approach a considerably less friendly gloss. He argues that the three volumes of *The Principle of Hope* represent an attempt to enthuse people into belief, rather than convince them by reasoned argument, and that this in turn reflects Bloch's lack of grip on reality; his wild and obscure hopes simply could not survive rigorous analysis:

> *The Principle of Hope* is not only not written with the reader's understanding in mind . . . it seems rather to be written to be *not* understood . . . Bloch's hope is never argued. It cannot be, it no longer corresponds to the real world . . . I would suggest that this is why Bloch bludgeons us with his hope and overwhelms us with his learning, rather than treating his reader with – shall I say it? – democratic respect.[146]

One does have sympathy for these critics. It is the case that Bloch's distinctive style does cause problems of comprehension; though he is far from unique in this – for example, Adorno's linguistic subversion springs to mind. It is also the case, as should become clearer in the course of this study, that Bloch did have a shaky grasp on reality, especially in matters social and political. There is also both pedantry and a degree of posturing, pseudo-profundity. However, it is not possible to agree with Aronson's thesis that Bloch actively sought incomprehension. Aronson's focus is on *The Principle of Hope*, but Bloch produced much clearer presentations of his ideas in many other texts, where understanding is undoubtedly the aim. Nor is Bloch an Anglo-American philosopher; his approach has its roots in an alternative tradition, with its own distinctive methodology. Bloch, furthermore, is attempting an extremely ambitious project, nothing less than a systematic mapping of being and its forms; a degree of complexity inevitably comes with this territory, even if it is accepted that Bloch's conceptual innovation degenerates on occasions into conceptual promiscuity, and a self-indulgent density of argument. Beneath the pomposity and the naivety there is both genuine profundity and conceptual sophistication of a high order.

The juxtaposition of Bloch's life and concepts prompts the

question of whether there is a relationship between Bloch's philosophy and his defence of Stalinism. His son, Jan Robert, has posed the question starkly: 'Does Bloch's conduct regarding the Stalin trials express the structure of his thought?'[147] To those who see Bloch as a blinkered, unrealistic intellectual, the answer is clear – a non-empirical, speculative dogmatism at the philosophical level is mirrored in his forays into the political. For Aronson, Bloch's dogged defence of Stalinism betrays the fact that his thought is closer to religion than it is to philosophy; a stubborn hope against all evidence to the contrary: 'Bloch's thought is ultimately an all-inclusive faith in the dawning of a better world, one neither demonstrated nor demonstrable . . . a hope without reason.'[148] Jan Robert Bloch's critique starts from a different basis: a belief that there is a tension between the underlying humanism of the Blochian system and Bloch's attitude towards Stalinism; hence the anguished question: 'How is it possible that the revolutionary Humanum went along with inhuman despotism, the upright gait with the execution of the upright by the upright?'[149] His answer implicates a moral perfectionism in Bloch's work; he posits 'a moral system which clung abstractly and therefore relentlessly to the upright gait, though humans broke under its force', and speaks of Bloch's 'application of an unshaded moral category', whereby he 'transfigured the USSR into a revolutionary emblem, regardless of her immanent bloody reality'.[150] The question of Bloch's imputed lack of empiricism can itself be partially resolved through empirical means. To anticipate Chapter 4, Bloch's attitude towards Stalinism was both more nuanced and mutable than Aronson's proposition suggests: for example, in his later years, Bloch penned highly critical views of Stalinism, and within the same broad system of thought as in the days of his 'defence' of Stalinism. At the very least this suggests that the issue of Bloch's Stalinism cannot be simplistically read back into some supposed fatal flaw in the broader philosophical system. Bloch plumbed depths of irresponsibility in his relationship with Stalinism, but this should not be made the basis for a general indictment of his thought.

2

CULTURE

Even the most cursory glance at Bloch's texts will reveal the sheer amount of space he devotes to cultural analysis. Not only does he dedicate many chapters and sections of his writings to music, literature, theatre and the like; but cultural allusions also abound in material which ostensibly deals with other matters entirely. Culture is one of the great themes of Bloch's work; in this respect, he is at one with the general 'Western Marxist' understanding that the cultural realm sensitively registers the complex contradictions of social life, and that analysis of this sphere can provide genuine and profound insight into the fundamental dynamics of society and history. Bloch's attempts to grapple with culture pre-date his Marxism. In his early work, which culminated in *Geist der Utopie* (*Spirit of Utopia*, 1918), he sought to combine cultural analysis with another important and abiding theme, religion, in an anatomy of the utopian impulse. Simply put, his claim was that significant works of art embody powerful human aspirations and are therefore in the very vanguard of utopian forms; and although his subsequent Marxism led to many changes in his analyses of cultural forms, this basic belief remained undimmed. These subsequent developments offered an increasingly sophisticated analysis of the modalities of culture. The issues with which he deals include the production of culture; the historical forms of culture; the nature of cultural heritage, and the role of popular culture, together with specific analyses of disciplines, art forms and genres. Ultimately all these analyses are informed by his underlying utopian project: that the true meaning of cultural history lies in the future.

There are also tensions, fractures and contradictions in Bloch's cultural writings. He has very firm ideas as to what is gold and what dross in cultural production. He does appear to be operating with a notion of authentic culture. As we shall see, this culture is given a relatively catholic definition, to the extent that it includes both the products of great bourgeois art and the Expressionist work of the early decades of the twentieth century. None the less, it could be argued that there is a highly subjective exclusivity in this canon, which sits ill with an attempt to understand the complex dynamics of modern cultural production. Even in his subtle analysis of popular culture, a lack of empathy with modern American culture results in the ferocious castigation of jazz, Hollywood films and the like. This hostility to much of the culture of America also involves the deep tension in his work between his political defence of the USSR and his utopian hope and aspirations: his willingness to use the political term 'fascist' to indict some of the cultural production of the USA is evidence of this. He also puts himself in the invidious position of defending the USSR when he has no time for orthodox socialist realism, and he is sympathetic to an avant-garde condemned in Soviet cultural policy. His cultural analysis is therefore a far from seamless web.

CULTURAL PRODUCTION

Bloch was very much aware of the dangerous predisposition within Marxism towards reducing the cultural to the economic, and argued that many Marxists had succumbed to 'economistic', 'vulgar Marxist' interpretations. In a late work, *Das Materialismusproblem* (*The Problem of Materialism*, 1972), the octogenarian Bloch looked back over the inglorious history of Marxist approaches to culture: to the Second International reductionism of Mehring and Kautsky; to the way 'the Soviets robbed themselves of their great writers'[1] in their crude economic labelling of, for example, the 'aristocratic' Tolstoy and the 'literary representative' of the landowners, Gogol; Lukács too, Bloch's early friend and intellectual influence, is deemed to have fallen on occasions into 'schematism'. What underlies the poverty of such analyses is failure to grasp the complex nature of the cultural realm, its subtle 'mediations' and profound dynamics. Bloch asserts that any sensitive account of the cultural production of humanity has to recognise that 'cultural shift shows a creative, reflecting consciousness that demonstrates manifold ways of transformation'.[2] In short, 'Economics by itself cannot explain cultural history'.[3] This, of course, is not meant to signal a regression to 'idealist' conceptions of culture as an entirely independent spiritual realm. Economism and idealism, taken together, merely reproduce the old dualistic notion of matter and spirit.

Bloch seeks to overcome this dualism by refurbishing Marx's concept of labour – the 'work process' as cognitive/physical activity. The historical development of this process – manifested, for example, in differing divisions of labour – brings the cultural into play. Using the Marxist distinction between base and superstructure, which he acknowledges has often itself been invoked in vulgar reductions, he argues that a 'cultural superstructure' does emerge in the work process. Bloch wishes to designate this superstructure as a place, a *'topos'*, to suggest the idea of an area or arena which, to an extent, has its own parameters and dynamics. Clearly the contents of this *topos* must be ultimately derived from the broader work process and its contradictions, but they have their existence in a distinct site. In this site, transformations of material occur – not arbitrarily of course – but with a complexity and diversity indicative of the complications of the underlying social field. Furthermore, this *topos* outlives the work processes which gave birth to it, not merely temporally but also in the sense that it is, and remains, an infinitely renewable and vital resource: 'the ancient slave and feudal societies no longer exist, but this is not the case with Greek and medieval art. Both have experienced numerous revivals in history that bring out new problems and continue to show their validity.'[4] Bloch refers to this afterlife as the 'relative return of the cultural superstructure',[5] which provides the material for what is commonly referred to as the cultural heritage. In other words, 'that which has been creatively transformed in the cultural superstructure and assumes a particular form does not exhaust itself in the final account.'[6]

Bloch is particularly interested in the mode of transformation which, in effect, creates true consciousness out of false consciousness; work, which while displaying the marks of the age, none the less transcends it: 'something that surpasses the particular epoch in a utopian way.'[7] Bloch also describes this process as the production of *cultural surplus* (or *ideological surplus*). Cultural products always reflect the ideology of their time, but great culture has something else, something which is more than, and cannot be reduced to, mere ideology. In describing the individuals who achieve this type of transformation, Bloch uses a term not usually found in Marxist discussions of art: 'genius'. Marx is credited with the rejection of both the 'sober' and the 'exaggerated' view of the individual in history, and Marxism itself, with its eponymous founder, is adduced as proof of this proposition. Not merely is a Marxist category of genius proposed, but the historical uniqueness of these individuals is also asserted; whereas military leaders such as Cromwell and Napoleon are replaceable, creative geniuses are not. In defence of this far from self-evident proposition, especially from a Marxist perspective, Bloch is prepared to argue that there have been historical periods whose cultural potential has not been realised due to the lack of geniuses: 'when the specific talents necessary for the tasks were missing, the tasks went unfulfilled.'[8] As an example he offers the 'empty spot' in German painting after Dürer and Holbein; here, where a cultural tendency does not encounter a creative genius there is simply a 'blank page'.

Genius is therefore the explosive intersection of subjective capacity with objective tendency. It is this meeting alone which produces something of lasting value. The resulting cultural products will mirror this age but also, and crucially, they will embody the straining tensions of that age: 'great art or great philosophy is not only its time manifested in images and ideas, but it is also *the journey of its time and the concerns of its time if it is anything at all*, manifested in images and ideas.'[9] This will appear to its own time as a novelty, the creation of something genuinely new; but from a Blochian historical perspective the underlying element present here is the 'not-yet', the utopian absence propelling humanity into the true being of the future: 'it is that which is not yet fulfilled.'[10] The historical context structures the relationship between ideology and its surplus. When an ideology is still in its progressive mode, there is clearly going to be less drag at the cutting edge of its surplus. Beethoven's work in the context of the radical liberalism of the French Revolution is cited: 'as a musician of an ideology that was still revolutionary, Beethoven obtained significantly less ideology in a static-harmonious sense than he did in a dashing utopian sense.'[11] The Marxist goal of the classless society is interpreted, here, as the point at which cultural production will continue its utopian function stripped entirely of its ideological dimension. Culture, not cultural surplus, will remain, but a culture entirely different from the specialist realm of class society. Genius will flourish: 'the production itself of genius can first attain the power of its complete force of production in the world only after the elimination of ideology and all interest in illusion.'[12]

Bloch's emphasis on the new, the forward-looking, the not-yet, raises the question here, as throughout his work, of the status of the old. In this case it concerns the nature of cultural heritage – a term, as he was to say on a number of occasions, with an impeccable Engelsian pedigree. As ever, Bloch firmly sets his face against recollection. Recollection when applied to cultural production is condemned as 'historicism'; and historicism is the enemy of novelty, in that it is locked into the forms of the past, mesmerised by their power, and quite unable to move beyond them. Bloch cites as an example late nineteenth-century revivalism in architecture, with its belief that 'the previous history of architecture had already provided the essence of all buildings'.[13] Historicism is, in turn, distinguished from an even more pernicious approach – that of 'the plunderer, the historical pirate'[14] who perverts the past for special interests. Examples of this include 'the Nazi desecration of the past', itself exemplified in the work of the Nazi ideologue Alfred Rosenberg, and the 'sublime and pretentious explanation of history' found in the Stefan George Circle. In historicism, one has 'the sterile incarceration of history'; in the historical pirate, the 'falsification of pedigree'; both are condemned as ideologies of decadence.[15] In contrast, the fruitful approach is to develop further the living spirit of all that is most vital in the cultural production of the past. There has to be both continuity with the rich and still unfulfilled tendencies of the past, but also the discontinuity of new forward movement: 'one does not discover new parts of the world if one does not have the courage to lose sight of familiar shores. But everything that is alive from the old shores comes along in the process of the new.'[16]

Bloch stresses the differing historical modalities of cultural heritage. Adapting the Marxist three-stage classification of the emergence, maturity and collapse of modes of production, he speaks of the transmission of cultural heritage in terms of the rise, flourishing and decline of epochs. The most palpable and energetic development of this heritage occurs with the revolutionary rise of a class, when there is a process of wholesale appropriation, transformation and further creation of potent symbolism and imagery. The great cultural efflorescence at the time of the French Revolution is deemed to be a case in point. The resulting surplus is in turn available to the new revolutionary class – the proletariat. In the flourishing moment of a society, Bloch posits the predominance of a seemingly static art of 'composure... equanimity and ... crystal clarity';[17] the monumental architecture of ancient Egypt, Byzantine mosaics and the work of Giotto and Dante are cited. Yet even here, the pull of the not-yet is apparent; undoubtedly marked by the prevailing ideology, but present none the less. Bloch referred readers to his own analysis in *The Principle of Hope* of these 'wish-fulfilment landscapes in the sedate works'.[18] In the period of decline, dominant ideologies fall apart, and the new (together with the new within the old) emerges from the wreckage. Bloch considered his own *Heritage of Our Times* (1935) to be a nuanced account of this process in the 1920s and early 1930s, and later quoted his characterisation of the time in that text: 'It is precisely here that the richness of a time that is falling apart is great, the collapsing times of the 1920s mixed with dawn and dusk.'[19] Tony Phelan has pointed to some remarks Bloch made in 1974 about *Heritage of Our Times*:

> a heritage can be taken not only from periods of revolutionary ascendancy (hence the word *inheritance* [*Erbschaft*] in the title – the expression comes from Engels, 'cultural heritage' [*Kulturerbe*], and it is not philistine in origin), and not only from cultural 'golden ages', but ... we can and must become the inheritors of periods of so called decadence.[20]

Phelan makes the ingenious suggestion that Bloch is here distinguishing 'inheritance' (*Erbschaft*) from 'heritage' (*Erbe*), where the former refers to what is available and the latter to what is actually inherited. In support he quotes Bloch's 1935 Preface to *Heritage of Our Times*: 'Of course the aunt whose estate one wants to inherit must first be dead; but one can have a very good look round the room beforehand.'[21] Phelan concludes: 'the actual inheritance, is what should first be considered, for it is from these particularities that the heritage will be distilled.'[22]

MUSIC

Bloch always prided himself on his musical knowledge. Music had been one of his subjects at university; in his youthful friendship with Lukács he claimed that he had been the musical authority; and in his first book, *Spirit of Utopia* (1918), musical concerns fill a significant part of the text. He numbered conductors and composers among his friends and listened to, and wrote about, music throughout his life. Certain pieces in particular, most notably the trumpet call from Beethoven's *Fidelio*, touched his deepest levels of emotion and belief. His son, Jan Robert, recalled this effect:

> Florestan, Bloch's matador of the upright gait, sings: 'Words of truth I bravely uttered, and these chains are my reward.' Whoever knows Bloch knows the meaning of the trumpet signal for him. Everything was in it. Nothing moved him more. Florestan's 'To Freedom, to freedom in heaven above,' Leonora's answer to 'O, my Leonora, what have you endured for me?': 'Nothing, nothing, my Florestan!' brought tears to his eyes, made his voice catch.[23]

This biographical importance of music enters his theory in two main forms. First, there is extensive discussion of music in his work, combined with frequent musical references in analyses of other matters. As Adorno noted: 'The sphere of music takes up more space in Bloch's thought than in almost any other thinker, even Schopenhauer or Nietzsche.'[24] Second, Bloch makes some very large claims about the nature of music. Music is credited with capacities absent, or more muted, in other art forms. There is a sense in which music is the supreme art for Bloch. One of Bloch's former students at Leipzig, Manfred Riedel, called his teacher 'an Orpheus of the Talmud'; in his lectures he 'swore by the utopian out of the spirit of music, he would intone Mozart's *Magic Flute* . . . and, over and over again, the trumpet fanfare from Beethoven's *Fidelio*.'[25] In *Spirit of Utopia* this is expressed in still very mystical language. Together with its profoundly utopian content, the ambiguous status of music as both matter and non-matter gives it a unique artistic power in human development:

> Only the musical note, that enigma of sensuousness, is sufficiently unencumbered by the world yet phenomenal

enough to the last to return – like the *metaphysical* word – as a final material factor in the fulfilment of mystical self-perception, spread purely upon the golden sub-soil of the receptive human potentiality.[26]

Or, put more plainly: 'Whereas paint still adheres very strongly to real things and can therefore join them in insignificance, be emptied of spirit, the clash and resonance of sounding brass will spill over.'[27]

The Principle of Hope (1959) presents these ideas in their mature form. In looking back to the origins of music in this text, Bloch distinguishes music from noise; and this distinction is couched in class terms. Noise is the sound of the cultic instruments: the crude, authoritarian, 'whirring, drumming, rattling'[28] of the ruling class. Music emerges from the lower classes, from the shepherd and the pipe. Drawing on anthropological and mythic sources, Bloch paints an Arcadian picture in which the shepherd used the pipe as a means of communicating over distance to someone who was absent, particularly the loved one. Desire for that which is missing is therefore present at the very birth of music. The sounds themselves embody both the loss, *and* the musically recalled presence, of the beloved – the 'contradictory-utopian goal'[29] of music. In contrast to noise, *tonality* begins to emerge – 'a drawing of lines in the invisible'[30] – music as human expression. Bloch also hears all of this in Berlioz's *Symphonie Fantastique*, with its evocation of the girl of the artist's dreams who is 'both absent and musically present.... It is the unenjoyed which fills this ... music; the Not-Yet, indeed even the Never, likewise has its most characteristic existence from the air-roots of sound.'[31]

Music is able to express such things because the psychical is able to charge the physical with audible, comprehensible material. In melody the skilful composer enables the listener to anticipate later tones in earlier ones, and thereby speaks to the audience. Music, for Bloch, is more directly social than any other art form, or as he puts it in *The Principle of Hope*, 'no art is as socially conditioned as ... music'.[32] He elaborates three main claims out of this contention. First, dominant social ideologies deeply structure musical production and consumption:

To incipient free enterprise corresponds the dominance of the melody-leading treble and the mobility of the other voices, just as cantus firmus in the middle and graded polyphony corresponded to society divided into estates. No Haydn and Mozart... without their respective precisely varied social mandate; it extends from the form of performance right to the characteristic style of the tonal material and its composition, to the expression, the meaning of the content. Handel's oratorios... reflect rising imperialist England.... No Brahms without the bourgeois concert society.[33]

Second – and here the contradictory nature of music is stressed once more – the immediacy and directness of music makes it the most sensitive register of the desires and aspirations of the marginalised and dominated classes: 'music, by virtue of its so immediately human capacity of expression, has more than other arts the quality of incorporating the numerous sufferings, the wishes and the spots of light of the oppressed class.'[34] Third, music is deemed to be much richer in cultural surplus than any other art: 'no art has so much surplus over the respective time and ideology in which it exists.'[35] This is through the capacity of music to express the deepest levels of hope in humanity. It was this which made Bloch so reluctant in his early *Spirit of Utopia* to engage in the type of sociological analysis of music he later displayed in *The Principle of Hope*; a belief that 'it is surely not the essential part of music... which can be classified in terms of economics and sociology.'[36] He had then argued that 'it would be shallow to claim Gluck goes with the Louis Seize style, or Mozart with the Austrian Rococo'.[37] In *The Principle of Hope* Bloch rejects interpretations which seek to confine expressiveness to romantic music alone. He ranges widely in preromantic music, ancient, medieval and baroque, to demonstrate that 'expression... is immanent to good musical form'.[38] Nor is this linked to musical conservatism, for Bloch does detect expressivism in modern atonal and twelve-tone music, as in the case of Schoenberg and Berg. Bad music, however, does not have this capacity, and Bloch excoriates the sentimental romanticism of, for example, Tchaikovsky; and, as ever, seeks social explanations for this phenomenon: 'the broad bourgeoisie of the large towns with its need for amorphous nerve-stimulation, and... above all the petit bourgeoisie with its cut-price consumption of feeling.'[39] That which good music expresses is more than mere human subjectivity, rather it is the articulation of the deepest social tendencies. In music the great 'not-yet' can be glimpsed, but, echoing Marx on philosophy, music's fulfilment is a social act of the future: 'no one has yet heard Mozart, Beethoven, Bach as they truly call, name, teach; this will happen only much later, in the fullest after-ripening of these and of all great works.'[40] Great music is, therefore, 'extra-territorial', it cannot die because its real life lies in the future; it has a 'core which, because it has not blossomed, cannot pass away either'.[41] This is the immortal element in music. Thus music is, for Bloch, the pre-eminently utopian art form, 'the most utopian of all arts',[42] the pre-eminent form of 'pre-appearance': 'music is that art of pre-appearance which relates most intensively to the welling core of existence (moment) of That-Which-Is and relates most expansively to its horizon.'[43]

POPULAR CULTURE

One of the most striking aspects of Bloch's work on culture is his analysis of popular culture. The theoretical underpinning of his analysis is the contention that utopianism is constantly bubbling out in society, and therefore it is necessary to be attentive to all the points of emission. Fredric Jameson perceives a great hermeneutical project at the heart of Bloch's work; and using Paul Ricoeur's notion of a double hermeneutic, he identifies in Bloch both a negative ideology critique and a positive search for hidden meanings; for Bloch was keen to isolate the worthless and the reactionary – the ideological as well as the ideological surplus. Jameson creates a compelling image of the Blochian universe, which rightly hints of Kabbalistic notions of a world of enigmatic signs waiting to be read:

> for Bloch the world is an immense storehouse of figures, and the task of the philosopher or critic becomes a hermeneutic one to the degree that he [sic] is called upon to pierce this 'incognito of every lived instant,' and to decipher the dimly vibrating meaning beneath the fables and the works, the experiences and the objects.[44]

One should not, however, push this too far. Bloch baulked at any suggestion that the world was a text. His insistence on the open-ended nature of reality meant that the world could never be reduced to the closed confines of a book: 'it is only because of the really possible that the world is not made into a sophisticated book.'[45] The world as text only had meaning for the philosophers of recollection, notably Plato and Hegel, for whom there is no world historical novelty.

While great art contains highly sophisticated and profound utopian contents, the utopian impulse can be detected in a variety of popular cultural activities. Bloch's early, and life-long, love of the adventure stories of Karl May is but one manifestation of an abiding sense of the potential in the apparently cheap and tawdry. His wish to decipher, to read and to interpret the rich, complex 'signs' of life was a point of intersection between himself and Walter Benjamin in the 1920s and 1930s; though the precise nature of their intellectual relationship is not entirely clear. In the 1930s, when they began to drift away from one another, Benjamin even complained that Bloch had purloined some of his ideas. For a period in the 1920s, however, there was a good deal of common ground and mutual influence: Bloch described their relationship in Paris in 1926 as symbiotic. In his 'Recollections of Walter Benjamin' Bloch spoke of 'our shared sense for the particular and for the so often overlooked meaning of the peripheral in our observations of the small and the unnoticed', and of Benjamin's acute sense of the extraordinary in the ordinary. However, even in this late encomium (1966), one senses a degree of unease in Bloch's description of Benjamin's method as 'slightly uncanny . . . as if the world were a text', and in Bloch's attempt to spruce up Benjamin's revolutionary credentials in the claim that in Benjamin's *One Way Street*, 'attention to the peripheral is extended from observation and theory to include praxis'.[46] Whatever the technical differences in their interrogation of everyday life, the principal difference lay in what Rolf Wiggerhaus has identified as 'tone and general perspective':

> Bloch was cheerful, Benjamin was bitter. Bloch trusted in the indestructible rebellious character of ' "life", which has not yet come to fulfilment' in any period; Benjamin observed with despair what Kracauer called 'the dangerous game of the historical process, in which ever more had to be saved with constantly decreasing resources'.[47]

Liliane Weissberg makes the same point in respect to their differing interpretations of Andrea Pisano's 1336 Relief, *Spes* (Hope) (which, incidentally, is used to illustrate the front cover of Volume 1 of the English translation of *The Principle of Hope*). Benjamin 'recalls the female figure's inability to reach a desired fruit and describes her helplessness as truth. Bloch refers to the same relief as an image of false hope only.'[48]

The third part of *The Principle of Hope*, entitled 'Wishful images in the mirror', contains a fascinating survey of phenomena as varied as fashion and fairy-tale, travel and dance. Throughout this section, his emphasis is on the role of dreams in the production of culture. These are the dreams of the day, in which the not-yet-conscious can emerge, not those of the night, the Freudian realm of the no-longer-conscious. He explores the dream world of modern society – good dreams, bad dreams, vicious dreams, corny dreams, noble dreams, tawdry dreams. He tries to pick his way through this diversity, isolating the particular configuration of dreams in a wide variety of popular cultural forms. The ultimate analytical and political aim is to identify both the repressive dross in these activities and the nuggets of pure utopian gold. Bloch's analyses reveal strong prejudices, and a pronounced cultural conservatism; there is a wide chasm between the sensitivity of his approach and the coarseness of many of his judgements.

His starting point is personal display. Grooming and fashion are double-edged phenomena. Bloch rejects simplistic analyses which entirely condemn personal display as false consciousness generated by the economic needs of consumer capitalism. The element of seduction is acknowledged, but its success depends upon the existence of genuine wishes and desires: 'Lipstick, make-up, borrowed plumes help the dream of themselves, as it were, out of the cave. . . . [It is not] possible for someone to make themselves completely false; at least their wishing is genuine.'[49] This wishing, however, takes place in a distinct ideological universe, and therefore usually develops in a conventional, non-threatening manner. Social mobility, not social revolution, is the goal. In this context there is both diversity and standardisation – a plethora of consumer goods pander to day-dreams and fantasies, but the employee looks in the mirror 'with eyes which tell him how the boss wishes him to be'.[50] Other potential sites for personal development are themselves rendered harmless; in sport, for example, 'genuine wishes are felt here at the start'[51] (the progressive dimensions of competition), but these are siphoned off into mere games and leisure.

In the case of popular literature, Bloch distinguishes between entirely passive magazine and 'bestseller' material and the very different category of popular reading he terms 'colportage'. The former offer the disadvantaged the promise of happiness within capitalist structures, either in the form of 'how to succeed' features or through fictional evocations of rags-to-riches stories. They take the edge off unhappiness and thereby help to stabilise the status quo. Colportage, on the other hand, comprises popular adventure stories and tales of the amazing and the miraculous; Bloch groups this type of literature with fairy-tales and the exotic, imaginary world of circus; they are united by their utopian charge, grounded in the popular imagination. The class and ideological dimensions of this distinction are revealed by the low esteem in which colportage is held, whereby in comparison with 'the kitschy happiness of the magazine story' it is 'the far less passive colportage, which is ... detested by noble bourgeois conformists'.[52] In fairy-tales the whole world is qualitatively – and strikingly – other: 'a more colourful or lighter Elsewhere.'[53] The poor and the weak do succeed, right and reason are vindicated, but not within the framework of the given; great tasks have to be undertaken, whole orders overturned, while the rewards are correspondingly magnificent. In fairy-tales, objects become magical; time and space cease to be barriers; wishes become commands. The utopian element is palpable, and becomes even more self-consciously so as the fairy-tale elements become embodied in 'literary fairytales' (Hauff, Hoffman, Keller), where the theme is the pursuit of dreams. In fairy-tales, utopian images of nature abound, and distant paradises become backdrops for extraordinary events. This is the link to the world of the fair and the circus. These shows and spaces are arenas for other-worldly displays of grace, dexterity, the abnormal, the exotic. As with all these forms of popular culture, there is much that is unpleasant and disquieting, but it could not be otherwise. The utopian flower grows where it can: 'A bit of frontier-land is there ... but with preserved meanings, with curiously utopian meanings, conserved in brutal show, in vulgar enigmaticness. It is a world which has been too little investigated in terms of its specific wishful regions.'[54] As with colportage, this neglect and low esteem is

not innocent; Bloch refers to 'the irritation the bourgeois con-
formist feels about this time-honoured pleasure of youth and
folk'.[55] Finally, in colportage itself, in works such as the adventure stories of Bloch's great favourite, Karl May, utopianism
manifests itself in the adventurous winning of a glittering prize:
'the dream of colportage is: never again the everyday; and
at the end stands: happiness, love, victory.'[56]

Travel can be a utopian experience, both in anticipation of a
freely chosen journey and in the changed perceptions of the trip
itself. Bloch claims that in travel there occurs a 'defamiliariz-
ation', which is the opposite of alienation. Objects experienced
in the new conditions of travel lose their familiarity and become
strange and vibrant – one begins to see with a painter's eye.
Travel also rearranges the relationship between space and time,
for as the scenery unscrolls before one, it is space that moves,
and time that is filled, as in the very best of adventure stories.
If the journey is with a loved one, utopianisation is reinforced
by an eroticisation of the landscape. Not surprisingly, therefore,
travel can unleash great artistic creativity. Even the experience
of homesickness can have a utopian dimension in that it defam-
iliarises one's habitual home and paints it in utopian colours.
However, travel has been corrupted by tourism which by organ-
ising it thoroughly, robs it of its utopian moments. In tourism
we take our home with us and there is thorough familiarisation:
'Since the journey has become comfortable, it does not take us
so far any more. It takes more homely habitual material with it
and penetrates into the custom of the land even less than
before.'[57] If the utopian can be found in geography it can also
be found in history. Bloch perceives in the collecting of antiques
a utopian protest against the mass-produced shoddiness of
modern consumer goods. Antiques 'are witnesses of a formal
certainty destroyed by capitalism, surviving flotsam from a lost
beauty'.[58] Bloch refers to the 'ruin-magic', the 'ruin-ciphers' of
these precious fragments and satirises the nineteenth-century
desire to reproduce the Venus de Milo with replacement arms.
Great antiques survive, modern production merely decays:

> It is the sign of something poorly built, therefore of most
> of the new gadgets and streets, that it cannot grow old,
> but only rots in the course of the years. And equally it
> is the sign of something innately precious that after an

appropriate time it joins up with the great old inheritance and is worthy of it.[59]

Dance, at its best, can be a richly utopian activity. In dance, the contours of a better existence are outlined in physical movement:

> The dance allows us to move in a completely different way to the way we move in the day, at least in the everyday, it imitates something which the latter has lost or never even possessed. It paces out the wish for more beautifully moved being, fixes it in the eye, ear, the whole body, just as if it already existed now.[60]

He is quite convinced as to which forms of modern dance do not manifest this quality. A tirade is launched against jazz:

> Nothing coarser, nastier, more stupid has ever been seen than the jazz-dances since 1930. Jitterbug, Boogie-Woogie, this is imbecility gone wild, with a corresponding howling which provides the so to speak musical accompaniment. American movement of this kind is rocking the Western countries, not as dance, but as vomiting.[61]

He detects a more promising, though still limited, development in the natural dance of Isadora Duncan, with its attempt to 'demonstrate a more beautiful image in the flesh'.[62] He is particularly drawn to folk dancing, where naturalness never left: 'the only place where people moved naturally . . . the content it signifies is joy beyond the day of drudgery.'[63] At the other end of the spectrum there is the authentic dance of the classical ballet, with its precise and graceful movements. If jazz provided him with an opportunity to express his dislike of modern American culture, folk and ballet allowed him to articulate his defence of Soviet Russia: 'the ballet is the school of every thought-out dance; it is no coincidence that it is flourishing in the Soviet Union together with the folk-dance, this other colourful-peasant genuineness',[64] and that the two forms mutually enrich one another. Not surprisingly he also sees some merit in Expressionist dancing, though he feared its 'night-side' linkages with Fascism, 'alongside its utopian glare or brightness'.[65]

Bloch also reflected upon the cinema. He considered the early silent films as a creative development of the ancient art of pantomime, an art which had declined in the mid-nineteenth century, but which had the capacity to express material that could not be uttered in words. He referred to Asta Nielsen, 'the first great film actress', who, 'with a flicker of the eyelid, a raising of the shoulder, possessed the art of expressing more than a hundred mediocre poets put together'.[66] Such silent eloquence was enhanced by the technical capacities of the new medium; Griffith's use of the close-up enabled the face to show a whole gamut of emotions in a way that was impossible in the theatre; objects themselves could become mimetic, as in Eisenstein's stamping boots on the Odessa steps. The addition of sound, paradoxically, increased the mimetic element in film as a whole new set of associations were conveyed via the soundtrack: 'drumming of raindrops on the window, a silver spoon dropped on a stone floor, creaking furniture reach into a micrological world of sensory perception and of expression.'[67] All of this is to be distinguished from the 'incomparable falsification'[68] of Hollywood; 'the dream-factory in the rotten and in the transparent sense'.[69] Bloch launches into another of his crude invectives against American culture:

> In Hollywood, as we know, it is so far removed from such work of enlightenment that it almost exceeds the crudeness and mendacity of the magazine stories; thanks to America the film has become the most desecrated form of art. The Hollywood cinema does not only supply the old kitsch . . . it also uses this kitsch for ideological stupefaction and fascist incitement. . . . [T]he dream-factory has become a poison-factory, no longer only for the purpose of dispensing escapist utopia . . . but also White Guard propaganda.[70]

The way forward for progressive film-making is to use the technical flexibility of the medium to articulate the fragmentary nature of the decaying bourgeois order. Film must respond to this 'period of cracked surface, of the previous groupings and identities decaying . . . the time of a not only subjectively, but objectively possible montage'.[71]

Popular culture is therefore a field of dreams. This gives Bloch hope, for although many of these dreams contain illusion, the act of dreaming is indicative of an inner vigour, a stubborn desire for happiness. The real enemy of humanity is therefore not illusory dreaming but nihilism, the loss of the capacity to dream at all. Good dreams can develop out of bad, but nothing

emerges from despair: 'artificially conditioned optimism . . .
is . . . not so stupid that it does not believe in anything at all. . . .
For this reason there is more possible pleasure in the idea of a
converted Nazi than from all the cynics and nihilists.'[72]

EXPRESSIONISM

It is worth looking at the relationship between Bloch and
Expressionism. Expressionism marked the young Bloch indel-
ibly, and this aesthetic of his youth reverberated throughout his
subsequent writing career. There is a continuing Expressionist
legacy in the style, form and content of Bloch's writing: the
prefatory gnomic utterances, the strange juxtapositions of
material, the recourse to the striking exemplar. Much of the
(frequently infuriating) oddity of Bloch's texts can be explained
in terms of this inheritance. Furthermore, Bloch's defence of
Expressionism, particularly in the 1930s, provides an insight into
his cultural theory, and especially into his work on literature
and painting.

Bloch's undoubted fondness for German idealist aesthetics
has misled some commentators into believing that he did not
appreciate modernism. Habermas, in a 1963 essay, 'Between
philosophy and science: Marxism as critique', claims that 'the
most recent developments in art, literature and music must seem
particularly unfruitful' for Bloch; this was because, 'like Hegel,
Bloch still adheres to the classicist aesthetics and to its central
concept of the symbolic'. Bloch's supposed position is unfavourably contrasted with the 'allegorical' approach of Walter Benjamin, with its focus on 'the cracks and crevices of a world torn
apart mercilessly into its representations'.[73] Habermas, in a later
essay, effectively subsumes the aesthetics of Bloch and Marcuse
under the same 'idealist aesthetics' category, in that, in almost
identical terms, he beats Marcuse with the stick of 'allegorical'
Benjaminism.[74] Whatever the truth of this assertion in respect of
Marcuse, it is entirely inappropriate in the case of Bloch; in fact,
as we shall see, Habermas' description of Benjamin's stance
could almost be taken as a summary of Bloch's own analysis of
Expressionism. Sándor Radnóti makes a different, but related
point. He acknowledges that 'Bloch is one of the first to give a
philosophical basis to avantgardism';[75] however (and here he
follows Habermas), because of Bloch's idealist aesthetics, differ-

ences in artistic form are of little consequence. Bloch's concern is with the substantive content of works of art – the passenger, so to speak, not the vehicle. His evidence, such as it is, is drawn from a passage in *Spirit of Utopia*: 'More important than the fact that the bystanders hear singing when a man cries out in the fiery belly of the Pharsalian bull ... are the cries themselves, their undeflected genuineness and depth.'[76] Radnóti concludes: 'Art as art interests Bloch very little in the philosophical context of *Spirit of Utopia*.'[77] Now, as we have seen, Bloch does, in this early work, resist all attempts to sociologise music; but it is highly improper to infer from this that Bloch was indifferent to form, then or subsequently. In short, one of the central attractions, possibly even *the* central attraction of Expressionism for Bloch, was its radical use of form.

Bloch's category of Expressionism is wide and elastic. Among the core group he includes painters such as Klee, Kandinsky, Chagall, Kokoschka, Dix and Grosz, and poets such as Trakl and Heym. Other individuals and movements are related in terms of association, parallels or affinities – the young Brecht, the photomontage artist Heartfield, elements of surrealism, Picasso's cubism, Schoenberg's serialism, and so on. This broadness reflects partly the diversity of the phenomenon itself and partly Bloch's broad use of the word: Expressionism as both historical movement *and* approach. There are the self-conscious members, and there are those who partake of its spirit. Bloch considers 1912 to 1922 to be the formative period, and includes his own *Spirit of Utopia* of 1918 as one of its products.

In the 1930s Bloch sought to defend Expressionism against Communist charges that it was essentially a reactionary movement. He found it paradoxical that this left-wing characterisation of Expressionism as 'Fascistic' or 'Imperialist' should occur at the very moment when the Nazis were condemning it as 'decadent'. His fire was directed at a number of Moscow-based writers, but his principal target was the person he considered to be the heavyweight among them – his former intellectual partner, Georg Lukács. Part of Bloch's critique was an attack on Lukács' sloppy methodology, but also, at a deeper level, his critique contested the Hungarian's very concept of 'realism'. In respect of the first of these, Lukács is criticised on a number of counts:[78] he fails to discuss a single Expressionist painter when, in Bloch's view, the painters are even more characteristic of the movement than are the writers; he considers a small, highly selective and consequently unrepresentative group of Expressionist writers, and even includes some who could not be so described, and he relies on literature about Expressionism rather than considering the art forms directly. Even more seriously, Lukács is deemed to have caricatured the ideological nature of Expressionism, ignoring the radical, even revolutionary aspects of the movement, relying instead on clichés about its supposed 'petit-bourgeois' composition. Bloch himself is aware of the darker side of Expressionism, but suggests that it merits a nuanced analysis and not mere undifferentiated sociological reductionism.

The more fundamental level of disagreement lay in what Bloch considered to be Lukács' inadequate understanding of realism. In a 1935 essay, 'Marxism and poetry', Bloch posed the question: why do so many Marxist creative writers feel that they are sacrificing imagination for reality? His answer was that here was a fundamental misunderstanding of what the 'real' comprised. A pernicious tendency had developed which reduced the portrayal of reality to semi-journalistic accounts of the surface level of life, and in particular, the 'real' life of the proletariat. Style, form and content were reduced to merely one dimension. 'Realism' and 'Naturalism' were the credo of this approach. For Bloch this was an entirely impoverished understanding of reality, for it excluded the incredibly complex and contradictory dynamics which make up the real. In terms of positive aspects, for example, such a flat view excluded the life of the imagination and of the emotions, the very real world of dreaming which had made earlier poetry such a vibrant and vital art form. Artists suffer, reality suffers. Today,

> naturalistic directness is praised as a manner of writing and as subject matter, the simple realism that kills the spirit, love and the same without much ado. Such writing and subject matter confine reality mainly to what has become real for the proletariat these days, and neither acknowledges any historical remains nor any dream, even if it existed objectively.... 'Leave everything behind' appears as a permanent inscription above the door to Marxism.[79]

Lukács' problem, Bloch maintains, is that he too has succumbed to an impoverished realism. Lukács enjoins a neo-classical realism to present the totality of modern capitalism. Unfortunately, capitalism is not the sort of closed totality which Lukács imagines it to be; rather, it is open-ended and fragmentary, and cannot therefore be captured by a form of classical realism: 'Lukács presupposes everywhere a closed coherent reality. . . . But perhaps Lukács' Reality . . . is not so objective at all . . . perhaps genuine reality is also – interruption.'[80]

From Lukács' 'realist' perspective, Bloch argues, Expressionism will seem chaotic and subjective, when in fact this approach has been the most successful to date in expressing the most profound dynamics of the modern era. Since for Bloch reality is an open-ended process which humans must complete, the poetic must be the creative interaction with the underlying movement of the period: 'Genuine poetry deals with *process*, isolating and manipulating the facts.'[81] In late capitalism the totality of the past, which classical realism ideologically expressed, has exploded, and bourgeois artists such as Joyce and Proust express this fragmentation from one aspect. The Expressionist inheritance provides the Left with a means to express this from a positive perspective. In this sense 'Expressionism is not yet at an end, because it has not yet been started on at all.'[82] Montage is the appropriate response to a fragmentary age: 'Montage can now do a lot, previously only thoughts lived easily alongside each other, now things do too, at least in the flood area, in the fantastic primeval forest of the void.'[83] Montage is the 'hollow space'[84] in which the new might emerge. At the time, Bloch saw elements of the new art for which he was looking in Brecht and Weill's *Threepenny Opera*. It expressed the contradictions of the era by mixing and subverting forms, simultaneously describing, satirising, undermining and hoping:

> Various features mingle, rub together. The angular tone and the bad atmosphere, the closed number and the rebellious content. The simplified means of expression and the extremely many-voiced dream of Pirate Jenny, the happy melodies and the blossoming desperation; finally a chorale that explodes. The song does not act, but reports on the situation, like the old aria; but without exception it reports a cursed situation.[85]

Of course, Bloch argues, such pieces might merely be received as enjoyment, and reality itself can only be changed by hard political activity; however, citing Adorno, he maintains that if revolutionary art 'cannot change society', it 'can nevertheless ... indicate its change in advance, by "absorbing" and speaking aloud what is dissolving and forming under the surface.' In particular, it 'illuminates the impetuses of those who march into the future even without music, but more easily with it'.[86] Adorno, in turn, recognised that Bloch's own *Spuren* (Traces) of 1930 was an Expressionist text, noting that:

> Bloch's philosophy is the philosophy of Expressionism. It holds to Expressionism in its idea of breaking through the encrusted surface of life.... The intention of his philosophy is objective, but its speech remains unabatedly expressionist. As thought, it cannot remain a pure verbal expression of immediacy.[87]

Lukács' response to Bloch later in the same year (1938) missed the point, but did so in an instructive manner. The Hungarian maintained that Bloch's defence of montage amounted to a relativist conception of cultural heritage, in which the various components were reduced to equivalent images:

> If one leafs through the writings of Bloch, one will find him mentioning [cultural heritage] ... only in expressions like 'useful legacies', 'plunder', and so on. ... In his eyes it is a heap of lifeless objects in which one can rummage around at will, picking out whatever one happens to need at the moment. It is something to be taken apart and stuck together again in accordance with the exigencies of the moment.[88]

This, clearly, is not what Bloch intended; he truly believed that he was engaged in the revolutionary appropriation of a living and historical heritage. Lukács' underlying argument was that Bloch's defence of Expressionism was an under-theorised privileging of a marginal artistic movement; Bloch had failed to look at the objective dynamics of modern capitalism:

> Bloch ... ceases to concern himself with the objective relations between society and the active men of our time.... Instead, taking the isolated state of mind of a specific class of intellectuals as his starting point, he con-

structs a sort of home-made model of the contemporary world. . . . Bloch fails to make reality his touchstone.[89]

Over twenty years later, Lukács was still making the same point when he described a book which Bloch had recently published, as being 'composed of a subjectivism which pretends to be objective and a very poor and abstract objectivity'.[90] Now, Lukács' 'objectivity' was itself grounded in a sterile Marxism-Leninism, but the observation is not without a sting. It does raise the question of the status of Bloch's notions of cultural inheritance and ideological surplus. We shall return to this question at the end of the chapter.

LITERATURE AND THE PORTRAYAL OF REALITY

The critique of Lukácsian realism was, therefore, an aspect of the broader issue of the artistic representation of reality. In a 1956 essay, 'On the present in literature', Bloch considered this matter with respect to literature. Drawing on a Marxist theory of ideology he makes an initial distinction between 'writing in keeping with the times' and 'writing according to life'.[91] The former type of writing responds to market needs and reproduces the belief system of the time in the form of the ideological 'period novel'. As this needs a degree of ability, it is therefore to be distinguished from a third category: literature so mediocre that it cannot even express these surface features. Since ideology is a category of historical materialism, Bloch wishes to set these distinctions into a historical framework. Given that Marxist insight into the nature of reality is a relatively recent occurrence, earlier writers clearly could not avail themselves of it. It is therefore a mark of greatness that some writers were none the less capable of penetrating deeply into the dynamics of their age; as in the case of 'Balzac's incomparable art of painting the attitude of *Enrichissez-vous* (Enrich yourself)'[92] of the bourgeois France of his day – though even he did not understand the true nature of the age. Such insight is possible because although knowledge of historical materialism is of relatively recent vintage, the process it describes is as old as reality itself; and therefore great artists are capable of perceiving and representing process movement. The hallmark of such endeavours is the

profound artistic expression of the critical and the utopian.
Balzac was thus

> helped by two resources that were also effective at a time
> when a Marxist analysis of the situation, or analysis of
> the 'current,' could not be applied. These resources were
> *Criticism to the point of satire* and *humane utopia*; both in
> fact were resources not just as mere subjective additives
> but at their best as the detected ingredients within the
> social reality itself.[93]

Satirical criticism reveals closeness to the reader, while the utopian adds the broader perspective and the longer view, and
together they comprise 'critical realism'.[94] The great writers of
this tradition, including Flaubert and Dickens, Dostoyevsky and
Tolstoy, were linked by a 'unifying theme: how to master the
present in a poetical way'.[95] In the fragmentation of the late
bourgeois period, latter-day adherents such as Robert Musil and
Thomas Mann found it increasingly difficult to hold the form
together. Critical and utopian artistic devices had to be used to
the very limit to cope with the ever-increasing gaps and silences:

> The socially determined lack of perspective in the late
> bourgeois novel brought about even more obstacles . . . this
> is why Robert Musil and Thomas Mann (in whose works
> the revolutionary proletariat is not even marginally visible)
> endeavoured even harder to employ the powers of critical
> satire and human utopia.[96]

Furthermore, the emergence of Marxism made this position less
and less defensible. Marxism presents the possibility of a new
configuration of the critical and the utopian; for 'only this analysis will have success in turning criticism that has mounted to
satire into something truly biting, which is to say, to lead it
beneath the surface of the symptoms and to make utopia concrete.'[97] As possible literary representatives of this new context,
Bloch suggests Gorky and Brecht – one representing the process
in the context of the Russian Revolution, the other in the context
of declining capitalism. However, in his writings of the 1950s
and beyond, the cultural excitement evident in his 1930s writings is no longer present. He acknowledges that there has been
very little good socialist literature. In the West, most literature
'regards only the grand hotel called sadness as the field mostly

for its muse',[98] while socialist writers, 'even in the great art of Anna Seghers ... do not come close to the other side of the homelessness'.[99] A self-consciously modern, critical-utopian (i.e. socialist) literature has failed to emerge.

Bloch also interrogates literature through an examination of specialised genres. Two companion pieces of the early 1960s are 'A philosophical view of the detective novel' and 'A philosophical view of the *Künstlerromans* (artist novel)'.[100] As with all of Bloch's literary analysis (and indeed, the entirety of his formal analysis) texts are treated as both material entities in a social and historical field *and* as bearers of more or less profound meanings. Appreciation of the complexities of the former makes him wary about over-schematising the latter. The questions he puts to the detective novel are therefore different from those he addresses to the artist novel. In the first case, he wants to know why the detective novel is so popular among all classes, whereas in the second, his work on the artist novel is primarily concerned with the genesis and form of this genre. None the less, he manages to unite the studies around two themes: the emergence of modern genres, and the nature of the distinction between critical backward-looking and utopian forward-looking.

The two genres are considered modern formations, the products of the period ushered in by the successful bourgeois revolutions of the eighteenth century. The detective novel was only made possible by the introduction of bourgeois juridical practices. Prior to this, evidence was considerably less important than confession and status, and without the centrality of evidence there was no overwhelming need for detection; there was, consequently, no space for the detective as hero. In the case of the artist novel, the ancient and medieval worlds had no imaginative involvement with the lives of their artists; it was only with the *Sturm und Drang* and subsequent romanticism of bourgeois individualism that the creative biography of the artist was explored. Bloch is even prepared to countenance the claim that both genres were first developed by the same individual – E. T. A. Hoffman – who 'created the first detective story in *Fraülein von Scudéry,* and then ... produced the first figures of the novel of the artist ... in *The Golden Pot*'.[101]

Bloch attributes the success of the detective novel to the attractions of its three main characteristics: guessing, discovering and what Bloch refers to as the 'un-narrated factor'.[102] Guessing provides intellectual excitement; it invites 'the reader's competition with the detective in the quest of the probable right clue'.[103] The act of discovery brings other factors into play. There is in the clue delight in the specific, the incidental, both as a pleasure in itself and as the royal road to the general, the big picture; in short, a whole host of pleasures at the 'micrological' level. The depiction of the detective as characterful (even eccentric), deliberative, moral and of a private status creates an attractive and imaginative contrast with the routine, possibly corrupt world of the official police force; it plays to fantasies of the triumphant outsider. The detective novel also grounds the method of detection in the models of the period:

> Holmes, *fin de siècle*, utilizes the scientific-inductive method ... Hercule Poirot, on the other hand ... intuits the totality of the case in accordance with the increasingly irrational modes of thinking characteristic of late bourgeois society. Thus Bergson and totality theory have triumphed over J.S. Mill and the mere aggregation of particulars in the realm of the detective novel as well.[104]

This type of novel is also in tune with the alienated conditions of modern capitalism. It is often the least suspicious person who proves to be the culprit, and their unmasking speaks of 'the interchangeability of all people who have become faceless'.[105] In a positive sense this links detective fiction with the critical dimension in great literature and science. In both Ibsen and Freud there is a refreshing uncovering of '*subjectively* false consciousness', while '*objectively* false consciousness' is unmasked by Marx. The detective glance therefore becomes a metaphor for the critical disposition; the probing of present and past for the authentic, the real, the progressive: 'detection techniques ... have the effect of nitric acid in the testing sense: they dissolve false gold, rendering that which remains ... unmistakably recognizable.'[106]

The third characteristic of the detective novel – the 'un-narrated factor' – is called 'that most decisive factor, which separates the detective novel from all other narrative forms'.[107] This is the fact that the crime has occurred before the narrative: 'the story arrives on the scene with the corpse.'[108] The theme of the detective story, its unique theme according to Bloch, is thus the discovery of something which has happened outside the narrative. A hidden internal/external reality has to be discovered. All other literary forms integrate such acts into the narrative, so that we witness them in real time, or deploy flashbacks or recoups, where the material is merely previously undisclosed, not hidden. Again, Bloch relates this element in detective fiction, 'the darkness at the beginning',[109] to more sophisticated cultural forms. He refers to the 'oedipal element' in such narrative – where a character finally comes to learn of some terrible or mysterious past event profoundly relating to themselves. More broadly it speaks of the condition of all those who grow up in a world not of their direct choosing, where knowledge of the truth is both necessary and frequently horrific. The critical backward-looking glance is therefore a fundamental component in any serious, radical project; and in detective stories, 'the poor relatives',[110] these signs are available to the general reading public.

The artist novel, in contrast, lacks a common form. The only exception to this characterisation that Bloch is willing to entertain is that the form has some unity because it does not depict the content of the respective artist's production – the 'omitting of the ending, of unproffered fruit';[111] yet on the other hand, as he admits, Mann's *Doctor Faustus* is able to *suggest* these contents. Bloch attributes this formal diversity to the lack of great defining exemplars. There is no *formal* equivalent to *Oedipus Rex*. This has cut two ways, for while the artist novel has never been as popular as the detective novel, neither has it been as generally debased as the more demotic form. Bloch situates the artist novel in the second part of the critical-utopian function. In the detective novel there is the interrogation of the past; in the artist novel there is the equally necessary creation of the future: 'Investigative uncovering is indeed only one aspect, aimed at the origin. Investigative edification is the other, aimed at the destination. There, the finding of something that has been, here, the creation of something new.'[112] Although Oedipus has no *formal* equivalent in this genre, he does have a parallel archetype in the figure of Prometheus. Prometheus, a figure frequently invoked by Bloch, is the great mythic exemplar of the pull of the not-yet, of *human* creativity, aspiration and daring. Bloch perceives the Promethean in these various fantasies of struggling artists. The two genres combined, the detective novel

71

and the artist novel, thus embody the figure of the critical-utopian:

> if the action of the detective story – from the beginning of
> *Oedipus* – is concerned with revealing a *past crime*, with
> revealing it, then the action of the *artist* story – from the
> beginning of *Prometheus*, even to the legend of the *building
> of the tower* of Babel – concerns itself with the *formation of
> the human*, with revealing this. The detective story depends
> on penetrating and digging up material, while the inven-
> tive story depends on revealing and shaping it in the not-
> yet and out of the not-yet that arises before us as that of
> the work.[113]

THE THEATRE

In *The Principle of Hope* Bloch begins his discussion of the theatre
by examining what people expect when they visit a theatre.
Some attend out of boredom, hoping to be diverted. Some,
however, 'a better active section',[114] seek something more – freedom; freedom in a positive not a negative sense: 'free, not
automatically, or simply free from something, but free to do
something.'[115] Both groups enter the theatre, however, because
they share a common need, called by Bloch the 'mimic need'.[116]
This is rooted in the desire to transform oneself; the actor too
possesses this desire, and acts out this wish for the audience as
a whole. In performance, the play gives 'a sensually colourful,
eloquently moved representation of something'.[117] The active
spectator is drawn in, and begins to participate in this remarkable, enhanced world:

> The curtain rises, the fourth wall is missing, in its place is
> the open proscenium and behind this show-side things
> must happen, in a pleasant, entertaining way, significantly,
> that is signifying Something. From the life we have had
> the narrowness disappears ... remarkable and decisive
> people, a further scene, powerful fates now appear. The
> spectator is prepared in an equally expectant and involved
> way for the things which are now to come.[118]

The performance of a play imposes activity on the audience. The
institution of applause (or its lack, or its opposite – the boo and

catcall) requires that a decision be made by the audience on both players and play. This involves a physical act of clapping or shouting. Thus for Bloch, it is a much more involved activity than is required to read a book. The live response to live activity is of a different order to silent reading, and in this sense deepens the judgement made. Judgement is also group judgement, it is not merely the response of an isolated reader; there is 'a formal assembly of voters in every theatre, whereas there is as a rule only a single reader confronting the book'.[119] Powerful theatre, and here Bloch has the work of Brecht in mind, builds on these aspects to reintegrate the theatrical experience into the broader world. The judgements generated, with their criteria of what could be, can re-enter the world, 'beyond the evening in the theatre... into life that can be better effected... into the things which in the bolder sense of the word are to come'.[120] Bloch endorses the basic Brechtian techniques: active but not direct engagement on the part of the audience; a degree of distance between actor and character; the estrangement effect whereby dramatic effects jolt the audience out of conventional responses; and the use of open-ended devices such as alternative endings so as to make the play a probing experiment. This approach is contrasted with 'schematism', which 'has already learnt the region that is accessible to it by heart with five or six formulas or hurrah-conclusions; which is also why it hates the Brechtian'.[121] No example is provided of 'schematism', but his use of the term elsewhere would suggest that he has socialist-realist theatre in mind.

Bloch believes that there are already pre-existing openings in drama. The intense portrayal of a character, as of Hamlet, brings out its internal contradictions – the possibility of different outcomes, different choices; great dramatic creations can, therefore, partake of the 'experiment of a Being-able-to be-different, Being-able-to-act-differently, Being-able-to-end-differently'.[122] Likewise, great theatre uses beauty and pleasure to open up the Promethean elements in those touched by its magic. And it is the sheer materiality of the theatre which brings this out – the physical, sensual, playing out and revealing:

Thus the theatre, in contrast to the book, is the sensual-reality in which unheard things are publicly heard, in which what is remote from experience-reality becomes vividly public, in which the composed-compressed, the full-filled really appears, as if it were in the flesh.[123]

It is above all 'mime' which is central to this experience. Mime articulates the poetry of the theatre. As in his discussion of film, Bloch extends the meaning of mime to cover the audible and the inanimate. There is thus besides the 'gestural mime' of the actors, the 'spoken mime' (a term he attributes to the philosopher and preacher Schleiermacher) of the text, and the 'aura mime' of the scenery.[124] 'Illusion' is of importance here; the 'stage is ... more appearance than any other mode of art'.[125] This is however deemed to be a source of strength, for, following the aesthetics of Schiller and Kant, illusion which is grounded in 'the reality of purpose' ceases to be mere subjective illusion; and it is precisely Bloch's contention that the 'sincere appearance of the stage is ... least detached from the reality of purpose; it is instead its promotion through festivity'.[126]

Bloch has decided ideas on how, in works of an earlier period, drama should be staged to bring out the gold-bearing seams. He distinguishes between false and genuine topicalisation. False topicalisation tries to ignore the historical dimension of drama by forcefully wrenching works out of context and artlessly modernising them. This is to be found in both modern bourgeois production and certain forms of socialist theatre:

> it is not easy to find a more fatuous piece of nonsense than the idea of playing Hamlet in a dinner-jacket ... or the idea of setting the first act of 'Tales of Hoffman' in a chrome-nickel bar. Or even of putting Schiller's robbers in proletarian garb and giving Spiegelberg a Trotsky-mask.[127]

Genuine topicalisation stages the piece in such a way that it speaks to the present age as a product of the past. This involves both preservation and novel artifice: 'a new perspective and one newly worked into it, but in such a way that the time-aroma of the writing and its stage-set never drifts away.'[128] The tendencies and contradictions written in by the original author are to be fully expressed via modern dramatic methods. The stage-set must therefore 'be changed to the point of recognition, to the recognition in fact of the class conflicts which take place in it and which have only now become ripe for expression'.[129] In the case of the stage-text, false topicalisation consists in modern interpolations and additions which try to turn the play into the 'modern and relevant' piece it clearly is not. In contrast it is legitimate to cut, adapt and even complete a play, if there are elements which are 'dusty . . . immature and unfinished',[130] so long as this is done by someone of the same stature as the author – as in Karl Kraus' rescue of Offenbach. Here, renovation is a form of 'after-ripening' of the work, enabling the emergence of 'the lasting resounding power and topicality of great dramas in the direction of daybreak'.[131]

Along with the sensitive renovation of old drama there must also be new plays. New, significant work cannot simply reproduce the old themes. These themes bear the ideological imprint of their age. The adherence of the classic tragedy to Aristotelian canons reveals the element of social repression. The arousal and catharsis of the emotions of fear and pity centred on the suffering hero, privileges suffering over rebellion and under the sign of fate. The proper themes of socialist tragedy are defiance and hope, which 'do not capitulate before so-called fate'.[132]

Doubts have been expressed about Bloch's technical knowledge of the various art forms he discusses. In a backhanded compliment, Adorno opined that 'Bloch's ear has no more patience with technical musical logic than with aesthetic refinement',[133] to which David Drew has impishly responded: 'Adorno's complaint . . . cuts both ways and draws some blood, not all of it Bloch's.'[134] Drew, in his introduction to an English translation of selections from Bloch's musical writing, discusses the hostile reaction of the music critic Paul Bekker to the publication of *Spirit of Utopia* in 1918. Bekker, says Drew, concentrated 'on Bloch's cavalier attitude to musical history, his shaky technical analysis, and his proneness to factual error';[135] Bloch was, however, defended by Margaret Susman, on the grounds that the musical dimension should be judged only as part of the overall philosophical content of the work, and consequently any technical deficiencies could not, in themselves, undermine the whole text. This is essentially Drew's own position: 'it is clear from the start that Bloch had no inhibitions with regard to academic proprieties in musicology, criticism and appreciation',[136] and his work is none the worse for it – which, in part, was what Adorno was suggesting.

Many will no doubt find Bloch's Marxist sociology of culture deeply problematic. Non-Marxists will find the historical periodisation and the characterisation of specific epochs inadequate and inaccurate. Even Bloch himself, in his early *Spirit of Utopia*, bridled at what he took to be the reductive implications of a sociology of music. Marxists too have detected in Bloch's own categories the very schematism he condemned in Lukács and the socialist-realists. In reading Bloch one cannot avoid passages where a piece of fine and subtle writing suddenly descends into the ugly class jargon of Marxism-Leninism. The extreme responses to this are either to dismiss such jargon as merely an ugly encrustation, or to argue that it fatally weakens the entire structure of Bloch's analysis. The particular form of his class analysis does render Bloch a highly questionable guide to art history, but the profundities of the informing analysis of the modalities of utopianism are not thereby compromised.

There is also the question of whether there is a tension between a theory of historical change (which stresses the dynamic, mutable nature of human productivity) and the idea of an ongoing cultural heritage – a golden thread linking disparate historical epochs. Is there an ahistorical normative element at work here? Has a template of *authentic culture* been imposed on history? Consider Bloch's allusions to archetypes. It is undoubtedly the case that he does believe in the historical ubiquity of certain archetypal dreams, activities and relationships. One can see the attractions of this device for his theory, since it appears to ground cultural authenticity not in the subjective judgement of modern radical intellectuals, but in the objective needs and aspirations of countless historical generations. But is this a legitimate inference? A counter-case would point to the immense diversity in social patterns, and to the fact (which Bloch himself acknowledges) that archetype theory has historically – as in the case of Jung – been used to legitimise some form of essentialist position, be it race, culture or whatever. Bloch's own horror of 'recollection' is of note here, for it speaks of his fear of the closure involved in most forms of memory. Are not the archetypes themselves being used to smuggle in highly subjective definitions of supposedly universal norms?

Bloch's definition of authentic culture is apparent in the

sweeping cultural exclusions he imposes. As we have seen, Bloch's sensitive method of cultural analysis is interspersed with ringing anathemas against a whole host of cultural forms – jazz, Hollywood films, tourism, magazine journalism, to name but a few. This cannot be attributed entirely to ignorance of these forms, though such ignorance is clearly present; rather these cultural forms represent for Bloch inauthentic developments, where authenticity is the socialist completion of the progressive bourgeois project. The dangers are historical distortion and political/cultural closure; an idiosyncratic account of cultural history, and a highly rigid understanding of 'progressive' cultural activity. His crude invective against American culture and laboured defence of the cultural policy of the Soviet Union are a graphic illustration of these dangers in action. It also meant that, the Soviet Union apart, the modern world seemed like a cultural wilderness; outside of Expressionism, one had to take solace in the culture of the past (and after the 1930s, Expressionism was itself the past), or in the trace-like utopian gleams thinly spread throughout a host of social and cultural practices. Even the Soviet Union was of limited comfort. His strictures against 'schematism', and his obvious dislike of socialist realism, meant that he could not have found much of Soviet culture in any way agreeable. In short, his particular understanding of cultural heritage and cultural authenticity meant that, inevitably, the twentieth century, as it developed, was going to be a great disappointment to him.

To conclude on a positive note: it is likely that Bloch's culture analyses will remain a major part of his enduring legacy, for culture is a field in which he is very much at home, and in which he frequently displays great descriptive and analytical virtuosity. The sheer breadth of his knowledge is quite phenomenal: he drifts effortlessly through the resources of western culture, and displays a truly encyclopaedic grasp of it. He is also sensitive to nuance, within cultural periods, between art forms, and in the very texture of works of art. There is, furthermore, a boldness to his analyses. He sets up challenging analytical frameworks, asks startling questions and fearlessly pursues the logic of his propositions. Even when he is wrong, the failure is attenuated by a breathtaking outrageousness. His cultural work also maintains a degree of independence from the specifics of his Marxism. He was an acute cultural critic before he became a Marxist, and many of the attitudes and the substance of the informing vision survived, with varying degrees of congruence, into his later work. It is not necessary, therefore, to be a Marxist to benefit from his cultural labours.

3

RELIGION

Bloch underwent confirmation and celebrated his bar mitzvah. Furthermore, if his later account is to be believed, during the ceremony of confirmation he made a private affirmation of atheism. We have in these three events, in symbolic form as it were, the principal ingredients of Bloch's religious thought; a refashioning of the Judaeo-Christian legacy into a radical atheism (or the development of the internal logic of this tradition, as Bloch would see it). Bloch was well into his twenties before he developed a positive appreciation of the value of religion. In a discussion with Michael Landmann he recalled that this had been brought about by his first wife Else von Stritzky. In Landmann's words, she 'awakened in him a sense for the religious, which as a young man he held to be a poor mixture of philosophy and art'.[1] This is apparent in his early works, *Spirit of Utopia* (1918) and *Thomas Münzer als Theologe der Revolution* (*Thomas Münzer as Theologian of Revolution*, 1921), where free use is made of the language and symbolism of theism. The flavour of the religiosity displayed in these texts is different to that found in his later works; the phraseology of personal piety and faith is deployed directly, as if out of the mouth of a believer; his emerging utopian metaphysics is couched in traditional religious language:

> God knows, or perhaps he doesn't know, what awaits us once the protecting walls of the body have fallen away from our dark inwardness, once we have been given up to the demons which have thus terrorized us already in our anxious dreams, to sink into the unprotected and unknown centre of our incognito. May the immortal soul give us the

power to be victorious there over its shadow state and powerfully to illuminate the dangers in it; and may God give us the grace to be there, where no less than here, the fortunate dream, the deepest of dreams, is already aware of him.[2]

There is nothing here, at the level of basic ideas, that the later Bloch would have found unacceptable (the darkness of the lived moment, the not-yet, extra-territoriality, the forward dream, the utopian resonances of the Godhead), but the tone and cast would be very different. It is as if in this early work he is trying to allow religion to express its subversive utopian core, spontaneously and unaided.

A number of scholars have sought to delineate the specifically Jewish aspects of his thought.[3] On the assumption of a basic biographical disposition, they point to the influence of early twentieth-century Jewish Messianism, with its reaction against both assimilationism and political Zionism; to Bloch's appreciation of the Kabbala, and the possible Kabbalistic provenance of some of his ideas and concepts; and to the, again, possible influence, both positive and negative, of Jewish thinkers such as Buber and Rosenzweig. Certainly in a letter of 1918, Bloch roundly asserts his Jewishness: 'I am a completely race-conscious Jew ... I am proud of this, my ancient mysterious people, and that in the best that I am, I am at home in my Jewish Blood and the great religious tradition of my people.'[4] Where this type of approach begins to go off the rails is when the undoubted, if difficult to define, Jewish dimension is credited with a disproportionate influence, as in Finkelstein's 'Bloch's kabbalistic Marxism'.[5] Such interpretations miss Bloch's deep grounding in the spiritualism, mysticism, theology and philosophy of Christianity. As we shall see, Bloch also followed the Hegelian/Marxist tradition of giving *historico-theoretical* primacy to Christianity. He was also hostile to interpretations which stressed the Jewish nature of his work; Wayne Hudson, who interviewed Bloch in his 91st year, and was convinced of his 'overwhelming Jewishness', found him to be 'concerned to reject any attempt to interpret his thought as essentially Jewish'.[6] In short there is a genuine, wide-ranging and fruitful interpenetration of Jewish and Christian elements in his work which precludes any notion of the hegemony of one or the other.

In the 1960s Bloch came to be an important influence on a number of radical currents in theology. The Lutheran theologian Jürgen Moltmann, a later colleague at Tübingen, was an enthusiastic advocate of Bloch's ideas; Moltmann's own work demonstrated the impact of the perspectives of *The Principle of Hope*. This influence can also be seen in the ideas of another Tübingen colleague, Johannes Metz, a Catholic theologian. But Moltmann and Metz were only part of a much wider body of theologians who saw in Bloch an exciting and radical perspective, focused on a refurbished Christian eschatology, which promised the opening up of new territory in theology. Where Moltmann recalled his fascination with Bloch's 'messianism',[7] Metz cited Bloch in the claim that 'Eschatological faith and earthly initiative go hand in hand';[8] while Wolfhart Pannenberg, another prominent theologian influenced by Bloch, wrote that 'Christian theology at some time will perhaps be indebted to Ernst Bloch's philosophy of hope if it again finds the courage to deal with its central category: the general concept of eschatology.'[9] In the Third World, liberation theologians such as Gustavo Gutiérrez used Bloch's work to help develop creative syntheses of Christianity and radical social theory.[10] From the perspective of the European theologians this was the period of 'dialogue' between Marxism and Christianity; in the words of Moltmann: 'in the 1960s Bloch came to the theologians, and the theologians came to him.'[11] 'Dialogue' is, perhaps, an inappropriate expression for what was largely a one-way flow of influence *from· Bloch* (he regarded Moltmann as more of a follower than an interlocutor). Wayne Hudson reports a conversation he had with Bloch in the early 1970s, in which 'Bloch defended his closeness to Christian thinkers in terms of revolutionary tactics and the need to provide bait for the theological fish'[12] – hardly what one could term 'dialogue'! It might be more accurate to describe this phenomenon as the harvest-time for ideas which Bloch had been developing for over half a century. As we have seen, religion had long held a fascination for him, and his earliest books on utopia and on Thomas Münzer reveal both impressive religious scholarship and a strongly developed religious sensibility. His religious thinking had evolved in subsequent years, but the main cast of his views was established before these theological encounters of the 1960s. Bloch's mature reflections on the nature of religion are to be found in the final volume of *The Principle of*

Hope (1959), and are expanded, rather than altered or developed, in his 1968 text *Atheismus im Christentum* (*Atheism in Christianity*).

For Bloch, religious consciousness has historically expressed many of the deepest and most profound aspects of human experience. Analysis of religion is therefore of fundamental importance in understanding not merely the past of humanity but its possible future, prefigured in religious longings. As a Marxist, Bloch acknowledges that he is a part of a particular trajectory of religious analysis, extending from Hegel, via Feuerbach to Marx. In the radical Hegelian culture out of which Marx grew, religious critique was the royal road to critique of the world. As Bloch notes: 'the whole analysis of alienation and the attempt to restore the alienated factors to the human subject began with the critique of religion.'[13] In this tradition of analysis, religion is considered as a form of mystified consciousness; humanity projects on to the religious sphere all those hopes and aspirations blocked by existing society. Religion is consequently a disguised form in which humanity talks about itself. The radical task was therefore to create a world in which there would be no need for a recourse to religious discourse. Bloch also argues that the God-figure has embodied the blocked potentialities of the world, referring to this process as the 'hypostatization' of God. However, he significantly develops this approach. He rightly distances Marx from vulgar interpretations of the oft-quoted 'religion is . . . the opium of the people' passage, noting that Marx was well aware of the positive dimensions in religion. However, he moves, in effect, beyond Marx's contention that the moment of religion had passed, for Bloch believes that not only has the religious legacy not been exhausted but also that this legacy is, in a sense, inexhaustible. This is still, however, within an atheist perspective – Bloch rejects the theistic basis of Christianity. The project here is 'to inherit those features of religion which do not perish with the death of God'.[14] This is presented, not as an extraneous, atheist reconstruction of Christianity, but as the development of the internal logic of Christianity itself. Atheism, in this sense, is the truth of the Bible:

> long before God as an existent object of being had been overthrown by the Enlightenment, Christianity put *man*, or more precisely the *son of man* and his representative

mystery, into the Lord of Heaven of former days. Feuerbach ... merely brought [this] to completion.[15]

In developing these ideas Bloch draws upon traditions other than the Hegelian-Marxist: the Judaic, mystical, heretical and nature-philosophy currents in which he had long immersed himself.

A NEW READING OF THE BIBLE

One fruit of this approach is that Bloch provides a radical exegesis of sacred texts. Although knowledgeable on a wide range of religions, his principal focus is on Judaeo-Christian traditions, and his one book-length study of religion *Atheism in Christianity* (if we exclude the politico-religious hybrid *Thomas Münzer as Theologian of Revolution*) deals exclusively with the Bible, its themes, sources and influence. In *The Principle of Hope* he justified this focus on theoretical grounds, stating that Judaism and Christianity are 'the highest religions'[16] – they contain a radical, human utopianism qualitatively different to the other great world religions: 'Moses ... forces his god to go with him, makes him into the exodus-light of his people; Jesus pervades the transcendent as a human tribune, utopianizes it into the kingdom.'[17] In Christianity indeed, with its radical man-God, there is the highest religious expression of human hope; a sentiment which both echoes the early Marx's claim that Christianity is the essence of religion, given its deification of the human, and registers Bloch's appreciation of the 'humane-eschatological, explosively posited messianism'[18] in Christianity. Bloch situates the modern, radical dismissal of the Bible in the hyper-rationalism of the Enlightenment. In their resolve to root out superstition and ignorance the enlightened savants were unable to see the ambiguous legacy of the Bible. They merely saw error, and were blind to the passages of gold in the text. They failed to see how deeply rooted the Bible was in the hopes and fears of ordinary people, and how biblical imagery had pervaded the social and political struggles of the rural and urban poor. The Bible was replete with archetypes which were 'through the ages ... uniquely native to all lands, striking home over the great distance of space'.[19] In what was an implicit attack on the subsequent hyper-radicalism of vulgar Marxism and, to some extent, of the element of closure in Marx's own work, Bloch affirmed the continuing revolutionary credentials of the Bible:

> The Enlightenment . . . will be all the more radical when it does not pour equal scorn on the Bible's all-pervading, healthy insight into man. It is for this very reason . . . that the Bible can speak to all men, and be understood across so many lands and right on through the ages.[20]

Bloch does not deny that the Bible is a double-edged weapon in that oppressive powers down the ages have found texts to legitimise their activities; the Bible has always been a contested document. This, however, is no reason to withdraw from the contest, for 'the counter-blow against the oppressor is biblical, too'.[21]

Bloch therefore approaches the Bible as a multi-layered, contradiction-riddled text, and speaks of biblical criticism as 'detective work'. This involves a sensitivity to the modalities of myth, and to the 'shades of difference . . . in the obscurity of myth'.[22] It also involves an awareness of the complex processes which produced the modern unitary text: additions and revisions; glosses and interpretations; changes from oral to written; differing sources and canons; distortions and corruptions: in short, the messy materiality of the text. Furthermore, it is not simply that some passages admit of contrary interpretation, which he concedes, but that the Bible text contains inherent contradictions which reflect conflicting principles and interests. His purpose is to lay bare the construction of the text, and thereby to reveal both radical and conservative inputs into the emerging document. Thus, for example, he considers creation and Apocalypse, creation and salvation, creation and Exodus to be 'contrary principles' in the Bible. On the one hand, there is the creation myth in Genesis. This, Bloch speculates, is of Egyptian origin, and a relatively late addition from a priestly code. Its centrepiece is the omnipotent creator exemplified in the text 'And behold it was very good'. It is backward-looking and closed. On the other hand there is the far earlier account of the God who delivered Israel out of Egypt. Its theme is the evil of the world to be overcome, the need for, and the historical reality of, Exodus ('the exodus-Yahweh, not . . . the creator-Yahweh'[23]). In the New Testament it became the Messiah's promise of 'Behold, I make all things new'. It is forward-looking and open. This is considered to be a dualism in the structure of the text, and not merely a question of interpretation.

The exodus motif looms large in Bloch's reappraisal of the Bible. As previously noted, when applied to God the term 'exodus' designates an alternative conception to the creator deity. Bloch identifies a more merciful God in the withdrawal of the curse on Cain, reinterpreting the mark of Cain as God's means of protecting Cain from violent death, and the refusal of the sacrifice of Abraham. Exodus-Yahweh also designates an open-ended conception of deity, of God as change and process rather than as timeless and unchanging. One passage in particular clearly so impressed Bloch that he refers to it time and again in works throughout his life. It is God's words to Moses in a fiery bush *'Eh'je ascher eh' je'* ('I will be what I will be') – a classic articulation in Bloch's opinion of the idea of definition lying in the future, of not-yet. As he put it in one gloss on this phrase:

> This is an early mythological and simultaneously no longer mythological determination of the essence, a determination which corresponds to the real condition of reality, a determination which posits no hereafter or 'above', but rather a possible 'before-us'.[24]

This is put in more religious and contextual terms in *Atheism in Christianity*: 'Exodus from every previous conception of Yahweh was now possible, with this *Futurum* as the true mode-of-being of that which is thought of as God.'[25] Bloch also uses exodus in the sense of the deliverance from Egypt. Here again the relative novelty of the God function is noted. God is no longer the distant and awesome creator-Yahweh, becoming instead the guiding light by which the Israelites escaped from oppression, and the sustaining presence in the long journey to the promised land – 'The God of Moses is the promise of Canaan or he is no God.'[26]

Bloch wishes to evince, chart and vindicate what he considers to be the utopian dimensions in what he sometimes terms 'the underground Bible'. This can involve a re-evaluation of biblical characters, as in the case of the serpent in the Garden of Eden. Although the serpent is presented as the ultimate fiend in Genesis, the ambiguities of the creature shine through the text. The incitement to Eve to eat the forbidden fruit of the Tree of

Knowledge, and thereby become like God, can be seen as a blow against the imperious creator-Yahweh. Time and again in his discussion of religious utopianism Bloch returns to the serpent's claim – *'Eritis sicut Deus'* (You will be like God) – seeing it as the leitmotif of the Promethean Bible. Bloch presents the serpent as the champion of the upright gait, who 'stands for an underground movement which has light in its eyes, instead of hollow submissive slave-guilt'.[27] It champions the divine potential in the human – 'the glint of freedom is ill-concealed'.[28]

Underpinning Bloch's image of a contradictory Bible and its underground strands is the idea that Judaeo-Christianity is a diverse field of religious experiences, which is itself part of an even broader field of religious impulses. Notions of tradition and the canonical are necessarily acts of power within, and selections from, this field. The relatively modern formation which is the Bible has therefore to be assessed in terms of the larger canvas of which it is a part, a process which should involve sensitivity to the various forms and instances of exclusion and inclusion. As a consequence, Bloch considers it entirely legitimate to interpret the Bible with the assistance of apocryphal texts, gnostic writings, heretical works as well as Judaic devotional and theological works. He refuses to see these sources as entirely external to the Bible, insisting that aspects of these traditions are in the very substance of the text. It is in this vein that he speculates about possible links between 'the serpent' and Jesus Christ. Using various serpent references in the Bible, the ideas of the serpent cult Ophites, Jewish esoteric speculations and other sources, Bloch advances the case for Jesus as the new serpentine opponent of the creator-Yahweh. It was the Ophites 'who definitively carried through the transvaluation of the serpent of paradise in relation to Jesus, as the usurper of Yahweh'.[29]

This is a part of a much broader re-evaluation of the figure of Jesus. Bloch sets the scene with a discussion of the 'Book of Job'. Job expresses radical doubts about the goodness of God, and although there is an element of submission at the end, Bloch characterises Job as one who has 'overtaken' his God. Job asserts the rights of the good and the poor to happiness against the cruel indifference of the creator-Yahweh. This itself is a form of exodus, for 'Job makes his exodus from Yahweh',[30] but it is not a regression into nihilism: 'this exodus is not one away from

Exodus itself.'[31] Bloch retranslates and reinterprets Job's famous 'For I know that my Redeemer liveth', viewing it not as a prophecy of the coming of Christ, but as a call for an 'Avenger' who will champion the cause of humanity against heaven itself. This is the bridge to the figure of Jesus:

> Job is pious precisely because he does *not* believe. Except in Exodus, and in the fact that the last human word has not yet been said – the word that will come for the Avenger of blood who puts an end to blood, the word that will come from the Son of Man himself, and not from any mighty Lord.[32]

Job's moral superiority over the creator-Yahweh prefigures Jesus' own advance beyond the 'Father' who would abandon him to a cruel death on the Cross.

Bloch stresses that Jesus was a real, historical figure, and rejects religious and mythic conceptions which seek to dematerialise him as mystical emanation, vegetation god and so forth. The humanity of Jesus links him with Moses. The reason why they are deemed to be the founders of their respective faiths and why those faiths represent something new in world history is precisely the radical, transformative relationships these two *human* beings had with their respective gods. Bloch's Jesus is an eschatological and revolutionary figure; an angry fighter ('I have not come to bring peace, but a sword'), one who would bring down the old corrupt, oppressive world and usher in the Kingdom, the New Jerusalem. The praise of meekness and peace, articulated in the Sermon on the Mount, refers to the Kingdom to come – the battle for that goal requires a much sterner approach. Along with the idea of the mild Jesus, also rejected is the notion of the interior, ethical Jesus (a thesis originated, Bloch claims, in the Enlightenment, and continued by nineteenth-century anti-Semitic liberal theologians). Bloch maintains that Jesus located himself in the Jewish messianic tradition, with its promise of an actual transformation of the world, not merely some transposed, heavenly after-life: 'the coming Kingdom is the primary thing in Jesus' mind, not love . . . [T]he Kingdom . . . is no psychological event, but a catastrophic, cosmic one, directed towards the new Jerusalem.'[33] Jesus' words on the Cross, 'My God, My God, why hast thou forsaken me?' and 'It is finished', are interpreted as the dreadful recognition of failure.

The morality of Jesus is also interpreted in this eschatological light: essentially these teachings were an 'advent morality',[34] either concerned with the impermanence of the existing world or advocating a communal ethic which prefigured, albeit in a pale fashion, the life of the Kingdom – 'like his love his morality can only be grasped in relation to his kingdom'.[35] The question of a continuing terrestrial morality only became an issue for Jesus' followers after the failure of his messianic mission.

Bloch sees great significance in Jesus' description of himself as the 'Son of Man', perceiving in it a utopian exaltation of the human, as distinct from the otherworldly, creator-Yahweh connotations of 'Son of God':

> 'Son of Man' . . . shows that the Messiah is no mere ambassador from on high. 'Son of Man' only appears modest or powerless when set alongside 'Son of God'. But in fact it is the highest title of all, and it means that man has got a very long way indeed: he has become a figure of final, all-conquering strength.[36]

In exploring this theme in the Bible and related discourses, Bloch draws out a further linkage, in the manner of the serpent/Jesus connection; only this time the link is between Adam and Jesus. In line with his thesis of the contradictory Bible, he points to the two accounts of the origin of Adam in Genesis. In one of these accounts Adam is merely created from dust and filled with life, whereas in the other (which he speculates may be of Iranian provenance), he is created in the image of God. Bloch calls this latter version the doctrine of the Heavenly Man (or Adam), and inserts it into his underground tradition, the human subversion of the imperious God. The heavenly Adam is a residual subversive fragment in a theocratic Genesis: 'the doctrine of the Heavenly Adam as the prototype of man belongs in its turn to the biblical Azores: to the remaining mountain-peak of a submerged, subversive, anti-theocratic tradition.'[37] Building on the Hebrew words for 'Son of Man', *ben adam*, Bloch posits a growing biblical linkage between the Heavenly Man doctrine and messianic expectations, until 'Jesus takes on the form of the returning archetypal Man'.[38] Jesus represents the most sustained, the highest form, of biblical rebellion against the creator-Yahweh. His link with divinity is one of equality, and he offers the promise of surpassing all that has gone before.

As 'Son of Man' he therefore embodies 'the realization that a man can be better, and more important, than his God'.[39] The human supersession of the creator-God consequently involves the humanisation of divine creativity: 'The creator, indeed the Pharaoh in Yahweh, falls away completely; he remains only as a goal, and the last Christ called only the community to be its building material and city.'[40]

Bloch sees a continuing conflict of principles in the biblical interpretations of Christ's death. Paul's doctrine of the sacrificial death is condemned as an anti-human regression, with deeply conservative connotations – 'the cross was to be *smashed*, not to be carried or to become the thing itself.'[41] The interconnected images of a sinful humanity, a God who required a blood sacrifice and the patient death on the Cross were entirely antithetical to the utopian humanity of the 'Son of Man'. The aim of this Pauline doctrine 'was to break the subversive element in the Bible once and for all, with the myth of the victim Lamb'.[42] But there is another image to be found in Paul of very different import, that of Christ triumphing over what Bloch calls 'the hardest of all forms of anti-Utopianism'[43] – death. Bloch explores this notion in connection with the resurrection, the ascension and the second coming (*Parousia*). He acknowledges that a shift has occurred in the Bible. It is no longer the arena of Jesus' *own* radical project which, at a personal level, had been cruelly voided on the Cross. Instead there is the utopian use of the supposed risen Jesus by the fledgling Christian community. This is the territory of 'wishful mysteries' and a 'second eschatology'. The utopian Jesus is himself utopianised. None the less, Bloch posits a deep level of continuity between the messianic goals of Jesus and the high utopian mysteries of the later books of the Bible. The resurrection of the 'Son of Man' was a ringing affirmation of the possibility of human immortality, a life-enhancing image of human transcendence, and a mighty blow against the forces of nihilism. Ascension could be, and in many places in the Bible was, interpreted as a vindication of a divine Christ, the return of the heavenly 'Son of God' to his proper realm, after his sojourn in the gross world of the fallen. A contrary strand, however, is the idea of humanity storming heaven – a usurpation of, or breaking into, the realm of the On-High. Jesus is here the tribune of the people fighting their cause at the highest level, and thereby revealing to people the legitimacy of their hopes and the possibility of their actualisation. Again, the linkage between the earthly and heavenly is firmly in terms of the former. The second coming also embodies contrary principles. There is the image of the divine Christ, the emissary of the Father, untouched by his period on earth, returning like an archangel Michael – an unreconstructed heavenly being. There is also, however, the image of the 'Son of Man' returning to his own people, particularly for 'the labourers and heavy-laden, the degraded and despised',[44] and re-establishing the just order of things. Heaven and earth finally meet in the form of a *human* new order: 'The point of the myth was the transformation of heaven as the preserve of God into heaven as the city of man, the new Jerusalem . . . : the new heaven and the new earth were fully anthropocentric.'[45]

JOACHIM OF FIORE AND THOMAS MÜNZER

Bloch's conviction that religious documents are pregnant with profound meanings, and that religious experience is a fundamental realm for radical analysis, informs his work on post-biblical religious life. Bloch interrogated Christian spirituality for traces of utopian content. He had long been fascinated by such sources and, for example, had seemed to Weber's circle in Heidelberg to be a religious and mystical thinker. He loved to wander through the byways of unorthodox religious speculation – gnosticism, the heretical Marcion, the great mystic Meister Eckhart, Jacob Böhme – convinced that they contained gold-bearing seams of utopianism. These religious currents, if correctly read, could yield profound insights into human possibilities. Two figures in particular frequently resurface in Bloch's work: the medieval Calabrian abbot Joachim of Fiore, and the sixteenth-century religious revolutionary Thomas Münzer. His fascination with twelfth-century apocalyptic spirituality and Reformation ultra-radicalism is indicative of Bloch's belief in the power of the margins. As with the 'underground Bible', Bloch perceived in subsequent Christianity alternative traditions which challenged dominant orthodoxies. Joachim's influence on the rebellious Hussites and Münzer's radical activities in the German Peasant War are seen as confirming the linkage between radical theory and objective radical tendencies.

Bloch credits Joachim with drawing up the 'most momentous

social utopia of the Middle Ages'.[46] Joachim's achievement was, 'in the full spate of revolutionary heresy',[47] to resuscitate the radical utopianism of the Bible in his doctrine of the three kingdoms: the former kingdom of the Father ('Old Testament . . . fear and . . . known Law'), the current kingdom of the Son ('New Testament . . . love and the Church') and the kingdom to come, the 'Third Kingdom' ('the Holy Spirit or the illumination of all, in mystical democracy, without masters and Church'). Further-more, Bloch maintains, Joachim grounded these stages in actual history, interpreted the coming Kingdom as a terrestrial and not a merely heavenly event, and made the poor the beneficiaries of this event, thereby revivifying the project of the 'Son of Man'. Jesus, too, effectively disappears as he is subsumed into the righteous community itself. Once more Bloch identifies an exodus:

> Its theme is precisely the exodus from fear and servitude or the Law and its state, the exodus from the rule of clerics and the immaturity of the laity or loving grace and its Church . . . [E]ven Jesus ceases to be a leader, he dissolves himself in the 'societas amicorum'.[48]

In *Heritage of Our Times* (1935) Bloch uses Joachim's image of the Third Kingdom as an example of the dangers of not engag-ing with the utopian imagery of past times. The failure of 'social-istic propaganda', which he describes as 'cold, schoolmasterish, and merely economistic',[49] to appropriate the deep resonances of Joachim's vision, was not repeated by the Nazis, who were aware of the emotive power of old symbols, and who made the 'Third Reich', with a changed and perverted content (and not directly from Joachim), a centrepiece of their effective propa-ganda. A previously revolutionary image was thus annexed by the forces of reaction: 'So the "Third Reich" came in time anew, but what a different one from that of Joachim . . . blazing dark-ness fell on the land, a night full of blood and nothing but Satan.'[50]

Bloch's fondness for Thomas Münzer was long-standing. Karl Mannheim, in *Ideology and Utopia*, spoke of 'an inner affinity' between Münzer and Bloch.[51] Bloch's second book, after *Spirit of Utopia*, had been the 1921 study *Thomas Münzer as Theo-logian of Revolution*. In the book he stressed the deep intertwining between the religious and the political in Münzer, who was simultaneously theologian and revolutionary.[52] Bloch sought to resist crude Marxist attempts to reduce the diversity of Münzer to sociological stereotypes, and criticised Kautsky for his narrow economistic reading. Bloch so frequently brackets together Joachim and Münzer because he does detect deep underlying similarities. This can be shown by looking at a passage of Münzer, which Bloch frequently quoted, taken from *Expressed Exposure of False Faith*. Münzer says that to many people his ideas must seem 'a powerful great fantasy'. This ability to be an adventurous visionary, out of kilter with prevailing orthodoxies, is for Bloch a source of strength linking Münzer and Joachim. A further link is Münzer's belief that humanity can aspire to the divine, and that earth can be transformed into heavenly dimensions – or as Münzer puts it: 'we men of flesh and earth are to become gods through Christ's becoming man ... indeed far more, we are completely changed into him, in order that earthly life may swing into heaven.' Again there is the belief that it is the poor that shall be exalted, for Münzer maintains that it is necessary to 'throw the godless from the throne of judgement and to raise up the lowly rough people'.[53] Finally, they also share a tolerant and internationalist definition of the Godly, embracing Jew and pagan and people of all creeds – a Joachite notion, which, Bloch shows, directly influenced Münzer:

> The citizenship of the forthcoming [Joachite] City of God was not determined by baptism but by perceiving the fraternal spirit in the inner word. According to Thomas Münzer's great supra-Christian definition, the future kingdom will be formed 'of all the chosen ones among all scatterings of races of every kind of faith' ... 'You should know', says Münzer ... 'that they ascribe this doctrine to the Abbot Joachim and call it an eternal gospel with great scorn.'[54]

Bloch makes the same point for Münzer in *Heritage of Our Times* that he does for Joachim – the Nazis have been more sensitive to the inheritance of the past than the Marxists: 'vulgar Marxism had forgotten the inheritance of the German Peasant Wars and of German philosophy, the Nazis streamed into the vacated, originally Münzerian regions.'[55]

COSMOS AND LOGOS

Bloch finds an echo of his own dynamic materialism in one approach to nature in the Bible. This enters the Bible via pagan astral myths, in which the natural has its own rhythms and importance and cannot be reduced to a mere backdrop, let alone a slave, of humanity. Thus although Bloch is hostile to attempts to reduce the entire Bible to a manifestation of an oriental nature cult, he is happy to acknowledge the solstice dimension in Christmas, and the sacred spring in Easter. As such, these festivals negate the conception that 'nature just lies at our feet and follows us'.[56] Unfortunately this disparaging attitude to nature is also very much apparent in the Bible, and becomes very influential in subsequent theological and philosophical thought. An important reason for this is the powerful role in the Bible of what he terms the 'logos-myth'. This myth of the ingression of the divine into the human could easily lend itself to a devaluation of the 'Cosmos': 'with its easily exaggerated slogan about man making the earth his "underling" ' and a conception of 'the cosmos which lay beneath and beyond the rule of the Logos'.[57]

Bloch explores a fruitful development of the logos myth in a discussion of Christian mysticism and Pentecost. The word 'mystic' he argues is derived from 'myein' which means 'to shut the eyes'. Since the fourteenth century, this has not meant a shutting out of the world but, on the contrary, has involved the development of an intense, internal vision in which the mystic gains knowledge of the objective via the subjective. Again, Bloch is impressed by the close associations between these mystics and rebellious social movements – the Lollards, Anabaptists, etc. What these mystics found was that God was not an external and remote being but was rather to be found at the very core of their own being – they discovered the divine spark *in themselves*:

> If the eyes were now shut to the Lord God it was because – to the newly awakened human subject – he was no longer strange: no longer an object held above us, but the very depths of our own subjective Self. He was the inmost *state* (not object) of our own misery, our own wandering, our own suppressed glory.[58]

Bloch takes this to be a religious formulation of his doctrine of the 'darkness of the lived moment' – the notion that the not-yet can be actually, if dimly, perceived in certain forms of consciousness, thereby linking subjective and objective. Such mysticism revealed the limitless possibilities in the human breast, or, as Eckhart put it: 'What the heavens could not contain lies now in Mary's womb.'[59] The Pentecost scene in Acts is also considered to be an instance of this type of moment. The descent of the Holy Spirit and the 'speaking in tongues' herald the last days and the coming of the Kingdom. This new member of the Trinity, 'God the Holy Spirit', represents the coming together of those old contrary principles, creation and salvation. Creativity is divorced from the old creation-Yahweh and enters the realm of human endeavour and aspiration. This novelty of the age of the Spirit is registered in Origen's 'Third Gospel', as well as Joachim's 'Third Kingdom'. Again, the subjective grounding is in the dark moment:

> the *infinite greatness* of a creative Beginning is lost now, with this future-facing *Veni creator spiritus*, in the *infinite smallness* of a Beginning. . . . It is the *Not-there of each present Moment*, which, still veiled to itself, and seeking itself, truly 'evolves' into being in and through World-process and its experimental forms.[60]

This conception points to the nullity of the question, Logos *or* Cosmos. Bloch appropriately turns to the final, apocalyptical book of the Bible, Revelation. The promised 'new heaven' and 'new earth' will not be sited in an otherworldly zone, but in the utterly transformed surroundings of *this* world. Logos and cosmos therefore meet in nature. It is a 'new Jerusalem', but it is still a Jerusalem; and it therefore occurs

> in a mythically and apocalyptically exploded world, but one which . . . belongs in the realm of nature, and one whose topos has remained within the fully logos-mythical but also meta-*physical* framework of an Eschaton of New Jerusalem.[61]

ATHEISM IN CHRISTIANITY

What then is to be the relationship between these religious images of liberation and a contemporary radical political project? Having rejected Marxist attempts to abstractly transcend religion, to mechanically read religion out of the revolutionary picture, Bloch is equally scathing about those who wish to re-inject religion into socialism in the form of ethical or Christian socialism – a regression from socialism to religion. Instead, he sees the utopian dimensions of the Christian tradition as 'unsettled debts', which can speak across the centuries to those who are still struggling for payment, and which therefore 'wait for us in the future rather than bind us to the past'.[62] The perennial conflict between oppression and liberation necessarily links historical glimpses of freedom, and endows the past with continuing potency. This, as Bloch describes it, seems to involve both cultural inheritance and structural similarity. That is, the explosive images of the past are available for echoing, and the desire for freedom over time necessarily replicates universal elements: 'not even freedom can help finding within itself images taken from the Exodus, or from the destruction of Baby-lon, or from the "Kingdom" of the free.'[63] This is not an attempt to collapse the distinction between past and present; for the confluence of biblical archetypes and modern needs is a process not of circularity but of novelty. The old material has to be worked upon and reintegrated into a modern context.

This requires that the future of religion be seen in terms of atheism. Only a Christianity stripped of its other-worldliness has a continuing role to play. On the other hand, an atheism without hope will degenerate into nihilism. Both elements can therefore be complementary: 'Only an atheist can be a good Christian; only a Christian can be a good atheist.'[64] Bloch believed that Marxism, grounded in objective social tendencies, would bring about the fulfilment of the ancient promise of the Bible:

> when dialectical materialism hears and grasps the import of the mighty voice of tendency in this world which it has made its own, and when it calls on men to work for the goal revealed by that voice, it shows decisively that it has taken hold of the living soul of a dead religion. . . . That is what lives on when the opium, the fool's paradise of the Other-world, has been burnt to ashes.[65]

Again, this differs from mainstream Marxist analyses in that the transcendence/fulfilment of religion is not conceived of in rationalistic terms, where to all intents and purposes religion vanishes. Religion has always been the sphere in which the profound mysteries of existence have been probed – 'the undischarged question, which has been a burning question only in religions, about the unestablished-meaning of life'[66] – therefore the ongoing salience of these matters guarantees the persistence of the stuff of religion: 'where there is hope there is religion'.[67] Bloch sees a continuing importance for the great themes of religion – mystery and resurrection, hope and morality – 'when the gods of taboo and fear have been abolished there is room for the advent of a mystery that is *adequate to the fearless man*'[68] (he called them 'red mysteries' in *Heritage of Our Times*[69]), or speaking of the historical development of religion in *The Principle of Hope*: 'the growing humanization of religion is not paralleled by any reduction in its sense of awe, on the contrary.'[70] Bloch's early book *Spirit of Utopia* countenanced a 'socialist-oriented Church facing new contents of revelation',[71] while in the much later *Naturrecht und menschliche Würde* (*Natural Law and Human Dignity*) he speculated that in a classless society 'the church is not going to become quite so rootless as the state'.[72] In short, religion becomes 'meta-religion'.

One religious theme that has continuing validity for Bloch is 'evil' – in biblical terms 'the Satanic'. Once more, Enlightenment optimism comes under attack. In its light-filled universe there was no place for the mighty Satan; evil was seen 'as something small and weak, a mere blemish on the beauty of an otherwise perfect world'.[73] This continuation of the creator-Yahweh's 'Behold, it was very good' extended into nineteenth-century notions of indefinite and ascending human progress. This was both a gross distortion of the actual state of the world and played directly into the hands of evil. In the first case the existence of phenomena such as Auschwitz belied the facile optimism of such pictures – the biblical Satanic, in comparison, provided a much more adequate distillation of such horror. Second, Bloch makes the point that unlike God – who does wish people to believe in him – evil prefers to keep a low profile, precisely because unlike the Divine there is so much obvious evidence for its existence. The marginalisation and devaluation of the diabolical therefore assists evil in the strengthening of its covert power. Bloch therefore wishes to distinguish his own atheism from a facile atheism which mechanically banishes not merely the positive aspects of Christianity, but also the potent negativity of Satan. If utopia is ever to be actualised, its dark opponent has to be acknowledged and fought against. An acute awareness of the presence and depth of evil is a prerequisite for any positive move forward.

Religion has also been an arena for what Bloch terms the 'life-force'. Religion at its best has faced the ultimate fears and dangers of life and death and has helped generate courage and vision. At it most basic, as in the religio-philosophical conception of stoicism, the 'upright gait' is vindicated; a fearlessness in the face of death is cultivated. With Christianity there is a move 'beyond imperturbability to the wings of indestructibility'.[74] Resurrection and Ascension proclaimed triumph over death, while mystical notions of a divine spark in humanity spoke of the immortal at the core of the mortal. The image of the noble, moral, upright person is clearly of continuing validity. The Christian promise of eternal life can be demystified without losing its mystery and profundity. It points to a deep level in humanity which Bloch terms 'extra-territorial',[75] and which is the basis for the only form of immortality open to *Homo sapiens*.

In *Atheism in Christianity* Bloch expands on this difficult concept of 'extra-territoriality' in a discussion of death. Can death really be overcome, or is it just metaphorically or mythically overcome? Bloch's affirmative answer to this question rests upon his notion of *homo absconditus* (hidden man). Individuals are not what they are, they are what they will be. They are not-yet, 'S is not yet P'. True identity must rest in the future; genesis is at the end, not the beginning. As a consequence, since death cannot destroy something in the future, it cannot destroy the identity of individuals:

> at the inmost kernel of our being we are *homo absconditus*, and that alone: we are the one authentic mystery of our own most immediate immediacy, and that mystery has never objectified itself. So, never having really come to be, it can never really pass away. . . . [T]he still infolded closest closeness of our deepest depths, is, *by virtue of being Not-yet-being*, utterly and completely extra-territorial to the great destroyer of being called death.[76]

The incompletedness of individuals and the world means that future struggle for completedness is a way in which earlier generations can live on and attain their identity – 'true being . . . waits, extra-territorially, in the wings.'[77] Recognition and anticipation of this can bring strength in the face of death.

The most profound images of the Bible point to this goal of true being. The God figure was the repository of these longings, but now 'the forward-look has replaced the upward-look',[78] the *homo absconditus* has replaced the *deus absconditus* (hidden God). The fact that the hypostatisation of God is no longer required means that that which was projected on to this mythical being can now inform a radical, transformatory project. A 'hollow space' remains which can now be filled:

> The place that has been occupied in individual religions by what is conceived as God, that has ostensibly been filled by that which is hypostatized as God, has not itself ceased after it has ceased to be ostensibly filled. For it is at all events preserved as a place of projection at the head of utopian-radical intention.[79]

There is now 'an as yet unrealized At-all, which men used to call God; but which a-theism sees as the Utopian Omega of the fulfilled Moment, the Eschaton of our immanence, the illumination of our incognito.'[80] It is thus a move from a being to a state of being: 'not God but kingdom.'[81]

Technical objections have been levelled at Bloch's reading of the Bible. It has been said that his lack of competence in biblical scholarship has manifested itself in erroneous or questionable construal; for example, doubts have been cast on Bloch's retranslation of 'Redeemer' as 'Avenger' in his discussion of Job,[82] and on his 'not-yet' translation of 'I will be what I will be'.[83] These claims, though very difficult for non-specialists to assess, are clearly potentially damaging to Bloch, given the weight he attaches to close biblical exegesis. It has also been said that, from a modern perspective, Bloch is reliant on rather old-fashioned traditions of biblical criticism, and that the resulting analysis bears the heavy imprint of old debates. In his defence, Richard Roberts has argued that Bloch's 'elderly' analysis, with its stress on the historical nature of the text, is closer to modern interpretations than the intervening radical readings:

> Bloch's discussion of biblical material is extremely dated

as it focused upon controversy that took place in the first two decades of the present century. In the light of this it is all the more remarkable that his presentation of the historical Jesus has gained rather than lost plausibility.[84]

Bloch's presentation of the Bible as a contradictory text prompts a number of questions. Modern scholarship would support Bloch's contention that the Bible is a complex amalgam of texts and traditions of varying provenance and consistency, but is Bloch's methodology fruitful and his specific characterisation accurate? Some might find an element of self-referential circularity in his approach. A dualistic reading of the Bible as the conflict between creation and salvation entirely structures his interpretation, and whenever a text appears which runs counter to his 'underground' Bible, it is 'explained' in terms of the counterveiling 'priestly code', or mistranslation or misinterpretation. Thus Job's final reconciliation with God, which is deemed to be at variance with the Promethean character of the rest of the text, is portrayed as a cover to allow the dangerous heresy through. It is difficult to lose at this type of game – any conflicting evidence can be easily assimilated. Furthermore, is the hypothesis of an underlying creation/exodus dualism sustainable? If the Bible is such a contradictory text, how could a plausible canon ever have emerged and be subsequently perceived as a satisfying unity by millennia of readers? Thomas West has suggested that criticisms of the deity in the Bible coexist with, and gain their legitimacy from, an underlying belief in the omnipotence and goodness of God, and that Bloch's 'effort to sharply divide the OT into two traditions – the protheocratic, which is archaic and conservative, and the anti-theocratic, which is utopian and revolutionary – results in a strained, unbalanced, and selective interpretation'.[85] The Bible is a remarkable text but the claim that a *structural* dialectic runs through it puts an intolerable strain on the document. Bloch also fails to provide any developed, let alone convincing explanation as to *why* the Bible should be expected to do so much work. The silence possibly reflects an awareness of the disparity between the adoption of what is in effect a radicalised version of Christianity's self-image (with its privileging of biblical tradition and of the 'founding' figures of Moses and Jesus) and Marxist historiography. As Wayne Hudson has argued, Bloch provides no Marxist explanation of why it was Moses who invented the idea of an exodus God, or why it should have been Jesus who 'made God man'. Moreover, he gives Judaism, Christianity and, above all, Jesus, a centrality in his treatment for which there is ... [no] methodological justification.[86]

One suspects the continuing influence of Kabbalistic notions of the Bible as a text of power!

In the case of Bloch's analysis of the religious inheritance, criticism can be roughly divided into the claim that Bloch collapses religion into Marxism, and the claim that he collapses Marxism into religion. We can identify a cluster of criticisms in the first of these claims. There are those which maintain that Bloch's atheistic appropriation of Christianity is a contradiction in terms, and that all that he has salvaged from the religious tradition are lifeless symbols. These criticisms usually originate from a theistic viewpoint, where it is the atheism at the heart of Bloch's Marxism that is deemed to be fatal. They deny Bloch's claim that Jesus was a failed Messiah, and that Resurrection, Ascension and the Second Coming were merely wishful mysteries, and argue that if this were true there could be no genuine continuing religious inheritance. The package is theistic or, ultimately, it is nothing. Bloch's use of Christianity without Christ is therefore akin to having a train without an engine. To take two examples from critics who are sufficiently sympathetic to Bloch to wish to engage with him. The Czech theologian Jan Lochman, while acknowledging the extent to which Bloch 'has pioneered so many of the themes of modern theology',[87] none the less concludes, contra Bloch, that 'Hope and God are inseparable'.[88] Or one could cite Wolfhart Pannenberg, who, although sympathetic to Bloch's eschatological concerns, finds a conflict between Bloch's process philosophy and the notion of the Kingdom. For Pannenberg the essence of the Kingdom is that it is entirely and ontologically new, and to make it merely the development out of existing tendencies is to rob it of this fundamental difference: 'The primacy of the future and of its novum is ensured only if the kingdom to come is founded ontologically in itself and only if it owes its futurum not merely to the presently existing wishes and aspirations of mankind'[89] – only a theistic ontology can provide this. From an atheist perspective

his theistic critics have only a counsel of despair to offer. However, even among those who are supportive of Bloch's atheistic
Christianity, worries have been expressed about what is seen as
the subversion of the religious dimension by his Marxism. The
claim here is that the wonderful open-ended contents of
religious hope are constrained in the strait-jacket of a Marxist
stages theory of history. Tom Moylan, for example, has argued
that there is a tension in Bloch's work between an orthodox
Marxist teleology and an unorthodox open utopianism, and that
religion has often been a casualty of the former: 'In his discussion of religion, he often presents a version of utopia that
draws on metaphors of *maturity* and *perfection* achieved at the
end point of the *totality* of history', and 'the careful interpretation and appropriation of religious space as a contested site
for the utopian impulse collapses in a heavy-handed imposition
of images of maturity and totality.'[90] Religion thus loses its
essence and is reduced to a lifeless Marxism. There is a good
deal of merit in this criticism. Here – as elsewhere in his work
– there is a yawning gap between the flexible, subtle and open
utopianism and a mechanistic and sometimes barbaric Marxism-
Leninism. It is also the case that Bloch does tend to assume an
identity between the Marxist vision of Communism and the
ultimate content of religious hope, between the two realms,
the realm of freedom and the Kingdom. The danger of closure,
Marx's own fear that 'utopians' might foreclose the future, is a
real one.

The other pole of criticism is that Bloch reduces Marxism to
religion. Critics often point to the mystical beliefs of the early
Bloch, and argue that an essentially religious vision informs all
his subsequent work and that Marxism was merely absorbed
insofar as it assisted this vision. There are, however, many vari-
ations in this type of criticism, coming from very different ideological traditions. At the time of Bloch's fall from grace in East
Germany, Marxist-Leninist ideologues asserted that Bloch's version of Marxism was just a form of mysticism 'which demands
no open break with Marxism, because it calls itself Marxism,
whilst allowing its adherents to detach themselves from Marxism',[91] and that 'Mystical philosophy of hope is irreconcilable
with Marxism',[92] while from an anti-Marxist perspective Leszek
Kolakowski has argued that 'Bloch's philosophy is in the last
resort a theogony, a fantastic projection of the God that is to

be'[93] and that Marxism was easily assimilated because it also had, via Hegel, deep roots in neo-Platonic gnosticism. A more nuanced approach is to be found in Wayne Hudson. Hudson suspects that Bloch 'confuses Marxism with a projective meta-religious outlook of an essentially religious kind'.[94] The great utopian goal is suffused with religious imagery, and is both 'moralistic and maximalist'. Hudson also points to the religious nature of Bloch's conception of good and evil, and to his concern to rehabilitate the religious notion of immortality via the concept of extra-territoriality. Hudson rightly finds this revamped version of eternal life deeply flawed, pointing out that real immortality refers to that which *is*, not to that which is not-yet, and that the destruction of the material process would simultaneously destroy the not-yet, thereby cancelling eternal life. Hudson seems to be inferring that Bloch's desire to validate an essentially religious vision drove him to propose such an unsustainable notion. Again, there are compelling elements in this type of criticism. Bloch does reformulate many aspects of Marxism, and some undoubtedly amount to a religious reformulation, but as a total judgement the claim of a religious 'reduction' of Marxism is clearly unsustainable and would involve a highly idiosyncratic and selective approach to Bloch's utterances.

There is a nobility and a profundity in Bloch's radical atheism. He has sensed that at a fundamental level the atheist and the theist are united in a perception of the richness and mystery of the universe. As Fredric Jameson has written of this approach, it recognises the self-contradictory and superficial nature of abandoning the miraculous and the awesome to the 'religious', especially when the most sophisticated representatives of the latter make no such exclusive claim:

> it has always seemed to me that the nonbeliever strengthens his adversary's case by his [sic] tendency (a properly superstitious one, we might point out) to attribute some unique and specialized, intrinsically *other* type of psychological or spiritual experience to the believer; and this, even though it is made plain in theological literature from the very outset that faith is to be described essentially as the longing to have faith, that the nature of belief lies not so much in some apprehension of the presence of God

as rather of his silence, his absence – in short, that there is basically no real difference between a believer and a nonbeliever in the first place.[95]

For Bloch, hope without uncertainty would not be hope, and therefore a superficial God of certainty is an affront to the hopeful core of authentic belief; and the vulgar, fundamentalist question – why believe in anything, or act morally, if there is no God? – simply reveals the spiritual impoverishment of the questioner. Bloch's recognition of the inexhaustible plenitude of being renders any distinction between atheism and theism a mere semantic quibble.

4

FASCISM AND MARXISM

The rise of the Nazis in Germany and the Bolshevik Revolution both powerfully mark Bloch's work. The 'triumph' of Fascism not merely revealed the terrifying dynamics of capitalism in crisis; it also revealed the deep inadequacies of much left-wing, including Marxist, analysis. Bloch responded both with subtle analyses and with a characteristic political toughness. The complex psychological and ideological wiles of Fascism had to be uncovered, and indeed countered, but the hard facts of the political climate had also to be recognised. This had important consequences in his approach to the Soviet Union. As we shall see, Bloch was a stern critic – at its very inception – of the autocratic aspects of the Bolshevik Revolution. However, his recognition of the constraints of Russia's underdeveloped economy, and a growing conviction that the Soviet experiment had to be defended against the hostile attacks of world capitalism, were part of his move, in the 1920s, towards a much closer attachment to the world Communist movement. Needless to say there was also a good deal of ignorance and naivety in this move. The rise of Fascism reinforced Bloch's belief that the USSR had to be defended, especially as it seemed that there was no plausible alternative bulwark against the menace of Fascist domination. Inevitably, this introduced tensions into his work. In the second section of this chapter we will deal with the theoretical basis of Bloch's Marxism, a basis deeply influenced by Marx's early radical humanism. Thus we shall be confronted with the incongruous spectacle of a humanist Marxism coexisting with a public defence of Stalinism.

THE ANALYSIS OF FASCISM

A witness of the rise of Fascism, Bloch had no illusions about its inhuman viciousness – the 'nastiness and speechless brutality . . . of the Germany of terror',[1] as he wrote in 1934. A Jew and prominent Marxist, he himself narrowly missed becoming a victim of Nazi violence. In 1933, in the wake of Hitler's electoral victory, a last-minute warning telephone call from Karola – his wife to be – enabled him to flee to Switzerland and narrowly escape arrest by the Nazis; yet he refused to become mesmerised by the gangsterism of National Socialism or to succumb to the crude, stereotypical 'explanations' offered by many on the left. Fascism, he argued, was a complex, contradictory phenomenon, in which there was light and shade, hope and despair. The description of Fascism as a product of capitalism had to lead to an explanation which could account for the relative independence of the disparate social actors, their varied ideological trajectories and the convoluted dynamics of their interrelationships. In line with his pervasive utopianism, he stressed, and displayed, sensitivity to the power and modalities of dreams. Fascism, unlike vulgar Marxism, understood the potency and ubiquity of dreaming, and moved with adroitness in this terrain. A topography of the dreamscape of the era of Fascism had therefore become a necessity, and Bloch's resulting analysis is incisive and imaginative. It is also relatively little known, even among *aficionados* of Marxist analyses of Fascism; set against the extensive coverage given to the relevant work by the Frankfurt School, Reich, Trotsky and Gramsci, Bloch's writing in this field has languished in undeserved obscurity.

Bloch's analysis of Fascism is to be found in *Erbschaft dieser Zeit* (rendered in the English translation as *Heritage of Our Times* [or more accurately, according to Tony Phelan, *Inheritance of This Time*[2]], 1935). The underlying argument is briefly sketched in the Preface. The current era is conceived, in explicitly Marxist terms, as a period of bourgeois decay. Put baldly, Fascism was allowed to flourish by dominant, though frightened, economic interests: 'the dupers . . . only have the character and function, for the capital that called them, of producing the most expedient degree possible of terror and confusion.'[3] However, the devil, as it is said, lies in the detail. For Bloch, the objectives of a Marxist analysis of Fascism must be twofold: first, to examine why it was that Fascism was able to mobilise significant social strata, and second, to identify the complex modalities of the New in the present, the foreglow of socialism amidst the decay of capitalism. Bloch is quite confident that the bourgeoisie has had its day, but the question as to what will replace the bourgeois order is open. These two analyses are interconnected, for, as Bloch contends, Fascism has been able to harness the anxieties and desires of diverse social classes, albeit in a corrupt and distorted manner. An awareness of the 'success' of Fascism is therefore a vital moment in identifying the transcendent elements of existing society. Achieving this awareness requires a much more sensitive and nuanced approach than is to be found in existing communist analyses. It is necessary to examine the experiential and ideological make-up of all social classes: identifying the point of entry of Fascist colonisation; separating the wheat of genuine novelty from the chaff of ideology, and rejecting the blinding methodology of schematic reductionism. This means that so-called 'reactionary' classes like the peasantry and the petit-bourgeois cannot be dismissed out of hand. The Fascist voice did make a sort of sense to these classes, but this is all the more reason to identify the authentic trajectory of the wishes and desires which Fascism has annexed. This in turn should lead to a new Marxist strategy which, instead of leaving a clear field to the Fascists, contests these disputed areas. It also requires a more discerning approach to the question of cultural inheritance. Schematic Marxism has talked too glibly of bourgeois ideology and reactionary culture, and has therefore missed the gold-bearing seams in the cultural realm, as well as failing to notice the canny use Fascism has made of this material. Battle must be joined here also:

> 'Life', 'soul', 'unconscious', 'nation', 'totality', 'Reich' ... would not be so one hundred per cent usable in reactionary terms if the revolution did not merely wish, with justification, to unmask here but, with just as much justification, concretely to outdo, and to recollect the ancient possession of these very categories.[4]

Thus Bloch believes that the rise of Fascism was both a disaster in human terms and an indictment of Communist analysis and strategy; it could, however, be turned into an opportunity to build a socialist society out of the ruins of capitalism.

Bloch's analysis does not take the form of a linear argument. Alongside systematic analysis he provides little illustrative vignettes, and short essay-length investigations of specific features and facets of Fascism. Thus in one short section of *Heritage of Our Times*, originally dating from 1929, he paints a picture of the horrors of an endurance-dancing competition to suggest both the poverty and the dangerously pent-up anxieties of the lower classes in Germany. Driven by indigence to take part in these 'competitions', the hapless participants provide a medium for discharging and dispersing the frustrations of the spectators: 'It is even nice to hound poor bastards just like the rich do to oneself. Brutal, but also merry rage then lets off steam. Passes on the kicks from above to those down below.'[5] Such spectacles are a sort of negative prefiguration of the institutional barbarism of the Fascist state: 'What the soul of the people is cooking up here will shortly be served up in quite an acceptable form.'[6] In an essay (also of 1929 vintage) evocatively entitled 'Saxons without forests', Bloch examines the contradictions of racist ideology. His starting point is the compensatory function of notions of 'the German', 'the Aryan', 'the Nordic', which provide a bogus nobility in times of want; the anxious petit-bourgeois is given a sense of self-worth and is provided with a Jewish 'counter-race' to denigrate: 'looking down in his blondness, he equally looks up to himself.'[7] For this trick to work however, given the palpably 'mixed' racial nature of German society, a plausible ideological narrative has to be constructed; a bizarre and ultimately murderous symbiosis has to occur between 'Germanness' and the 'Jewish other'; with a terrible irony, the notion of the chosen people is appropriated, and then substantiated by the extermination of the perceived competitor: 'if the swastika crusader wants to be the chosen people, he must slander the original today, crush it under his boots, make it into a "world plague" and exterminate it, in order to be "chosen" himself, to have any "race" at all.'[8] Bloch also examines the relationship between town and country in Fascism: he detects, in the rural distrust of the town, elements of a long-standing and genuine hostility to the dehumanising effects of urban capitalism. Fascism has distorted this hostility into a reactionary rural romanticism for use in both rural and urban constituencies: a responsive rural base is established, and urban dissatisfaction is channelled into a rural utopianism. The inability of vulgar Marxism to respond to the genuine elements in these various wishes assists this process:

> the capitalist factory dams up 'soul', and it seeks to flow away, indeed to explode against dreariness and dehumanization; but ... vulgar Marxism ... cordons off their 'soul' for them again, even theoretically, and thus drives them back to a reactionary 'idealism'.[9]

Hence the alliance of a town-hating country and a country-loving town. In line with his belief that to be successful Fascism must first tap into, and then distort, positive drives, Bloch looks at a wide range of such appropriations. In Chapter 3 ('Religion') we discussed his examination of the Nazi appropriation of the once radical image of the Third Reich. Other Nazi appropriations include the red of the Socialist flag; the use of street processions; the May Day holiday; the designation 'worker', and a fraudulent use of *praxis*, turning it into an anti-intellectual activism:

> Thus the enemy is not content with torturing and killing workers. He not only wants to smash the red front but also strips the jewelry off the supposed corpse. The deceiver and murderer cannot show his face other than with would-be revolutionary speeches and forms of combat.[10]

The name 'National Socialist' is also clearly fraudulent. Its *class-based* and *international* mission of destroying socialism both precludes any possible rootedness in a genuine nation (and its corollary, real internationalism), and belies its so-called 'socialist' credentials:

> it is ... eminently international, in so far as capital in all fascist states must develop the same kind of national feeling and national ideology, namely against class-conscious proletarians. ... So-called National Socialism is ... neither national nor socialist, but a deception or mistake in both. Only the International causes the National to seize possession of itself, and makes of meagre and ideological 'national souls' national bodies of nearness. In class society up to now nation has been at best a fragment or the particularly cunning use of a revolutionary motif by the

ruling class-ideology. Only in the actual national unit, not in the romantic-deceptive one of 'patriotism', does nation thus become real.[11]

Having examined various planes and sections of the Fascist experience, Bloch develops a more systematic analysis around the concept of non-contemporaneity. He begins with a psycho-historical proposition: 'Not all people exist in the same Now.'[12] We will perhaps understand this proposition more easily if we think of it in terms of the horizontal and vertical axes of social life. If at the horizontal level, people are clearly contemporaries in the sense that they palpably inhabit the same space, this contemporaneity vanishes when the vertical dimension is taken into consideration, for people may be intellectually, emotionally and culturally rooted in earlier times. This comes about because of the uneven development of capitalism. The capitalist mode of production has been incapable of integrating all of society into the contemporaneity of the modern. In varying degrees, indi-viduals and classes have not been fully absorbed, and therefore retain elements of the mentality of earlier ages. In short, 'various years in general beat in the one which is just being counted and prevails.'[13] This sets up contradictions capable of regressive and progressive use. The achievement of Fascism, given Marxist dereliction, has been partially to master even the most progress-ive of these non-contemporaneous remains. When contemporan-eity is a hostile world, the Fascist promise of a return of the supposed good old days meets a ready response: 'because at least the intolerable Now seems different with Hitler, because he paints good old things for everyone.'[14]

Bloch provides three initial examples of non-contemporaneity at work: in youth, in the peasantry, and in the impoverished middle class. In the case of youth he makes a number of psycho-logical and sociological assumptions. Young people tend in gen-eral to be out of sympathy with the age they inhabit, a process heightened by the dehumanisation of modern capitalism. In this context a form of psychological atavism can come into play – 'an element of prehistoric life'[15] – in the form of bonding and the need for surrogate fathers. Sociological factors intrude here, for Bloch maintains that the cultural inheritance and disintegrat-ing class position of the bourgeoisie make bourgeois youth more susceptible to these developments than proletarian youth. Atavism also joins forces with a more familiar form of historical non-contemporaneity – as youth can be drawn to a whole range of cultural memories (the resonances of traditional clothing, for example). Fascism responds to, and further cultivates, these primitive and historical fantasies. It combines contempt for the modern world with a confected tribal, hierarchical past ('blood-based, tangible life in small groups, with a known leader'), and an assertion of authentic, 'decent' human values ('manly qualities . . . strength, openness, decency, purity'[16]); an attractive, though ultimately bogus, alternative to the undoubted inadequacies of the present. This process is, of course, assisted by the very tangible financial benefits the Right can offer to youthful would-be supporters. On the other hand, these energies and desires, if properly handled, can help energise a very different type of movement: 'the keen air of youth causes left-wing fire, when it burns, to burn even more strongly.'[17]

The peasantry are still rooted in ancient ways, and this makes them resistant to capitalist integration. Bloch quotes an old peasant proverb: 'work to which you are whistled is no good.' This ideological distance is grounded in the continued existence of peasant ownership of land. Unlike the relatively weak craft labour which capitalism could easily supersede, peasant ownership has provided strong bulwarks against the process of capitalisation. The peasantry has taken elements of urban capitalism – accounting methods, elements of mechanisation, some consumer goods – but on their own terms and in the service of traditional ways. A residual communality in rural life also helps attenuate and mask the undoubtedly great economic differences in the countryside; the peasantry feels itself to be a relatively unified 'caste'. Fascism has moved into this territory. Economic crisis has already made the peasantry susceptible to rightist nostrums. Furthermore, there is a great deal of suspicion, petty individualism and general conservatism in the peasantry. Fascism has thus found a degree of receptivity for the anti-modern and anti-urban elements in its ideological repertoire. The peasantry's

> tied existence, the relative ancient form of their conditions
> of production, of their customs, of their calendar life in the
> cycle of an unchanged nature, also contradicts urbaniz-

ation, unites with the reaction which is expert at non-contemporaneity.[18]

But, as this list suggests, Fascism is not the most appropriate home for these elements. Bloch refers to the 'cultural ground water' lying beneath such ancient ways:

Despite the radio and newspapers, couples live in the village for whom Egypt is still the land where the princess dragged the boy Moses out of the river, not the land of the pyramids or the Suez Canal; it continues to be seen from the viewpoint of the Bible and the children of Israel, not from that of the Pharaoh.[19]

As such, a very different future from one the Third Reich has here prefigured (or a very different Third Reich).

While the poverty of the indigent middle class makes it potentially revolutionary, its position in the process of production and its cultural memories make it fertile territory for Fascism. In this class a reactionary nostalgia dredges up old hatreds and old ideals: the 'Jewish usurer', the golden 'Germanic' past. All kinds of primitive desires well up to the surface: a patriotism 'reminiscent of primitively atavistic "participation mystique", of the attachment of primitive man to the soil which contains the spirits of his ancestors';[20] a credulous belief in Jewish and Masonic world conspiracies and in the mystic properties of the 'Blood'; a militarist regression into a thoughtless world of .obedience and violence; feudal and hierarchical fantasies born of fears of proletarianisation: 'the employee's desire not to be proletarian intensifies into an orgiastic desire for subordination, for a magical bureaucratic existence under a duke';[21] a transformation of ignorance into an anti-intellectual assault on 'mere' reason, and a retreat into earlier forms of consciousness. All of this is facilitated by the distance of the middle class from the act of production (unlike the proletariat), creating a gap in which the absurd can flourish. There is 'such a distance from social causality that an illogical space can develop . . . in which wishes and romanticisms, primeval drives and mythicisms revive'.[22] Even the specifically economic wishes of this stratum, encapsulated in the Fascist doctrine of the Corporate State, is an attempt to turn the clock back to the period of small-business early capitalism. However, there are different modes of irrationality, just as

111

there is the rationality of capitalism and the rationality of socialism. Bloch detects in the impoverished middle classes, 'in the
rage of millions, in the landscape which has become archaic
around them . . . fields of a different Irratio. . . . Living and newly
revived non-contemporaneities whose content is genuine.'[23] The
strategic implications are reiterated: 'fanaticism. . . . still benefits
the White Guards . . . as long as the revolution does not occupy
and rename the living yesterday.'[24]

Owing to its distinctive trajectory into the modern world,
Germany is particularly awash with non-contemporaneity:
'Germany . . . is . . . the classical land of non-contemporaneity.'[25]
Having only experienced a bourgeois revolution as late as 1918,
it has retained a mass of old economic forms and accompanying
ideology, from the poor peasantry at one end of the spectrum
to the aristocratic Junkers at the other. Unlike England and
France, German capitalism failed to integrate at the social, political or economic levels. This failure of integration, this fundamental weakness, allowed not merely the continuation of old
practices and mentalities, but created a vacuum into which very
old, barbaric material was sucked. Bloch employs vulcan imagery to portray this unequal capitalist development. Germany
is more 'volcanic' than, say, France; its thin crust cracks, and
material from very great depths comes to the surface: 'Precisely
this relative chaos then also rolled towards National Socialism
"untimely", non-contemporaneous elements from . even
"deeper" backwardness, namely from barbarism.'[26] Feeble, frag-
ile civil society is rapidly overwhelmed by a return of the most
primitive of impulses:

> a totally non-contemporaneous, indeed disparate insanity.
> We recall the tune: 'When Jewish blood spurts from the
> knife', which drifts over the SA troops as a swastika in
> music, we feel the dream of preserved insanity, preserved
> overcompensations from puberty in this kind of National
> Socialism . . . we find age-old sadism even at funeral cere-
> monies, in oaths of revenge or in the ceremonial rage at
> the 'memorial'.[27]

Unable to assimilate its past, Germany is being torn apart by it.

Bloch distinguishes the 'subjectively non-contemporaneous'
from the 'objectively non-contemporaneous'. The former is a
feeling of being historically out of joint with the contemporary

world; a dislike of, or unease in, the present: a 'muffled non-desire for the Now'.[28] The objectively non-contemporaneous is the continuing existence in the present of earlier modes of existence; a concrete historical residue: a 'remnant of earlier times in the present.'[29] In the case of the German petit bourgeoisie, as their position has worsened so the subjectively non-contemporaneous has changed from being merely a sense of embitterment with the times to being 'accumulated rage'[30] against the present. The objectively non-contemporaneous aspect of this is the declining and anachronistic way of life of the petit bourgeoisie which capitalism is slowly strangling, though it has yet to complete the job: 'an unrefurbished past which is not yet "resolved" in capitalist terms.'[31] However, there are both positive and negative aspects to these contradictions. Objective residues can indict both the present and the past, in that they represent a contradiction not merely of the capitalist present but of historical inadequacy in general. Thus the objectively grounded notions of 'home, soil and nation' testify to past as well as contemporary unfulfilment:

> they were contradictions even in their origin, namely to the past forms which never in fact wholly realised the intended contents of home, soil, and nation. They are thus already contradictions of unfulfilled intentions ab ovo, ruptures with the past itself ... throughout the whole of history as it were.[32]

The petit-bourgeois opposition to the present mixes this deep level of contradiction with images of 'the good old days' and produces its characteristic reactionary fantasies. None the less, the nuggets of gold are still there. The rage against the modern contains an element of rational anger against blocked historical potential. Fascism is only able to capitalise on the slogan of 'home, soil and nation', because of the deep and genuine longings tapped by those words – longings for security, rootedness and community.

Non-contemporaneous contradictions assume their current shape as a result of an 'objectively contemporaneous' contradiction – namely, the fundamental contradiction lying at the heart of the capitalist mode of production. It is precisely the underlying crises of capitalism which stimulate the reactionary fantasies of anachronistic classes. The class on the receiving end of the objective contradiction – the bourgeoisie – uses non-contemporaneous contradictions to hold back the disintegration of its mode of production and the advent of socialism: 'it uses the antagonism of a still living past as a means of separation and combat against the future dialectically giving birth to itself in the capitalist antagonisms.'[33] At the ideological level, nihilism, itself a contemporaneous product of the commodification of people under capitalism, is filled by petit-bourgeois 'harmonistic images of the past which merely seek to revoke the excess of capitalism or to subordinate it to themselves'.[34]

Bloch defines the objectively contemporaneous contradiction as the 'prevented future contained in the Now', and the subjectively contemporaneous contradiction as 'the free revolutionary action of the proletariat'.[35] Bloch's hope was that a 'Triple Alliance' could be formed, consisting of a proletarian leadership, the peasantry and impoverished middle class. For this to be achieved, the genuine anti-capitalist dimension in non-contemporaneous contradictions had to be identified and refunctioned into a broad revolutionary movement. And for this in turn to happen, Marxism itself must reject its vulgar dismissal of all forms of non-contemporaneous contradictions. In its analysis of Fascism, Marxism should be aware that 'whilst it is part of the nature of fascism to incorporate the morbid resources of all cultural phases . . . it is wrong to say only the morbid ones . . . as if the healthy ones were not accessible at all to the ideology of decay'.[36]

One can, of course, applaud Bloch's virtuoso exploration of the dreams of Weimar Germany, without necessarily accepting in its entirety the sociology in which it is encased. The proletariat inhabit the analysis in a highly stereotyped manner. As the bearers of the contemporary contradiction, they apparently have no rotten, reactionary dreams, and would seem, as a consequence, to be in no way implicated in the emergence of Fascism. Instead it is in other classes, the peasantry and, above all, the petit bourgeoisie that the problem is deemed to lie. Bloch's failure to explore the complex and less-than-spotless dream world of the working class deprives his analysis of comprehensiveness, and weakens it as a plausible account of the rise of Fascism. This is compounded by an inadequate awareness of the role of gender. Bloch does talk about the role of women, the oppression of women and of some women's fantasies, but his analysis is usually and unselfconsciously focused on male social actors, and even here, he does not seem to recognise the cross-cutting effect of gender on class relationships. The notion that specifically 'male fantasies' (to use Klaus Theweleit's expression[37]) could be a significant variable is simply not entertained. (This is, after all, the man who was to write in *The Principle of Hope* that 'the Soviet Union faces no question of women's rights any more, because it has solved the question of workers' rights'.[38]) His interpretation of the petit bourgeois is, here again, stereotyped; one detects a sneering and highly condescending tone in Bloch's remarks about 'the little man' and 'the shop-girl', which amounts, at times, to a collapse of political and social categories into those of manners and taste; a supercilious definition of 'vulgarity', its lazy equation with reaction, and a simplistic grounding in the caricature of a class. The importance of the petit bourgeois to the rise of Fascism is undeniable; it is Bloch's assessment of the degree of culpability of this class that is questionable.

Bloch's blinkered solicitude for the proletariat extends to a distinct soft-pedalling of criticisms of the workers' party – the German Communist Party (KPD). Despite all the criticisms he makes of vulgar Marxism in *Heritage of Our Times*, Bloch could still make the astonishing claim that 'what the party did before Hitler's victory was completely correct, it was simply what it did not do that was wrong'.[39] This is pure sophistry; for does not the failure to identify, analyse and recolonise the vital realm of dreams and fantasies vitiate the entire strategy? The claim concerning the 'correctness' of the party is also highly dubious, and again casts doubts on the explanatory value of his analysis. It passes over the role of Stalinist theory, strategy and tactics in the dividing and consequent weakening of working-class resistance to the rise of Hitler. It is difficult to see what was 'completely correct' in the KPD's designation of Social Democracy as 'Social Fascism', its bitter campaigns against fellow leftists and its tactical alliances with the Nazis. Bloch's characterisation of alternative leftist approaches as 'social democratic dilution' and 'Trotskyite obstructionism'[40] gives some insight into the fatal sectarian stance which underpinned his claim about the KPD. For Bloch to suggest otherwise might have entailed recognising a degree of personal culpability in the rise of Fascism.

There are significant gaps and unevennesses in his description of National Socialism. First, there is what one might term the absence of the Fascist in Bloch's analysis. There is no systematic analysis of the real National Socialist; Fascist ideology is described, its attractions highlighted, and potential and actual support is analysed, but the genuine Fascist is substantially missing. The 'duped', 'seduced' and 'intoxicated' (to use Bloch's terms) have a great deal of space devoted to them, but the duper, the seducer and the intoxicator do not. They only appear as fragments in analyses and descriptions – no sustained, three-dimensional presentation of a representative of the species ever appears. Second, there is an element of inconsistency in Bloch's portrayal of Fascism. He wished to suggest the strengths and dangers of Fascism *and* to convey a sense of the movement's fundamental absurdity. As all the opponents of Fascism found at the time, this was a very difficult balancing act. *Heritage of Our Times* oscillates between an appreciation of the cunning and skill of the National Socialists and a contemptuous dismissal of the movement. As a result there is a certain incoherence in his characterisation of Fascism. Third, there is a narrowness of focus in his description of the skills of the Fascists. Bloch is sensitive to the psychological dynamics of the transmission of Fascist ideology. However, as Anson Rabinbach has pointed out, there is relatively little focus on the technical/technological aspects of this process. By giving insufficient attention to how Fascism manipulates modern propaganda media, Bloch largely ignores a vital component in the strength and novelty of Fascism. In this respect Rabinbach contrasts Bloch with Benjamin unfavourably:

> Bloch ... does not go as far as Benjamin in identifying what is fully new in fascism: that the technical capabilities of the fascists make possible the actual participation of large masses of people in events. ... [H]is theory seems only indirectly concerned with *how* fascism organizes and maintains its hold.[41]

This element of distance between *Heritage of Our Times* and its ostensible object of study may possibly explain Walter Benjamin's own unfavourable reaction to the book. For Benjamin, *Heritage of Our Times* 'in no way corresponds to the circumstances

116

under which it has appeared', and is like, Benjamin tells us, a fine gentleman visiting an earthquake site who can do nothing better than surround himself with his faded finery.[42] Finally, Bloch uses the term 'Fascist' to do different types of work. There is the usage deployed in detailed historical analysis, as in his account of the emergence of German National Socialism. But there is also a looser, more functional deployment, where Fascism is used as a virtual synonym for a reactionary blockage, or mischannelling, of the new. The impulse here appears to be the desire to put Fascism in its place as a mere sub-system within capitalism; refusing to exceptionalise Fascism in order to emphasise the primacy of the capitalist mode of production. This latter approach permitted a rather promiscuous use of the term in inappropriate descriptions of a range of disparate phenomena. The 'functional' usage became debased, in later works, to a catch-all insult for any supposedly reactionary element of advanced capitalism, be it US foreign policy or the films of Hollywood.

MARXISM

Bloch had reached his late thirties by the time he began to develop a self-conscious Marxism. The first edition of *Spirit of Utopia* had already been published. There was thus a pre-existing body of ideas, a youthful system in place by the time of his voyage into Marxism. Thus although Marxism was to have an immense effect on his subsequent work, the earlier thinking had its own impact on the way Marxism was absorbed into the emerging system. Bloch began to appropriate Marx as a way of adding a deeper social dimension to his utopian philosophy. Initially, therefore, the process was viewed as the synthesis of two insufficient systems. From this perspective Marxism's socio-economic depth was not matched by insight into the profound motivations of the human subject. In the second edition of *Spirit of Utopia* (1923), for example, Bloch is openly critical of Marx's deficiencies; historical materialism contained a one-sided determinism which excluded the crucial, free creativity of the individual:

People, not things and not the mighty course of events outside ourselves (which Marx falsely places above us), write history. His determinism applies to the economic future, to the necessary economic-institutional change; but the new man, the leap, the power of love and life, and morality itself, are not yet accorded the requisite independence in the definitive social order.[43]

Lukács detected the same approach in Bloch's book on Thomas Münzer, and asserted the sufficiency of Marx, against Bloch, in *History and Class Consciousness*:

> When Ernst Bloch claims that this union of religion with socio-economic revolution points the way to a deepening of the 'merely economic' outlook of historical materialism, he fails to notice that his deepening simply by-passes the real depth of historical materialism.[44]

This criticism is interesting, because it anticipates a path Bloch was himself soon to tread. In the late 1920s and early 1930s he replaces the earlier 'synthesis of insufficient systems' approach with the notion that Marxism *was itself* the most advanced embodiment of the theoretical and practical tendencies of the age. Bloch therefore appears to collapse (or possibly inflate) his own system into Marxism. In reality, of course, under the rubric of 'Marxism', Bloch inserted Marxism into his own philosophy; though admittedly the form of this philosophy was itself heavily marked by the Marxist infusion.

The historical Marx is considered to be a point at which both subjective and objective tendencies creatively meet. The young Marx subjectively grasped the underlying, objective tendencies of the age, and began to work with the grain of history. Marx possessed the quality of 'genius', which enabled him both to bring the not-yet-conscious to consciousness, and to understand that this process was grounded in the objective movement of reality itself. Marx was

> a young genius who ... began to accomplish the objectively necessary in a particular sphere as his individual destiny, and who experienced the inspirational breakthrough of his work as no other could in fully grasped concurrence with the socio-historical tendency of his time.[45]

While necessary, Marx was by no means inevitable. Bloch's conception of genius, and his overall open-ended theory of history, precludes any notion of timetabled world-historical figures. It is the fact that the true and the real are not immediately apparent which makes the genius so precious. In his work on cultural geniuses, Bloch pointed to cultural gaps where the requisite genius simply failed to appear. The degree of his enthusiasm for Marx is a testimony to his belief that it could have been very different; one could not simply assume that a Marx would emerge. There is an explicit devotion to Marx which verges on the pious; the highest compliment he could pay his own work was to show that it was in accord with, or represented a development of, the work of Marx. Quite simply, Marxism was, for Bloch, the royal road to truth; as he told the audience at his inaugural lecture in Leipzig: 'whoever is seeking for *truth* must enter the realm opened up by Marx. There is no further truth, there is *no other.*'[46] Only towards the end of his life was he willing to develop an explicit critique of Marx, and even this was delivered in the context of sustained devotion.

Bloch's Marxism is a *humanist* Marxism. There is an inclusive and exclusive element here: Marxism is *merely* the latest phase in a long campaign for humanity, but *it alone* can claim to be continuing the fight; Marxism is both the cutting edge of the current struggle against dehumanisation and the true heir to the earlier phases. At the *theoretical* level, Marxism is the contemporary embodiment of a tradition of historically sensitive philosophical humanism: 'Marx kept alive an historical evolutionary humanism which derived from Leibniz, and which was mediated to him through Hegel';[47] while at the *political* level it has taken over the torch of humanity from the radical bourgeoisie:

> because Marxism in general is absolutely nothing but the struggle against the dehumanisation which culminates in capitalism until it is completely cancelled out, it follows . . . that genuine Marxism in its impetus, its class struggle and its goal-content is, can be, will be nothing but the promotion of humanity . . . it alone is the heir of the humaneness which was intended in the earlier, revolutionary bourgeoisie.[48]

Not surprisingly, Bloch rejects any attempt to divide Marx's work into an early humanism and a mature non-humanism. He denounces those 'who seek to split Marx in half',[49] and asserts that 'the mature Marx ... is the truth of the young Marx'.[50] He distinguishes abstract from concrete humanism, where abstract humanism is an indiscriminate and undifferentiated proclamation of 'goodwill to all', while concrete humanism is 'addressed' to those who most need it, and contains hostility towards those who are perpetuating dehumanisation. The goal of humanity requires action against those who, by their class activity, postpone everybody's humanity. Revolution is thus the realisation of humanity: 'the arch-humanistic element in social revolution finally removes the covering of self-alienation from all mankind.'[51] The transition from early to mature Marx is presented as a growing insight into the socio-economic dimensions of this fundamental humanist struggle: 'Marx transfers what he earlier called "real humanism" into the materialist interpretation of history.'[52]

Bloch's appreciation of the early Marx is indicative of a broader sympathy for the Hegelian dimension in Marxism. This, in turn, reflects a sensitivity to the positive aspects of the idealist tradition in general. In his work of the 1940s one detects a crusading zeal to vindicate the idealist heritage in Marxism. In his inaugural lecture at Leipzig (1949) he expressed the view that 'Idealism is a category, a very significant one ... and therefore is not yet a completely exhausted mine' and referred to 'the gigantic stretch of idealism, and ... the ferments working toward truth that are contained in the husks of idealism'.[53] In the case of Hegel it was his dialectical idealism which most excited Bloch. His 1949 text *Subjekt–Objekt. Erläuterungen zu Hegel* (*Subject–Object. Commentaries on Hegel*) highlights the debt which dialectical materialism (a term which Bloch uses in an entirely positive sense) owes to the great idealist dialectician, Hegel. Hegel is therefore of fundamental importance because 'for Marx, a concretised dialectics controls all his analyses, and overlays all his hopes'.[54] One can see in Bloch's presentation of Marx's 'correction' of Hegel the hand of Marx *and* Bloch himself. Thus there is the acknowledgement of Marx's undoubted jettisoning of Hegel's quasi-mystical universal spirit: 'Hegel's interpretation of dialectics is a mere to-and-fro conversation in a cosmic discourse, so to speak, of a world architect with himself.'[55] However, Bloch perceives in a second rejection a theme very close to his own heart – the incompatibility between 'recollection' and open system. Recollection (*anamnesis*) is both an epistemological and an ontological concept for Bloch. In epistemological terms, it refers to the Platonic theory of knowledge as memory, and is rejected because of its exclusion of genuinely *new* knowledge. In the case of ontology, Bloch sees it in the assumption that a pre-existing substance lies at the heart of reality, the result of a past and completed creation. Once again there is no place for the truly new in this model, for there is no open process. He credits Marx with perceiving this in Hegel, and abandoning it:

> Another Hegelianism dropped by Marx is that of mind doubly spiritualised as reminiscence which, in the dialectical procession of minds, ultimately eliminates *not* minds but, on the contrary, the course, the process, or – as Marx says – the space of production, which is Time. Yet the real totality and its really universal substrate now become really visible – as *dialectical, processual matter which retains its openness*. This does not reduce the fundamental essence to something past or to some substance which in every aspect has been wholly 'ready' from the outset.[56]

The new materialism is therefore not a mechanical materialism of inert, unfruitful matter but a dialectical materialism, which 'envisages matter as being dynamically active in the direction of the future, to which the past itself refers'.[57] This is the crux of Bloch's reference to the continuing validity of idealism – its exploration of dynamic openness renders it an enduring resource; Engels' *Dialectics of Nature* is cited as an example of the creative development of this legacy, and Bloch clearly placed his own work in the same tradition.

Bloch believed that he had found in Marx a sensitivity to the future-in-the-past that matched his own. Again the allure of the early Marx is evident. Marx's early work on religion, and the critique of Hegel, are invoked when Bloch claims that 'setting things on their feet' is not the same as stripping phenomena of their sublimity; nor is 'correcting' the historical inheritance the same as attenuating it; that, on the contrary, 'a good substance is in fact not weakened when it is corrected, and even more obviously it is not secularized when, once set on its feet, it is realized'.[58] A text he never tired of quoting was Marx's 1843 letter to Ruge claiming that 'the world has long possessed the dream of a thing of which it only needs to possess the consciousness in order really to possess it. . . . [H]umanity is not beginning a new work, but consciously bringing its old work to completion.' Marx was thereby enlisted as a champion of Bloch's long-standing belief in a protean and cumulative heritage stretching across the centuries towards ultimate fulfilment in the future. Marx's formulation in the Ruge letter, according to Bloch, 'transforms history from the temple of memory into an arsenal'.[59]

For Bloch, Marxism is unique in that it has the capacity to allow the combination of scientific analysis with utopian longing; analysis schools the dream, while the dream energises the analysis: 'Reason cannot blossom without hope, hope cannot speak without reason, both in Marxist unity – no other science has any future, no other future any science.'[60] Bloch also expresses this through two further pairings – sobriety and enthusiasm, and cold and warm streams. Sobriety is a necessary component of any revolutionary struggle, for it asks hard questions and demands rigorous analysis. What Bloch terms the 'bon sens' of genuine sobriety is distinguished from mere common sense which is deeply imbued with ideology and prejudice. Enthusiasm is defined as 'imagination in action',[61] it is the future-oriented zip and vigour, the speculative élan required to give any movement real momentum. The Marxist task is to maintain a varying balance between these elements, so as to assist the development of underlying objective tendencies:

> it is equally unwise and alien to Marxism to reach under reality with nothing but sobriety, as it is to overreach it with nothing but enthusiasm; the Real, precisely as that of tendency, is attained only by the constant oscillation of both aspects in *trained perspective*.[62]

Likewise there has to be both the 'cold stream' of painstaking analysis and the 'warm stream'[63] of revolutionary rapture. In short, 'only Marxism is both the detective and the liberator'.[64]

Once Bloch became a Marxist, the revolutionary proletariat formed the centrepiece of his politics. Unlike many Western Marxists who sought to transform, diminish or drop the role of proletariat in their socio-political theory, Bloch kept faith with Marx's 'universal class'. He held on tenaciously to Marx's belief that the proletariat was the only class in capitalist society whose socio-economic position forced it to confront and unmask the deceptions of capitalism, and usher in the liberation of both itself and the whole of society. Even in the late 1960s, while accepting that the proletariat had not become progressively impoverished in advanced capitalism, he none the less maintained that Marx's impoverishment proposition had merely been 'suspended until a fresh crisis hits the employed much harder than the big employers'.[65] He was prepared to acknowledge that 'some manifestations of the essential nature of capitalism have changed' *but* 'the essential nature of capitalism has not changed, and re-establishes itself time and again'.[66] The category 'proletariat' was still at the heart of his analysis.

From the beginning, Bloch had to fit his belief in the revolutionary role of the proletariat into his broader perception that utopian yearnings were to be found across social classes and in diverse cultural forms. In *Heritage of Our Times* he developed the notion of the 'multi-layered dialectic'.[67] The contemporaneous contradiction in capitalism is *subjectively*, proletarian revolutionary activity, and *objectively*, the socialist mode of production gestating in the womb of capitalism. Alongside this are the non-contemporaneous classes and their hybrid ideologies. A Marxist strategy has to yoke the anti-capitalist dimensions in the latter to the fundamental, contemporaneous contradiction in capitalism. In dialectical terms, this means that 'the entirety of earlier development is not yet "resolved" in capitalism and its dialectic'; that capitalism is 'not the only house of history to be dialectically inherited',[68] and that therefore, a new 'totality' has to be created which can release all the trapped potential of past and present moments. This Bloch distinguished from 'historicism', which treats all past and present voices as having equal value, and 'sociologism' which imposes schematic laws on the past. Sensitivity to differing times, locations and rates of change is essential: 'A multi-temporal and multi-spatial dialectic, the polyrhythmics and the counterpoint of such a dialectic are thus precisely the instrument of the *mastered* final stage of totality.'[69] In practice, this means a critical, and activist, proletarian hegemony over the classes of non-contemporaneity. Bloch employs a choral metaphor:

> The proletarian voice of the contemporaneous dialectic firmly remains the leading one; yet beneath and above this cantus firmus there run disordered exuberances which are to be referred to the cantus firmus only through the fact

that the latter – in critical and non-contemplative totality – refers to them.[70]

It is not easy to characterise Bloch's broader Marxist political perspective: his views were not static, and there were complicated internal differentiations. After two initial phases (pre-Marxist until about 1918, and the transitional synthesis which lasted until the mid-1920s), one can identify three broad Marxist phases: (1) his period as an independent Marxist (mid-1920s until 1949); (2) the GDR experience (1949–1961); and (3) the subsequent West German period (1961–1977). In Bloch's first Marxist period, it is necessary to distinguish between his views on the Soviet Union and his analyses of Marxism in the West. Oskar Negt has called Bloch 'the German Philosopher of the October Revolution';[71] but this is a misleading description, which occludes what was a changing and nuanced approach to the Soviet Union. In 1917 and 1918 Bloch's response to the Bolshevik Revolution had very much stressed its otherness. His head filled with Dostoyevsky and Tolstoy, he had welcomed the revolution as a kind of semi-mystical emanation from Holy Mother Russia, though he was hostile to the godlessness and inhumanity of the Bolsheviks, and used atavistic labels such as the 'Red Tsar' and 'Ghengis Khan' to refer to Lenin. There was an implicit contrast between a primeval Russia and a modern Europe;[72] furthermore, his whole orientation during the First World War had been, contra Lenin, one of support for the advanced western democracies of Britain, France and America against backward Prussian militarism. As he wrote at the time:

> As certain as it is, for example, that Lenin's dictatorship can be explained by the absence of an industrial proletariat forming the majority, so little does this by itself explain everything. As certain it is that definite czarist tendencies with the flag of freedom on the bayonet are being carried on in present-day Bolshevist Russia, just as certain does the sense of the following pro-Entente and not only abstract radical socialist principle apply, that each people can expect a kind of socialism according to the measure of its former bourgeois freedom, of its degree of recognition of persons, suspicion of the state and liberalism.[73]

Once a Marxist, however, Bloch's public characterisations of the

Russian revolution and its leadership reflected the Soviet self-image. Even in his final period, when he was out of sympathy with developments in the East, he could claim that the problems of the revolution were 'masterfully reduced by Lenin's call for electrification plus Socialism' and that 'long into Stalin's regime, Marxism was at home only in the Soviet Union'.[74] Bloch would have seen his response to the Soviet Union in the 1930s as embodying the unity of enthusiasm and sobriety. Enthusiasm could be found in an unstinting rhetoric: 'If Lenin was the Caesar of the Soviet Union, then Stalin became its Augustus, its "augmenter" in all respects', or 'It does one good, after all the wavering of the West, to see an achievement about which one can say with all one's heart, yes, yes, yes'.[75] In the 1930s he doggedly defended the USSR against its various critics. His 1937 article 'A jubilee for renegades' is a ruthless defence of the Moscow show trials. He makes it quite clear that he accepts the Soviet State's version of events: that 'this 20-year-old bolshevist child must rid itself of so many enemies',[76] and that this is the 'moment the Revolutionary Tribunal put[s] enthusiasm to the test'.[77] The need for trials is not traced to any fundamental defect in the system but to the worsening international situation which, linked with internal subversion, was thereby threatening the security of the revolution (hence his readiness, at the time, to accept that Trotsky was a Gestapo agent). However, his undoubted naivety and willingness to defend the USSR publicly should not be seen as indicating either an entirely uncritical stance towards Soviet Russia nor an unwillingness to criticise the German Communist Party (KPD). Bloch's first Marxist period was dominated by the struggle against a Fascism unleashed, he maintained, by capitalism, and it was his belief that the Soviet Union represented the only hope for Socialism in such a perilous world. In these circumstances, as he put it, 'anti-bolshevist statements serve only the devil himself' and 'senselessly exaggerated criticism of the homeland of the revolution will not benefit the ideal of revolution'.[78] There was thus a real reluctance on Bloch's part to say anything which would play into the hands of the enemy. This was revolutionary 'sobriety' standing firm in the face of 'renegade' loss of enthusiasm.

When it came to criticising the German Communist Party, or when discussion was concerned with less 'direct' theoretical issues, Bloch was not so reticent. Although he absolved the KPD of errors of commission, he had no doubts as to the grave errors of omission. The failure to cope with Fascism owed a great deal to the abstract, schematic and rationalistic approach of the Party, which had failed to lock into the contradictory particularity of the various social classes:

> The position of the 'Irratio' within the inadequate capitalist 'Ratio' has been all too abstractly cordoned off, instead of its being examined from case to case and the particular contradiction of this position being concretely occupied.[79]

Likewise, in his debates over Expressionism with Lukács and other Moscow-based theoreticians he had polemicised against the reductionist theory of 'realism' evident in their aesthetics, and had championed western avant-garde art. We should also recall that Bloch at no time became a member of the KPD.

The two positions can be reconciled if we assume that, during this period, Bloch already held a theory we know he was later to hold explicitly – that the different historical trajectories of Russia and the West created entirely different fields of operation. Such a theory would also display a degree of continuity with his 'primeval Russia' notions of 1917 and 1918. If this supposition is correct it would mean that he held, on the one hand, that the underdeveloped base of the revolution had forced the Soviet Union to pull itself up by its bootstraps, and it therefore needed unstinting support from its friends in the West (including, of course, the avoidance of the 'insulting' view that there might be something 'backward' in its development); while in the developed West, on the other hand, with its own traditions and inheritances, a different style of politics was the order of the day. This is not to say that Bloch was a Marxist-Leninist only with respect to the Soviet Union; rather, he believed that Marxism-Leninism had to be sensitive to differing contexts. The reconciliation was clearly not perfect. Bloch's silences are deafening. If the KPD is in error, where does the ultimate fault, in a 'World Communist Movement', lie? If Lukács' 'realism' is reductive, what does this say about Soviet 'socialist realism'?

These problems came to a head in Bloch's second Marxist period – his years in East Germany. If Bloch had been working with a East/West dualism, he now had to confront, and physically live in, the place where East met West – a Soviet Marxist-Leninist regime established in the homeland of high German culture. His initial response was to embrace enthusiastically the self-image of the new polity. Under the theoretical guidance of Lenin and Stalin, the political guidance of the party and the administrative guidance of central planning, the society was advancing towards the goal of full communism. In his 1949 inaugural lecture in Leipzig Bloch maintained that 'the always keen and well-thought-out, open and concrete wisdom of Lenin and Stalin,[80] watches over the path to the classless society',[81] and that 'out of this non-schematic approach new intermediate analyses of situations, always more concrete and expanded two-year, five-year, plans of theory and practice are always arising. . . . But to this end all faces must be turned in one and the same direction.'[82] In *The Principle of Hope*, a thoroughgoing Leninism is evident:

> it is no accident that apart from the tolerant element as it were that expresses itself in the realm of *freedom*, Marxism is also animated by the cathedral element as it were, which expresses itself precisely in the *realm* of freedom, in freedom as a *realm*. The paths to it are likewise not liberal; they are the capture of power in the state, discipline, authority, central planning, a general line, and orthodoxy.[83]

Capitalist encirclement was still deployed to justify continued support for the Soviet Union; only now it was the 'Imperialist' USA, rather than Hitler, that spearheaded the capitalist onslaught on the home of socialism; in fact Bloch's functional definition of Fascism allowed him on a number of occasions to directly use the term 'Fascist' in relation to America. The 'capitalist threat' also enabled him to take a 'sober' stance on the problems of socialist construction in East Germany – defence against Imperialism was not without cost; sacrifices had to be made. In the opinion of his son Jan Robert, who was a schoolboy at the time, Bloch became blind to the oppression before his eyes: 'all around him, the injustice was tangible. It did not have to be transmitted, but Bloch's telescope did not see it.'[84] However, the increasing pressures which Bloch began to experience, culminating in his public denunciation by the state, combined with an inexorable disillusionment, forced Bloch to reassess the East/West dualism. The inadequacies of the GDR not only reinforced his belief in the need for sensitivity to local conditions, but finally forced him to develop an open critique of the inadequacies of the Soviet system itself. After a period of semi-covert existence, these ideas came to be stated explicitly after Bloch had left the GDR in 1961 – they constitute his third Marxist period.

In a 1968 speech given to celebrate the 150th anniversary of the birth of Marx, Bloch shared his reflections on the history of Marxism. The Bolshevik Revolution was now to be seen as a brave attempt to build Socialism in conditions which favoured the emergence of a Stalinist tyranny. On a tsarist base, a tsarist 'socialism' had triumphed over the best intentions of Lenin. Stalin was no longer to be bracketed with Lenin:

> It should be clear that the absence of bourgeois revolutionary modernisation in Czarist Russia necessarily had specific consequences in the new Russia. There the springs of social wealth ran not richer but poorer than in more developed capitalist countries. In the absence of long-standing forms of bourgeois freedom the predicted dictatorship of the proletariat had to be established directly on the basis of the Czarism that had immediately preceded it. Among the results were the personality cult, an extensive and absolutist centralisation, lack of room for any except a 'criminal' opposition, the terror and the police state, and an all-powerful state police. . . . In short, besides many excellent Marxist achievements, a wholly undemocratic 'Socialism' was established on the historical basis of Russian reaction.[85]

Bloch also now displays a more relaxed attitude to Marx, which is less defensive and more questioning; he asks if there was perhaps something lacking in Marx's own work which might have prevented such a perversion of his essentially open and undogmatic system: 'it is pertinent to ask why certain purely theoretical features in Marx did not hinder the emergence of such practices, even if they did not evoke them.'[86] Thus he asks whether there was a lack of rigour in Marx's conception of the dictatorship of the proletariat which allowed Stalin to turn it into a tyranny; he begins to quote with increasing frequency Rosa Luxemburg's phrase: 'No democracy without socialism, no socialism without democracy.' His long-standing criticism of 'realism' is now directly related to Marx, as he asks whether there was a connection between Marx's own neo-classical aesthetics and 'the dictatorship of utterly uncreative functionaries over artists and writers that could so affect the evolution of Soviet art'.[87] Finally, and of particular relevance after his own brushes with a Marxist state, he wondered aloud about the relatively weak presence of Enlightenment liberalism in Marx's work: 'Undoubtedly, there is in Marx a certain lack of emphasis on, and sometimes also an absence of, enlightenment, which certainly served to reinforce the centralizing tendency in Stalinism' and 'in addition, hindsight shows [a] comparatively weak emphasis on personal freedoms in Marx'.[88]

If there is too little Enlightenment in Marxism regarding personal rights and freedoms, there is, in a sense, too much in the excesses of its scientism. Bloch now deems Marx's critique of utopianism to have been too severe and to have assisted the development of a hyper-rationalism in subsequent Marxism, which thereby went against the grain of Marx's most profound ideas: 'Marx was a scientific iconoclast who prepared the way for the commonwealth of freedom. Nevertheless, the advance from utopia to science was too extreme.'[89] Building on long-expressed criticisms, Bloch excoriates the abstract models, spun by Marxists, which had failed to engage with the complex lived experiences of actual people. A living Marxism therefore had to set its Enlightenment legacies in order. Hence Bloch ends his lecture (and his reflections on the fate of twentieth-century Marxism, in which his life had been so bound up) on a positive note. His was no trajectory out of Marxism – 'In 1968 we celebrate the one hundred and fiftieth anniversary of the birth of Karl Marx. We still have reason to hope for a *concrete* celebration in 2018.'[90]

The political theorist and Labour Party activist Harold Laski, when challenged at a public meeting, retorted: 'Yes, my friend, we are both Marxists, you in your way, I in Marx's.' This was Bloch's position also. He claimed not to be merely interpreting Marx, but to be developing the essence of Marx's own work – not simply because he believed Marx to be 'right', but because Marx's theory was itself the expression of objective tendencies in reality. Such a claim places a great obligation on Bloch to present an accurate account of Marx's work. As one might expect in such a creative thinker, Bloch's Marx says infinitely more about Bloch than it does about Marx; or as Wayne

Hudson more delicately puts it: 'As an interpreter of Marx, Bloch is original but idiosyncratic.'[91] Although Bloch asserts the continuity of Marx's output, he himself is heavily grounded in the early Hegelian Marx, and he makes relatively few forays into the output of Marx's maturity. He also tends to repeat a relatively few quotations from Marx, and these are not always mainstream. The overall impression is not of a detailed and exhaustive portrayal of the whole project of the historical Marx, but of a very selective use of aspects of Marx's work in the development of a distinctively Blochian theoretical system.

Selectivity might also reflect a certain tension between Bloch and Marx. As we have already noted, Bloch came to Marxism with an existing body of thought; initially at least, he found Marx's work wanting on the nature of human intervention in history. Although subsequently united in an all-embracing 'Marxism', Bloch's earlier, pre-Marxist perceptions still exercised an influence, and constantly introduced sympathetic material, as it were, into the ongoing system. Clearly then, there was ample scope for tension to arise within the Blochian system between the early utopian philosophy, and the historical materialism, however humanist, of Marxism. The question of the compatibility of Bloch and Marx is a difficult one to resolve. Bloch claimed he was developing Marx's work, not slavishly copying it, and obviously we have no way of knowing what Marx's attitude to such subsequent developments as the notion of 'Reimannian time' might have been. On the other hand, Bloch did maintain that he was in harmony with the essence of Marx's thought, and he also ventured into areas in which Marx could have 'anticipated' him – but did not. Thus Bloch grounds his entire worldview on a radical-Aristotelian materialism; Marx, who was undoubtedly familiar with Aristotle, did not develop such a notion. Indeed, Bloch has to turn to the work of Engels to find anything remotely adjacent to his own dialectical materialism in the classic corpus of Marxism, although Engels' compatibility with Marx in this area has itself been questioned. The absence in Marx's work of a developed materialism was not a mere oversight, but reflected precisely the 'humanism' which Bloch so admired. Marx was concerned with the historical modalities of *human* production – matter, as in the form of nature, was of interest only insofar as it intersected with the human domain. Bloch's immersion in esoteric nature philosophy might, of course, make him a more interesting figure than Marx, but it is difficult to see him as cut from the same cloth.[92] Marx's own mature *magnum opus* is a painstaking and rigorous analysis of the anatomy of capitalism; Bloch, in contrast, simply takes Marx's social categories as self-evident givens. Bloch displays little of Marx's socio-economic sensitivity; he *is* sensitive to social manners, style and beliefs, but this co-exists somewhat uneasily with a rather crude, derivative class taxonomy. For a thinker who stresses dynamic processes, there is a curious rigidity and sluggishness about his economic classes; his social world is populated with '*the* bourgeoisie', '*the* proletariat', '*the* peasantry' and '*the* petit bourgeoisie'; there is a relative absence of delineation, of internal differentiation, or of a sense of mutability.

What are we to make of the political aspects of his Marxism? In his first Marxist period Bloch frequently displayed ignorance, naivety, double standards and a coarse and vituperative, polemical approach to political opponents. It was not simply that he was empirically mistaken about the Soviet Union; there was an element of ideological ignorance, an unwillingness to probe too deeply, as well as an outward suppression of those doubts that did exist. Any doubts which he may have entertained did not, however, prevent him from using such emotive terms as 'renegade' against those who voiced their own doubts. In this first period, if what we have argued above is true, he could at least console himself with the belief that the Soviet Union was attempting to build socialism in a backward society, and where the alternative was Fascism. Once he was in East Germany after the war, the situation was different. True, he could use the argument of 'American Imperialist' pressure, but Germany, though devastated by the war, was no backward society. One suspects that Bloch had to develop all kinds of psychological devices to block out, explain away, or live with, the gap between his continuing Stalinist rhetoric and the by now quite undeniable degradations of the reality. The balancing act could not last and, under pressure himself, Bloch began a process of fundamental reassessment. However, he undertook this in a curiously detached manner. His son, Jan Robert, recalled Bloch's blasé response to Khrushchev's denunciation of the Stalinist era in 1956:

Bloch took the 20th Party Congress's political measure in his own way: 'How simply getting rid of something can enrich us' . . . as though a relieved, observing cavalier was speaking and not a philosophical protagonist of precisely that which had been 'gotten rid off', as though it were not an issue of facts but of opinions.[93]

Once in West Germany, Bloch did develop a critique of Stalinism, and of Marx himself. Here again, however, there was a degree of reticence about his own culpability. There was both silence, and an attempt to historicise and generalise his response to Stalinism. Thus in a conversation with Michael Landmann in 1968, he implied that his defence of the Soviet Union was typical of left émigrés in 1940:

> In 1940 we (the leftist emigrants) in the USA all thought that fascism was the inevitable last stage of capitalism and that Russia would never become fascist. This prognosis turned out to be false. The *citoyen* of the French Revolution became the *bourgeois* of capitalism. Who knows what the Soviet *comrade* will become?[94]

Any guilt was thus to be dispersed in the supposed, shared beliefs of long ago. This lack of sustained self-critique tarnishes the greater political clarity of his final years.

5

NATURAL LAW, UTOPIANISM AND NATURE

This final chapter deals with three perennial themes in Bloch's work. The first of these, natural law, is not one normally associated with the Marxist tradition, and its long-standing strictures on 'bourgeois' rights. For Bloch, however, the natural law tradition was rich in humanist values, and was therefore a far from spent force. Its central concern with human *dignity* placed it at the forefront of the struggle for a genuine socialism, and Bloch's own experience of the indignities of the 'socialism' of the GDR certainly reinforced this conviction. The concern of utopianism is with human *happiness*. Bloch's entire philosophy is utopian, but it is worth examining his specific analyses of the various *forms* of utopianism. For example, in *The Principle of Hope*, Bloch develops a vast taxonomy of manifestations of the utopian, encompassing a quite extraordinary range of phenomena. Alongside the exuberant open-endedness of this approach, one can also detect the desire to discipline the utopian in an attempt to develop a politically realistic utopianism. This said, Bloch was not always successful in avoiding an authoritarian utopianism. Finally, we shall consider Bloch's thoughts on nature. In a sense, this will bring the study full circle, for Bloch's philosophical starting point is the dynamic creativity of the material. It was his conviction that the adventure of this material universe had only just begun, and that the production of humanity, though nature's most spectacular feat to date, was by no means its last. It is therefore appropriate to finish with Bloch's spectacular cosmological speculations.

133

NATURAL LAW

In 1961, Bloch's *Naturrecht und menschliche Würde* (*Natural Law and Human Dignity*) was published in West Germany. The theme of the book is the continuing validity of the natural law concern with human rights and dignity. The fact that this was the year Bloch himself moved from East to West Germany inevitably suggests two tempting, and interrelated, hypotheses: first, that the book was conceived in response to his disillusionment with the GDR, and second, that it represents a fundamental break with the orientation of his previous Marxism. Both these hypotheses should be resisted. *Natural Law and Human Dignity* itself started life as a manuscript of Bloch's American period (1938–1949) and was provisionally entitled *Naturrecht und Sozialismus* (*Natural Right and Socialism*); in other words, *before* Bloch's sojourn in the GDR. In a 1939 address to German émigré writers in America he had extolled America's 'democratic' and 'humanistic' ideology, the importance of ancient republican ideals in the period of George Washington and the effect of the Enlightenment, and had ended the address thus: 'We, German writers in America . . . are working at the one necessary task: the realisation of the rights of man.'[1] Even in his notorious 'A jubilee for renegades' of 1937 with its defence of the Moscow Show Trials, in which one might have expected a certain reluctance to discuss natural rights, Bloch commended the natural law tradition. The central theme of the article was the parallel between the 'renegades' of the French Revolution and those of the Bolshevik Revolution. The German writers who had deserted the earlier revolution in the face of popular disorder had failed to grasp that it was the bourgeoisie who had destroyed the promise of their revolution: 'the songs of mourning delivered by Klopstock and Schiller were directed at the wrong corpse – at the broken palm branch rather than the perished citoyen.'[2] Even earlier, during the First World War and prior to his Marxism, Bloch had aligned himself with the democratic powers against the autocracy of the German state. He had also linked the dictatorial elements of the young Bolshevik state to the lack of a strong tradition of 'bourgeois freedom' in Russia. In short, Bloch had long been interested in the natural rights tradition and the humanist heritage it embodied; and he had clearly integrated this into his Marxism from the very start. None the less, the East

German experience had a clear influence on the development of his ideas on natural law. He emerged with a heightened sense of the distinct nature of having one's humanity insulted; his firsthand experience of a 'socialist' police state undoubtedly brought home to him the horrors of the practical denial of human rights, and provided him with a greater appreciation of the natural law lacunae in the Marxist tradition.

In the Preface to *Natural Law and Human Dignity* Bloch considers it paradoxical that socialism (by which he really means Marxism), given its humanist basis, has been so hostile to the natural law tradition. As with all his analyses of intellectual heritage, Bloch wishes to identify, in the midst of manifold ideological forms, the progressive core of the tradition. Liberalism has merely been the most recent vehicle for the eminently human concerns of natural law. The image of the upright gait haunts the tradition, and links it to the essential interests of a humanist Marxism:

> To this humanism there belongs the question of the *genuine* intentions of the old natural law, to it there belongs the task of a socialistic heritage in these formally liberal, but not merely liberal, *human rights*. The establishment of honesty and uprightness against a well-padded, re-christened, and retrogressive subordination is a postulate of natural law that is found nowhere else.[3]

This inheritance is to be found in Marx, who, we are informed, 'is not merely giving economic advice when he teaches us "to overthrow all relations in which man is a degraded, enslaved, abandoned, or despised being" '.[4] Natural law cannot be outdated, because the object of its critique – dehumanisation – is itself alive and well; but it has to be integrated into a framework which recognises that 'human dignity is not possible without economic liberation, and this liberation is not possible without the cause of human rights'.[5] Bloch emphasises that this does not mean that the two elements are 'automatically born of the same act'[6] – rather, that they require one another to flourish.

Bloch distinguishes the heritage of the natural law tradition from that of social utopianism. Both were concerned with the human world, and with making it more humane; but unfortunately they had different foci, and therefore pursued independent paths; there was no co-ordinated attack. Social utopias were concerned with happiness and the removal of toil and burden, and tended to deploy an enthusiastic mode of anticipation. Natural law, in contrast, was concerned with dignity and the removal of degradation and insult, and tended to deploy a sober mode of anticipation. However, the natural law tradition is not, at its best, a merely passive, moralistic approach. Natural law does not coincide with justice; rather, it has been the banner of those attempting to achieve justice; it can therefore be located in the historical struggle of the downtrodden to move beyond a mere abstract justice, grounded in an external authority, towards a concrete just society:

> Genuine natural law, which posits the free will in accord with reason, was the first to reclaim the justice that can only be obtained by struggle; it did not understand justice as something that descends from above and prescribes to each his share, distributing or retaliating, but rather as an active justice of below, one that would make justice itself unnecessary. Natural law never coincided with a mere sense of justice.[7]

Understood in this way, Bloch believes, the natural law tradition can be fruitfully combined with the resources of social utopianism.

Natural Law and Human Dignity presents a historical account of the emergence of natural law doctrines from the ancient world into the modern, and it attempts to chart the complex ways in which natural law can be both affirmative and subversive of the social order. The periodisation is Marxist. The historical watershed is the gathering pace of the bourgeois assault on feudalism from the seventeenth century onwards; from this point, natural law is drawn into the fundamental social dynamics of modernity. In the earlier modes of production Bloch particularly singles out the achievements of the Stoics. They are credited with the earliest doctrine of an essentially humanist natural law, and are related by Bloch to that other great ancient source of radical thought, the Bible:

> Stoicism had taught equal rights for all on the basis of the unity of the human race. The contact with the ancient prophets of Israel, who were the first to lay claim to an analogous position, was a singular event full of conse-

quence. The unity of the human race, the natural right to peace, formal democracy, mutual aid – through the Stoics, all of these principles came to be the beginnings of a more or less definite concept.[8]

It was not, however, a radical reading of the Bible which infused natural law theories in medieval western Europe. In a negative appraisal of Thomism, Bloch posits an ideological reduction of the tradition to the oppressive needs of a corporate society. The stirrings of the modern are detected in the divisions of the Reformation and Counter-Reformation, as both Calvinists and Jesuits confront states hostile to their own beliefs; natural law doctrines appear, embodying notions of popular sovereignty and rights of resistance. This leads on to a lengthy analysis of the complexities of the bourgeois restructuring of natural law, and encompasses a wide range of thinkers from Hobbes and Grotius to Kant and Fichte; the section ends with a discussion of what Bloch saw as the decrepitude of bourgeois natural law in German juridical liberalism – where the terminus was the Fascist 'assassination' of natural law. In a discussion of the function of positive, or state law, Bloch takes the opportunity to ventilate, albeit in a slightly oblique fashion, some thoughts on socialist violation of legality. His theme is Zola's melding of natural and positive law in *J'accuse*; Bloch comments:

> one finds here moral, methodological elements . . . of a will to scientifically establish the facts that are to serve as instructions for locating justice. That no one who is innocent may be condemned, that one who is guilty and revealed as such must be struck down without any possible protection, that no important document may be based on falsehoods, and that no document that may exonerate someone may be kept secret or only treated as a small matter: These 'self-evident truths' are not historically transient or subject to fluctuations like stocks on the market, which rise and fall according to the military or governmental state of affairs. . . . The path that leads to the classless society will not be permitted to be distinguished from this image of the impartiality of the consciousness of law and the rigor of a legality that is not merely formally democratic. Revolutions overturn the old positive law, but

if they remain revolutions they do not create a new injustice.[9]

The voice of bitter personal experience would appear to be speaking here.

Bloch explores the resonances of the term 'natural' in natural law. He detects a link with, or an echo of, early myths of a maternal nature in formulations of natural law from the Stoics to Rousseau. Bloch plunges into the space created within Marxism by Engels' *The Origin of the Family, Private Property, and the State*, though the point of entry is Bachofen rather than Morgan. It is a world of conflict between feminine and masculine principles. In these ancient images, a maternal law embodies the values of blood ties, of protection and nurture, of harmony with nature; a 'humanist' value system in opposition to the artificial and domineering world of the masculine; the goddess Demeter is the symbolic form of this primordial mother – Demeter as legislator. For the Stoics the dignity of nature in its maternal form extends to the dignity of the individual, of the person who must be respected because they embody the status of nature herself. Well over a millennium later, maternal images of nature abound in Rousseau – not just in *Emile* but also in *The Social Contract*. The persistence of images of nature as a 'great mother' across the centuries has refreshed the humanist agenda in the natural law tradition: 'the traits of the ancient maternal law have remained recognizable in the many formations of philosophical natural law insofar as nature conserves, or presents anew, the face of a *magna mater*.'[10] Again, Bloch stresses the centrality of dignity; this is not a social utopian vision of happiness.

The high point of bourgeois natural law, for Bloch, was the period of the French Revolution. He notes the deficiencies of the revolutionary slogan of liberty, equality and fraternity, the ambiguities and the actual and potential distortions; yet he asserts, contra Horkheimer, that the genuine heritage of the Revolution is ultimately socialist: 'Freedom, equality, fraternity, the orthopedia of the upright carriage, of human pride, and of human dignity point far beyond the horizon of the bourgeois world.'[11] Marx is read as displaying an ultimately positive attitude towards this inheritance. The Marx of *On the Jewish Question* (1844), with its hostility to the 'rights of man', is seen as reacting to the hypocrisy of the bourgeois masking of the profit motive with fine talk of 'rights'; the unmasking required a critique of the ideology of human rights. Even here, however, a more positive appraisal of the bourgeois heritage is to be found; for Marx argues that the abstract rights of the citizen, isolated and limited in bourgeois society, need to be reappropriated and refunctioned by the concrete subject of a rational society. Marx recognised that the bourgeois image of the citizen contained more than a legitimation of the free market. Once he had passed this early period of a hypercritical approach to rights, Bloch argues, 'Marx permitted a warmer light to fall even on human rights'.[12] Marx, in this interpretation, appreciated the 'futural content' and 'forward effect' of rights; that, for example, 'freedom is criticised so little that, quite the contrary, it is that human right whose radiance and humanity provide the standards for Marx's critique of private property'.[13] In political terms, this translated itself into support for proletarian attempts to gain freedom of assembly, rights at work, and so forth. Bloch also interprets Marx's conception of the programme of socialism as including 'the search for the rights of an uncompromising practical criticism that intervenes in the interests of the goal of socialist construction within the framework of solidarity'.[14] This enables Bloch to ground both his defence of natural law and his critique of Stalinism in Marx's own work:

> But it should be the same banner of human rights that exalts the workers of capitalistic lands to their right to resist, and that opens the way for them in socialistic lands by means of the construction of socialism, and the right (and even obligation) to criticise. Otherwise, authoritarian socialism would prevail – *contradictio in adjecto* – even though the Internationale fought for the human right of organised maturity and responsibility.[15]

Bloch is adamant that in a socialist society, *positive law* will disappear. This is because private property is the basis of such law, and its abolition deprives positive law of its content and function. As a consequence, jurisprudence is singled out as the one ideological activity that has no ideological surplus; it has nothing that a future rational society can take over:

it is the only one to die in this way (instead of being

liberated from its evil ideological character). Morality, art, science, philosophy, and certainly the humanism of religion are emancipated from the ideological superstructure in which they dwell in the class society; they are freed from illusion and establish themselves in reality. For the most part, however, jurisprudence withers away here.[16]

The slight caveat at the end refers to activities which Bloch clearly thinks may not be entirely attributable to the existence of private property – but even here, he thinks there will be a degree of attenuation:

All that remains – after the removal of the protection of profit and the governmental apparatus for oppression – is sexual offense and crimes of passion (although even in this instance, the abolition of the category of property completely transforms passions such as envy, ambition, and, most of all, jealousy).[17]

His conclusion is unambiguous: 'Marxism has merely a historical interest in positive law.'[18]

In contrast, natural law will continue to have relevance in a socialist society. This means that the self-image of classical natural law cannot be sustained; natural law is not something eternal, fixed and transcendent; its legacy will be reworked in revolutionary practice; even its most enduring image – human dignity – will be construed differently in the ongoing historical context; abuses, ancient and modern, will still need to be guarded against:

The inventory of theories of natural law that have existed hitherto do not become museum pieces with the approach of the classless society, as positive law does. For a long while it continues to contain prophetic advertisements and useful instruments even if they must be reassembled if they are to be efficient. This sphere is so little abandoned that for a long while, and occasionally more than ever before, it is sensible of and an instruction against all usurpation from above, all reification of the means of power, and all exercise of uncontrolled power.[19]

The implication, of course, is that the more advanced the society becomes the more natural law becomes concretely and routinely embodied in social relationships.

Bloch approaches the nature of socialist society from another angle in a discussion of the distinction between subjective and objective right – between the rights of the individual and the rights of the society. Although in a capitalist society subjective right is deeply marked by property relationships, there is also a humanist dimension, the right of the upright gait, which will be taken over into socialism:

> In a classless society without money markets there are no owners of merchandise, but there are producers of goods who are legal subjects (juridical persons), and not least among their rights is the right not to be compelled to be a producer of goods. Thus the *ultimate subjective right* would be the license *to produce according to one's capabilities, to consume according to one's needs.*[20]

The ultimate goal is, of course, the elimination of the difference between subjective and objective right, where a non-antagonistic society would undermine the dualism. In the meantime the two spheres continue to have their separate legitimacy: an excess of the private or the abuse of the public require countervailing forces. Stalinism is condemned as a statist abuse of objective right. The Soviet jurist Vyshinsky is critiqued for his reversal of the Marxist strictures on the progressive withering away of the state; instead, Vyshinsky mounts a defence of the expanded state; objective right becomes a bloated tyranny; as a consequence, 'not only civil law, the right to a trial, but also the right to work is completely limited and dominated by the objective sphere of right'.[21] For Bloch, it is essential that objective right become detached from the idea of the state: 'a "true state" ... is a contradiction in terms.'[22] Objective and subjective right will merge in a stateless society – 'the first polis'.[23]

The defence of natural law is grounded in Marx; it is later 'distortions' that are held to blame. By the late 1960s Bloch is more prepared to include Marx himself in the indictment. Gaps in Marx's own work are now highlighted: a lack of appreciation of the insights of Enlightenment liberalism; too little emphasis on personal freedoms, and an inadequate formulation of the concept of the dictatorship of the proletariat. The later 'distortions' are now perceived as, in effect, pushing at an open door.

Marx's strength lay in the analysis of exploitation – degradation, on the other hand, was undertheorised. A critical remark Bloch made at a lecture in 1968 can be taken as encompassing Marx also: 'There are men who toil and are burdened, those are the exploited. But in addition there are also men who are degraded and offended. Of course the exploited are also degraded and offended, but a distinction must be made between these two aspects.'[24]

Bloch is entranced by Marx's vision of the classless society, and portrays the end of positive law as a society of fundamental harmony:

> With this metamorphosis of causes fraud, theft, embezzlement, trespass, murder, and robbery all become more than outdated, they become as good as prehistoric; the framework and edifice of distinctions, and of judicial nuances, become museum pieces.[25]

This seems to sap his ability to ask hard questions; enthusiasm gets the better of sobriety. In his depiction of both Communism and the period leading up to it, there is no analysis of, or even speculation about, the forms in which administration will replace the state, or the institutional ways in which private right will be able to withstand a statist abuse of objective right. As Wayne Hudson has noted:

> Bloch fails to descend to the technical legal and administrative procedures which could perhaps allow the norms he prescribes for a socialist society to take effect. Indeed, he provides almost no practical indications about how this socialist society is to be organised; and no procedural suggestions as to how a socialist society, committed to high moral goals, is to be prevented from resorting to amoral means to achieve them.[26]

If the vision is realisable then there would seem to be no reason why the main features of an appropriate socialist administration could not be specified; if, on the other hand, clear doubts might be anticipated, a not unreasonable assumption, then the need to provide a plausible framework would appear to be even greater. All we have is a pretty picture and a yawning theoretical gap.

A corollary to this silence is the lack of empathy with the

Anglo-American tradition of the rule of law and 'due process'.
Bloch displays some scholarly knowledge of this approach, but
there is no appreciation of its strengths. The only English theorist who has any space devoted to his work is Hobbes. The
discussion is abruptly terminated with a dismissive assertion of
English exceptionalism:

> Such an unusual detour to the path of equal rights for all
> does not detain us long. It was too closely tied to the
> situation in England, and did not relate itself to anything
> either before or afterward. The feudal Magna Carta, which
> had restricted the royal power, entered into bourgeois-
> parliamentary order. Hobbes was unintelligible on the
> Continent because he presupposed too much that was
> English.[27]

If Hobbes was too English, Locke was merely the pale follower
of Continental trends; Bloch refers to him as 'the Grotius epi-
gone'.[28] The American Declaration of Independence is noted,
and there is a brief discussion of the English common law, but
there is no suggestion that there is a rich and distinctive field
to be explored here. Instead, Bloch's socialist vision draws on
the imagery of direct democracy, of unmediated sovereignty
of the people; and he notes with approval Rousseau's critique of
representative government. Positive law is the first victim of
Bloch's revolutionary firing squad and jurisprudence the second.
We are left with a nebulous image of 'rights' without a state or
a positive law.

None the less, Bloch is to be applauded for exploring a new
terrain in Marxism. *Natural Law and Human Dignity* presents
Bloch's long-maturing thoughts on the validity of the natural
law tradition within Marxism, sharpened by his personal experience of 'socialist legality' in the GDR. His presentation of the
tradition is scholarly and subtle, and the interweaving of the
analytical, the critical and the speculative deftly achieved. The
moral voice of the work is clearly expressed: Bloch is able to
convey the humiliation and degradation attendant upon a denial
of human dignity. The book is an important contribution to both
socialist theory and to the study of natural law. As Peter
Osborne states it in a review of the English translation:

> in both the richness of its treatment of its historical material

and the subtlety and force of its dialectic, it provides an account of the radical implications of natural law theory which remains far superior in both its philosophical and political acuity to the majority of more recent, more direct analytical accounts.[29]

In subsequent reflections Bloch deepened the analysis further by exploring weaknesses in the conceptions of Marx himself.

UTOPIANISM

No major philosopher or social theorist has devoted as much time and space to the phenomenon of utopianism as Ernst Bloch; it is no exaggeration to call him the philosopher of utopia. Within Marxism he rehabilitated utopia into a positive concept, after its almost terminal decline in the scientistic Marxism of the Second International; while, more broadly, he demonstrated the continuing validity of utopianism within modern social theory. His work is thoroughly saturated with utopianism. It is not simply that he explicitly and self-consciously reflects on utopianism, its history, conceptual structure, theoretical and strategic utility and so forth, but that his own concepts are themselves utopian. Concepts such as 'not-yet', 'novum', 'front', 'latency', 'tendency', are meant to register the dynamic pull of the future. He rejects the conventional 'realist' critique of utopianism; since reality is itself incomplete, and thus 'not-yet', any realism worth its salt has to have utopia at its very heart:

> So far does utopia extend, so vigorously does this raw material spread to all human activities, so essentially must every anthropology and science of the world contain it. *There is no realism worthy of the name if it abstracts from this strongest element in reality, as an unfinished reality.*[30]

This fundamental future orientation is the uniting factor in Bloch's immense theoretical output, linking the early *Spirit of Utopia* (1918) to his very last works. In all of his analyses, and whatever phenomenon is under investigation – be it a work of art, a religious text, a social structure or a political context – a point is reached where the dimension of the future is isolated and reflected upon. In *The Principle of Hope* Bloch referred to the ancient grammarian M. Terentius Varro, who was said to have omitted the future tense in his grammar; in a sense it is only the future tense that energises Bloch; the past and present are investigated for the openings and blockages of the future. For Bloch, however, this merely registers the interconnectedness of present and future, for while the present is pregnant with the future, the future is also the royal road to an understanding of the present: 'utopian conscience will not be fobbed off with what is poorly existing ... the furthest-reaching telescope is necessary to see the real star of the Earth.'[31] This unity of the anticipatory and the critical enables utopianism to keep alive a historically tested and changing vision of the highest good in the teeth of the resistances and inertia of existing institutions and structures:

> It is *rectified* – but never *refuted* by the mere power of that which, at any particular time, *is*. On the contrary it confutes and judges the existent if it is failing, and failing inhumanly; indeed, first and foremost it provides the *standard* to measure such facticity precisely as departure from the Right; and above all to measure it immanently: that is, by ideas which have resounded and informed from time immemorial before such a departure, and which are still displayed and proposed in the face of it.[32]

For Bloch, utopianism emerges from people's capacity for, and need of, dreaming. He distinguishes the night-dream, with its journey into the repressed material of the past, from the day-dream where:

> the day-dreaming 'I' persists throughout, consciously, privately, envisaging the circumstances and images of a desired, better life.... It is concerned with an as far as possible unrestricted journey forward, so that... the images of that which is not yet can be phantasied into life and into the world.[33]

The Principle of Hope is a vast compendium of these day-dreams, from little private reveries, through formal utopias to the most sublime visions of art and religion. Bloch, while wishing to make analytical distinctions between types of day-dream, does not want to create Chinese walls between them. His whole point is to suggest a free-flowing utopian energy which can be channelled into a multiplicity of forms, some reactionary, some progressive; utopianism is therefore not confined to 'the Utopia': 'the utopian quality is found in many more areas than its restriction to the so-called utopian romance or novel would allow'[34] – or as he put it in *The Principle of Hope*:

> to limit the utopian to the Thomas More variety, or simply to orientate it in that direction, would be like trying to reduce electricity to the amber from which it gets its Greek name and in which it was first noticed. Indeed, the utopian coincides so little with the novel of the ideal state that the whole totality of *philosophy* becomes necessary . . . to do justice to the content of that designated by utopia.[35]

In *The Principle of Hope* he devotes a whole section to what he terms 'little daydreams'[36]. He examines the hopes and fantasies of people at various stages of their life, and focuses on the range of wishes which motivate them, from love and altruism to egotism and the desire for revenge: childhood fantasies of safe hiding-places and adventures in foreign lands; adolescent dreams of love and parental appreciation; the vengeful or sexual fantasies of adulthood, or the rewriting of personal history where the right decision was made; and the elderly images of wisdom, rest and evening.

The 'Utopia' is discussed under the rubric of 'Outlines of a better world'. Here again his categorisation is flexible and eclectic. He uses a thematic approach, subsuming whole utopias or elements of utopias under broad themes. There is thus the 'medical utopia' which works on the fantasies of the removal of disease and pain, and the possibility of combining youth with longevity; Thomas More's hospital provision in *Utopia* (1516) is one cited example, as is Sweven's *Limanora, The Island of Progress* (1903), where the inhabitants 'intervene in the mere laissez faire, laissez aller of the body, restraining, promoting, stimulating, arranging and re-arranging'.[37] In the 'technological utopia', the human will develops techniques, and an appropriate instrumentation, with which to transform nature and society, as in the alchemical utopia of Andreae's *Chemical Wedding of Christian Rosenkreutz anno 1459* (1616),[38] and the 'utopian laboratory' of Bacon's *New Atlantis* (1623).[39] Throughout his discussion of types of utopia, Bloch casts his net far and wide, and includes material and forms which would not normally be discussed under the heading of utopia. He thus includes very old or marginal forms

like the fairy-tale, non-literary forms such as painting and architecture, and remarkable and striking elements from a variety of
past visions, regardless of their provenance. Thus, in the case
of medical utopias, he presents the fantasies of the mentally ill
and the exotic claims of quack doctors, while his discussion of
technological utopias notes the significance of Aladdin's magic
lamp! These latter instances would appear to be examples of
medical and technological *utopianism* rather than utopias in their
own right. An example of his exploration of non-literary forms
is provided in a section entitled 'Buildings which depict a better
world, architectural utopias'. Bloch sees in Egyptian and Gothic
architecture two archetypes of utopianised buildings; they
express in their proportions and dimensions an imitation of a
longed-for perfection; in Egypt this produced a cosmic 'crystal
of death utopia', while in the Gothic form it generated a Christ-
like 'tree of life utopia':

> In the architectural will of Memphis stood there and then
> the utopia of an *aspiration to become and a being like stone,
> of a transformation into crystal*. In the architectural will of
> Amiens and Reims, of Strasbourg, Cologne and Regens-
> burg sprouted there and then the utopia of an *aspiration to
> become and a being like resurrection, of a transformation into
> the tree of the higher life*.[40]

Other artistic forms of utopianism are explored in painting,
opera and literature (i.e. outside explicit utopian literature). He
perceives a utopian 'wishful landscape' in two versions of Watteau's painting, 'Embarkation for Cythera'. The subject of the
painting is young men and women waiting to take a boat to
the island of love. Its utopian quality comes from the *anticipation*
of erotic pleasure, and is to be distinguished from the less
effective *portrayal* of such pleasure in Rubens' 'Garden of Love'.
Watteau plays with possibility, Rubens merely depicts the 'habit
of happiness'; openness triumphs over closure. 'Embarkation for
Cythera' is thus:

> an archetype of the romantic journey ... an enchanting
> landscape surrounds the couples, the contours of the park
> have already become blurred, the love-barque waits on
> the silver water, distant mountains stand in the twilight,

invisibly but directly the night of the island influences the movement and fore-pleasure of the picture.[41]

Bloch was clearly entranced by this image, for he uses it on many occasions as a broader metaphor of the utopian journey. One such use occurs in his discussion of 'geographical utopias', as exemplified by the voyages of discovery; in these the explorer (Marco Polo, Columbus) has, amidst the various economic motives for the journey, a utopian purpose also; a desire to discover the splendid land – 'the finding of the earthly paradise itself';[42] 'for each of them has at the centre of its positive hopes the topos: land of gold, land of happiness. It allows each of them to be called an embarkation for Cythera, an expedition to Eutopia, an experiment of the New World.'[43] Philosophy also is explored in the 'perfect wishful landscape of philosophy', as Bloch examines the visions of the Stoics, Spinoza, Kant and others.[44]

In his analysis of the more familiar 'social utopias', Bloch combines a Marxist historical approach with a thematic classification based on a dualism of freedom and order. After a survey of ancient and medieval utopias Bloch counterposes the social freedom utopia of More's *Utopia* to the social order utopia of Campanella's *City of the Sun*, and makes them respectively the ancestors of liberal-federative socialism (Owen and Fourier) on the one hand, and centralist socialism (Saint-Simon, Cabet) on the other. Needless to say, Marx is deemed to have subsumed the best elements of both into his own work: 'Marx equally connected and overcame the free-confederative element in More and his successors, and the ordered-centralist element in Campanella and his successors.'[45] All of these pre-Marxian visionaries are categorised as 'abstract' utopians in that, following Marx's analysis of utopian socialism, they were created in times preceding the emergence of the revolutionary proletariat and historical materialism; their work is necessarily confined to historically specific good intentions. In *The Principle of Hope* Marx is portrayed not in the familiar Marxist terms of rejecting utopianism in favour of science, but as seeking to move from *abstract* to *concrete* utopia. Anticipation and goals are deemed to be both legitimate in Marx's work and central to it. Marx's own dismissive remarks about utopianism are firmly put in their place:

if instead of such ideals . . . Marx teaches the work of the next step and determines little in advance about the 'realm of freedom', this does not mean . . . that these goal-substances were missing in his work. On the contrary, they move within the entire dialectical tendency as its ultimately inspiring purpose, they establish the spirit of the entire revolutionary work. Marx likewise uses ideals as a measure of criticism and direction, only not transcendentally introduced and fixed ideals, but those to be found in history and thus unfinished ideals, i.e. those of concrete anticipation.[46]

As we have seen, by the late 1960s Bloch was arguing that even Marx had not quite got the balance right, and had moved too far towards scientism. In *The Principle of Hope* there is no such suggestion; the criticism is ventilated only in relation to *Marxism*. Marx's achievement was thus to show how the kernel of social truth in the great abstract utopians could be finally realised via concrete social tendencies; abstract utopianism would then be replaced by the concrete utopia. Dreaming is to be fulfilled, not rejected: 'The very power and truth of Marxism consists in the fact that it has driven the cloud in our dreams further forward, but has not extinguished the pillar of fire in those dreams, rather strengthened it with concreteness.'[47] This is a utopianism which is 'transcendent without transcendence'.[48]

Since Marxist concrete utopianism is the cutting edge of reality, then necessarily, alternative utopias developed since Marx must either (at best) dovetail with Marxism or (at worst) be antithetical to Marxism in varying degrees. Bloch places 'bourgeois group utopias' into the former category. These are visions which, unlike the great social utopias of the past, do not seek to change the whole of society, but wish rather to promote a group interest; the group interest is defined by some common characteristic in the context of perceived oppression or persecution. The examples given are youth, women and Jews. In reality their interests are best served within Marxism, but their vision, insofar as it contains progressive elements, is to be sharply distinguished from late bourgeois reactionary utopias: 'they really wanted to reach the light. Once again a dream of the better life surfaced here, even if by unsuitable means, on soil that had become wholly unsuitable.'[49] The days of the abstract social utopia have passed, argues Bloch. He is thus dismissive not simply of the radical utopias of Henry George and Carlyle, but also of the state-socialist vision of Bellamy, and even William Morris' *News from Nowhere*. They are condemned as either misleading or irrelevant: 'If a tomorrow is pictured as a whole however, then this mostly becomes deceit in late bourgeois terms, and at best it becomes a game, or romantic.'[50]

The most advanced elements of all the various types of utopia are tending towards the concrete utopia – towards the finishing of unfinished business. In medical utopias, 'a long painless life to a ripe old age, culminating in a death replete with life, is still outstanding';[51] in technological utopias, it is the notion of a non-exploitative and co-productive relationship with a nature which is itself a subject; in architectural utopias, 'a protective sphere, a homeland built in advance'.[52] In painting, opera and literature there is the 'wishful landscape of beauty, of sublimity';[53] geographical utopias point to a golden space, and philosophy to a will for the essential: 'Verum Bonum [true good]. Man as a question about it, a world as an answer to it.'[54] Finally, in the case of social utopias, 'Utopia that has become concrete provides the key to this, to unalienated order in the best of all possible societies';[55] Marx's realm of freedom, where *realm* provides the complementary order to freedom.

Bloch's historical and functional analysis of utopianism brings a number of conceptual problems in its wake. His historical taxonomy of social utopias, for example, is entirely dependent on historical materialist assumptions. Although, as we have seen, he distinguishes between utopias of order and of freedom, this is a very rough-and-ready classification, which creates some very unlikely bedfellows (e.g. More with Owen and Fourier). The real basis of differentiation is in terms of the class dynamics of various modes of production. Thus in his *Tübinger Einleitung in die Philosophie* (*Tübingen Introduction to Philosophy*, Vol. 1, 1963) he could write:

> the great Utopians spoke out on behalf of the *coming* bearers of society, and for the particular *tendency to come*. Obviously the interest they assume is no existing, ruling one, but one on the ascent. With Sir Thomas More it is a freer market system, with Campanella the period of absolutist

manufacture, and with Saint-Simon the new, more social-ized, magical *'de l'industrie'*.[56]

Without an alternative analytical framework the whole classifi-cation rises and falls with the validity of the underlying Marxist historiography. He has, of course, his broad thematic differen-tiation when it comes to distinguishing types of utopia, or themes within utopias. However, his impressive and wide-rang-ing categories – 'medical', 'geographical', etc. – suggest further problems. They ultimately rest on a functional definition of utopianism; the production of utopias is a response to funda-mental desires and dispositions in individuals across time and space. This leads to an extremely Catholic assemblage of utopian forms and contents, to the point where it is difficult to see what *does not* count as utopian. The ubiquity of the category begins to undermine its explanatory value. Adorno perceived the dan-gers of this approach in a review of Bloch's *Spuren* (*Traces*):

> For just as there is nothing between heaven and earth that cannot be seized upon psychoanalytically as a symbol of something sexual, so there is nothing that cannot be used as symbolic intention, nothing that is not suitable for a Blochian trace, and this everything borders on being nothing.[57]

Furthermore, there is comparatively little intermediate categoris-ation to introduce a more detailed internal differentiation. Bloch produces a wealth of material but not the conceptual apparatus to do justice to it.

Bloch produces some odd readings of a number of his utopian examples. In the case of More's *Utopia*, for example, Bloch is so focused on the humane and democratic communism of the text that dissonant elements help propel him to the view that ' "Utopia" is most probably a hybrid creation with two authors'.[58] Another instance is his hostile treatment of William Morris, whom he describes as a 'homespun socialist', a 'machine-wrecker' and the creator of a 'backward-looking utopia'.[59] He is clearly ignorant of Morris' actual views and, in any case, is disinclined to find anything of much value in formal utopias post Marx. His analysis of women's group utopias con-tains some of the silliest sentiments he ever penned, including, in proletarian idolatry mode, the statement that 'the female worker does not feel discriminated against by the men of her class'.[60] A number of his interpretations are thus blighted both by ignorance and by his own ideological assumptions.

The concept of concrete utopia is also problematic. First, it is rooted in an implausible theory of proletarian revolution. Second, there are elements of closure in both Bloch's articulation of the concept and his use of it in his social theory. His belief that 'concrete' utopia is somehow 'grounded' in 'objective tendencies' does seem to rob it of those elements which make utopianism such a vibrant phenomenon. As Bloch himself acknowledges, the great 'abstract' utopians produced exciting and stimulating visions; in effect, by accepting that they were beyond their times, he recognises their relative autonomy. Concrete utopianism, on the other hand, seems locked into contemporary social trends to a far greater degree. While there is a defence of vision, anticipation and ideals, this is in the context of a much more disciplined approach. His dislike of post-Marxist formal utopias such as Morris' *News From Nowhere* well illustrates this closing down of the space for exuberant, imaginative speculation. This is compounded by a normative presentation of the content of concrete utopia. Despite Bloch's methodological warnings about not foreclosing the future, he cannot resist draping his own speculations with the purple of objectivity. Bloch seems to be quite clear as to what the broad outlines of concrete utopia will be, and is quite prepared to use this vision as an 'objective' critique of mere 'subjective' visions. The openness of Bloch's sensitive portrayal of the manifold forms of human dreaming thus narrows into a one-way street. As Ruth Levitas has noted, Bloch ends up with 'a teleology which suggests that history has a goal rather than simply that human beings have purposes'.[61]

None the less, Bloch's work on utopianism is a mighty achievement. Others have written on the subject before and since, but none approach the monumental nature of the Blochian investigations. It is not simply the sheer volume of the material, nor the expanded definition of the utopian which thereby opens up a new continent for exploration; it is, in addition, Bloch's attempt to place utopia as a central, possibly *the* central, category of modern social theory. As Adorno remarked: 'Ernst Bloch is the one mainly responsible for restoring honour to the word "utopia".'[62]

NATURE

For Bloch, utopian movement is not confined exclusively to the social or human sphere. His radical materialism expresses a belief in the natural element in human dynamics, and the dynamic element in nature. Since he rejects theistic notions of creation, humanity must have emerged within nature; matter itself must have the capacity for creative movement and change. A dualism of an active and creative humanity and a lumpen and essentially static nature cannot be sustained; nature is not the mere site of, or backdrop to, the only play in town – the rise of humanity. Nor should nature be viewed as mere raw material for human purposes, though this is often how the relationship is perceived; humans are in no position to look down on a nature which should be treated with the very greatest of respect. For Bloch the great material drama, of which humanity is a part, is far from over; the processes which gave rise to human consciousness within nature have not exhausted their creativity. The utopian tendencies within the human world need to be related to an even larger and more awesome process – the onward development of the material universe itself.

Bloch was always to retain an affection for Engels and his *Dialectics of Nature*, and was happy to refer to 'dialectical materialism' even after his move to West Germany in the early 1960s. Engels had not only taken radical materialism seriously, but he also, in the process, added a further link in a venerable tradition of active nature philosophy. As Bloch claimed in 1972 in *Das Materialismusproblem* (*The Problem of Materialism*):

> as far as nature is concerned, does not dialectical material-
> ism rely on a depiction of nature like Engels' depiction
> in *Dialectics of Nature*, which goes back beyond Hegel to
> Aristotle's stages of nature with its entirely own qualitative
> groups of a physical, chemical, and organic kind and its
> own spheres?[63]

The Principle of Hope provides a breakdown of this tradition from Aristotle to the Renaissance: in the ancient world – Strato and Alexander of Aphrodisias; and in the middle ages – the Arab Aristotelians, Avicenna and Averroes, the Jewish Avicebron, and the Christian heretical writers Amalrich of Bena and David of Dinant.[64] The Renaissance period brought forth Bruno, Böhme and Paracelsus, and classical German philosophy produced Leibniz, Hegel and Schelling. To this philosophical tradition Bloch added his usual diverse sources: fairy-tales, literature, music, religious thought and the like; a great utopian storehouse of the future potentialities of nature.

In one section of *The Principle of Hope* Bloch approaches these ideas via a discussion of technology. He posits the emergence of a non-Euclidean technology, as indicated by twentieth-century developments in atomic physics, and argues that such a technology can only flourish in a society that has transcended not merely the abstract bourgeois approach to humanity, but to nature also:

> this shift will no longer be able to occur on the basis of the bourgeois relation to human beings and to nature, i.e. within that component of the relation to nature which belongs to bourgeois ideology and thus shares the rest of the *abstractness (alienness) of the bourgeois material relation*.[65]

Capitalist society has, over time, not merely reduced people to things, but has made things interchangeable; the actual content of things has gradually lost ground, as a form of universal commodification has occurred. The distinctive qualities of the natural world have been swept aside, and ideologies have grown up which replace qualitative approaches to nature with quantitative ones; a move from Giordano Bruno to Galileo.

Bloch identifies three principal omissions in this new world-view. First, no amount of abstraction, no artificiality, however perfect, can achieve genuine independence from nature; raw materials still are, and always will be, required. The need for a sound relationship with nature remains as necessary as ever: 'However synthetic the chemistry, no cornfield will grow on the flat of the hand, which is to say: the link with what has prevailed, which can only be better managed when allied with itself, still does not come to an end here.'[66] Second, the phenomenon of natural laws has been omitted. Bloch wishes to reject theories which either turn natural laws into mere subjective constructs or into iron objective laws. Natural processes have their own dynamics; humanity is a part of that process, but it is also able to participate creatively in the movement of the whole:

all recognized laws reflect objective-real conditional connections between processes, and human beings are
thoroughly embedded in this element independent of their
consciousness and will, yet capable of being mediated with
their consciousness and will.[67]

If this element of the subjective mediation with nature is not
acknowledged, the danger is that nature will be perceived as
an alien, external force, and attitudes of hostility will emerge.
Thus in a discussion of Hegel, Bloch contrasts the sound
approach, which 'makes nature into a collaborator', with the
false and exploitative one of 'colonial cunning'.[68] A final omission is the creativity and productivity of nature – 'the manufac-
turing element in nature'.[69] Here, Bloch picks his way critically,
though sympathetically, through ancient animist notions, and of
nature-philosophy with its image of a 'natural subject'. These
notions are discussed in relation to left-Aristotelian notions of
the creativity of matter, and of *natura naturans* (nature
naturing). In a reference to the methodology of the early Marx,
he argues that 'natura naturans can be set on its feet',[70] stripped
of residual mystical and pantheistic elements. As in the human
realm, the natural subject is not-yet; it is unfinished, incomplete,
and its genesis lies at the end and not the beginning:

> Not even the so indubitable subject of human *history* exists
> as already realized of course, although it increasingly
> manifests itself in empirical-organic terms, and above all
> in empirical-social terms as working man. How much more
> therefore may that which is hypothetically described as the
> *nature-subject* still have to be a predisposition and latency;
> for the concept of a dynamic subject in nature is in the
> final instance a synonym for the not yet manifested That-
> impulse (the most immanent material agent) in the real as
> a whole.[71]

From the perspective of human technology this means that a
new non-exploitative approach, based in social solidarity, will
help unlock the potentialities of nature; this is conceived of as
a Marxist project:

> *in place of the technologist as a mere outwitter or exploiter there
> stands in concrete terms the subject socially mediated with itself,
> which increasingly mediates itself with the problem of the natural*

subject.... [I]t is probable that Marxism will also advance in technology to the unknown, in itself not yet manifested subject of natural processes: mediating human beings with that subject, that subject with human beings, and itself with itself.[72]

The cosmological aspects of this process are discussed in *Tübingen Introduction to Philosophy*, Vol. 1 (1963). Bloch proposes a new conception of time to comprehend the trajectories of the natural and the human. He adapts Riemann's notion that space is structured by context into a theory of 'Riemannian time', where time is likewise affected by local variables. Armed with this approach he makes an initial distinction between pre-human and human history. His purpose here is to emphasise the qualitative leap represented by the emergence of humanity. Thus although the preceding geological time was of infinitely greater duration than the brief span of human history to date, it was in terms of time and being considerably poorer:

despite its formally so very much longer duration, natural time is *less dense* than *historical-cultural time*. Though hugely inflated in comparison with the latter, natural time contains less intensive-qualitative time – just as pre-human Nature contains less developed being.[73]

However, this distinction is not meant to imply a further one between a natural past and a human future; the emergence of humanity is in no way an adieu to nature. Bloch seeks to characterise this erroneous view:

natural time must be *pure past*, having no more specific novelty concealed within itself. Only thus can it lie actually before human history: as a husk from which the grain has been taken; as a slave whose duty is done and whose capacity is exhausted; prodigious pre-history, but prodigious in no other way. Only thus does the history of Nature make a unilinear advance into the history of mankind, which succeeds it and 'crowns' it historically, in development. Accordingly there was once a popular scientific book entitled *From the Nebula to Scheidemann* (O Scheidemann, core and crown of history now revealed!).[74]

This unilinear model is entirely inappropriate; a 'topology of times'[75] is required which can encompass the relative thinness of pre-human history, the plenitude of human history, *and* the *continuing* temporal modalities of nature. Bloch considers absurd the notion that nature has no rich future ahead of it, that the production of humanity was its final creative act; that:

> the 'Iliad of Nature' would literally have found its home and termination in the human 'Odyssey of the Spirit'; and accordingly, the time of the previous history of Nature would appear empty, and – in contrast to the time of human history – without any noteworthy future mode of its own? And therefore without progress *sui generis*, without real possibility in regard to that very far distant future, still so distant from *given* history; in regard to that profundity which as yet can hardly even be probed, and which *Marx* so recently pointed to as the humanization of Nature?[76]

Bloch deploys his distinction between the natural past and the natural future to make a further point about quality and quantity. Pre-human nature displays a very prominent mechanical and quantitative aspect; and this has not disappeared with the arrival of humanity. On the other hand the future potentialities of nature suggest a strong symbolic and qualitative dimension, and this too must have its reality acknowledged. There are thus two modes of natural time present, in a sense 'alongside' human time, but also bound up with its potentialities, just as human time is bound up with them:

> The two modes of time do not, however, flow simultaneously yet separately; and the second does not simply cancel the first, *pro rata* valid mode: instead, both natural times are polyrhythmically *enwreathed in one another.* Consequently the *natural time of the dawning morrow-to-come*, as a time of the humanization of Nature, *is particularly bound up with the tendential contents of cultural historical time.*[77]

Bloch's remarks on nature are, perhaps, the most spectacular manifestation of his distinctive cast of thought. A number of commentators have used these remarks to characterise the Blochian project in general. In *The Concept of Nature in Marx*, Alfred

Schmidt perceives a fundamental difference with Marx's own approach to nature in Bloch's musings about a natural subject:

> Bloch's nature-speculation, which is meant to be an inter-pretation of dialectical materialism, does not simply go beyond Marx's thought, with its metaphysical and cosmo-logical extension of the Marxist problem of nature; it also leads directly away from it.[78]

Marx, in this reading, treats nature as an external and complete phenomenon, upon which humanity imposes its purposes: the very approach which Bloch polemicised against in his critique of capitalist technology. Schmidt seeks to edge Bloch into the camp of idealism, for a natural subject smacks suspiciously of Hegelian notions of spirit's odyssey towards self-identity:

> Bloch ... inclines – at least hypothetically towards Hegel's view that the total reality is an absolute Subject which mediates itself with itself. ... The phrase about the [not yet manifested That-impulse ... in the real] ... makes it quite plain that Bloch professes the idealist belief that 'at the basis' of the world there lies an ultimate, self-reproduc-ing principle of being. However, such a principle is foreign to Marx's whole way of thinking.[79]

Schmidt's point about the difference with Marx is well made; even though his assumption that this is to Bloch's discredit is not. Less defensible is the charge of Hegelian idealism. Bloch refers to a natural subject as something lying *in the future*. It is *not-yet*, and not an underlying substance or entity. Furthermore, the process requires the 'co-productivity' of nature and humanity – it is not some inexorable purpose of nature working itself out through various manifestations. Nature has produced humanity, and therefore humanity's future co-operation with the potentialities of nature is nature assisting itself. Bloch had not polemicised against pantheism and animism to reinstate these conceptions in however 'dialectical' a form. Matter is the source of all creativity, but the emergence of humanity irrevoc-ably alters the field in which all future creativity can take place. On the other hand such misinterpretations are partly Bloch's own fault. One senses a sort of visceral attraction to the visions of Bruno, Böhme and Paracelsus, a deep sympathy for an active, subjective nature; it is therefore possible to confuse Bloch's utopian hope for a true natural subject with a supposed description of an actual subject.

Habermas is also sceptical of the compatibility between Marx and Bloch on the question of technology and nature, though he does not thereby question Bloch's Marxist credentials as did Schmidt. For Habermas, Bloch 'calls into question the innocence of the forces of production, whose innocence was guaranteed by Marx's philosophy of history'.[80] More broadly, Habermas points to parallels not so much with Hegel but with the nature philosophy of Schelling, and calls Bloch 'a Marxist Schelling'. However, there is no suggestion that Bloch has somehow regressed to Schelling, as Schmidt suggests Bloch has done with Hegel; Habermas accepts that 'Bloch gives Schelling's doctrine of the potencies a Marxist interpretation'.[81] In fact Habermas' main critique of the whole Blochian system is that it is *insufficiently* grounded in the German philosophical tradition; it has 'leapt over Kant' and is 'in some way precritical'.[82] In the specific case of Bloch's concept of nature, Habermas objects to the undertheorisation of the issue; Bloch, he contends, accompanies his speculations with merely a few references to utopian anticipations of this concept in, for example, art:

> only the reference (once again reminiscent of Schelling) to the cognitive mode proper to the experience of natural beauty, a sort of knowledge of nature within works of art, disguises, in a makeshift way, the embarrassing lack of a methodological introduction to the 'doctrine of nature as expression'.[83]

None the less, Habermas displays a degree of sympathy for Bloch's basic hope of a 'technology without violence', and takes Bloch's part in the dispute with Marx; Bloch, he says, 'holds onto utopia by promising a socialist resurrection not only to capitalism but to the technology brought forth by it'.[84]

Bloch's speculations on nature reflect his belief that genesis is at the end, and not in the beginning. His system starts with matter and its potentialities, and ends with a utopian vision of a supernature where humanity, itself a natural product, co-produces with a still dynamic nature. He seeks to give both nature and humanity their due; humanity is the greatest product of nature to date, but it forgets its natural origins at its peril. Humanity is thus exalted *and* humbled.

CONCLUSION

Throughout his life, Bloch had been concerned to identify the heritage of earlier ages; it is therefore appropriate to enquire into the nature of Bloch's own heritage. He certainly shows no signs of passing into obscurity, in fact the contrary is the case. This is not simply because there has been a continuing scholarly interest in his work since his death, but also because his influence has permeated into a very wide range of disciplines, which range from the study of folklore and science fiction to theology and political philosophy. Furthermore, as more and more of his work is translated, this tendency seems set to develop an even greater momentum.

The term 'epic' springs to mind in considering Bloch's life and work. His life was long, and bound up with the significant events of the century. He produced a large body of work which ran to seventeen volumes in the Collected Edition, including the mammoth *The Principle of Hope* which weighed in at 1,655 pages in the German text! Furthermore, even the most cursory examination of these texts will reveal the immense range of his interests, for there were few disciplines that he had not explored and deployed. Confronted with such diversity, reviewers will tend to fall back on the amazed list, as witness Eric Hobsbawm's appreciation of *The Principle of Hope*:

> How many philosophical books, marxist or otherwise, contain analyses of the relation between music and medieval scholastic logic, discussions of feminism as a variant of Utopia, of Don Juan, Don Quixote and Faust as myths, of Natural law in the eighteenth century, the evolution of Rosicrucianism, the history of town planning, yoga, the

baroque, Joachim of Fiore, fun-fairs, Zoroaster, the nature of dancing, tourism and the symbolism of the alchemists?[1]

Hobsbawm indeed confirms the epic scope and ambition of the work. Bloch was attempting to construct a system in the grand manner of an Aquinas or a Hegel; an all-encompassing account of the dynamics of the universe itself. His system is not, however, a closed one: his universe is incomplete, its genesis is at the end not the beginning. He attempts to refurbish metaphysics for the twentieth century – an audacious challenge to the modern loss of philosophical nerve. He is simply not prepared to limit himself to the actual, or the particular, or the sayable, nor to abandon the normative, or the speculative, or the mysterious. In this respect his work is gloriously out of kilter with the times; a postmodern nightmare incarnate – a veritable mother and father of a metanarrative. Anyone who deems him to be behind the times might well recall his own concept of 'non-contemporaneity', where the past defends the future in the teeth of a false present.

Bloch's feel for the micrological is strikingly modern. While his one time friend Walter Benjamin has become the subject of a minor industry, Bloch's equally sensitive feel for the small scale, the ephemeral, the marginal and the fleeting has suffered relative neglect. The superiority of Bloch's approach lies in his determination to locate the small in the context of the grand; to move effortlessly from exhausted competitive dancers to the genesis of Fascism, or from a Jewish folk-tale to the heights of theological speculation. Fredric Jameson refers to 'the future which stirs at its convulsive but microscopic work within the smallest cells of the vast universe itself', and notes of this Blochian concept of 'traces' or 'spoor' (*Spuren*) that:

The centrality of this concept in Bloch may be measured against Benjamin's brittle world of script and allegorical fragment, in which the incomprehensible sign alone survives as the mark of a forgotten disaster; or against Derrida's theory of the 'trace', where only the pure temporal movement of signification itself, as it deposits itself in object or in letter, is retained, without any ultimate sense of the direction or meaning of that movement.[2]

Bloch's evocative vignettes of the extraordinary in the ordinary are amongst the most memorable aspects of his work.

All of these factors reinforce the sheer distinctiveness of Bloch. He is a true original, his work quite unlike any other. He laboured on his great enterprise with dogged perseverance, ploughing on regardless of neglect, criticism or fashion. The resulting body of work is therefore both intensely personal and powerfully independent. George Steiner has spoken of 'Bloch's essential aloneness' and of 'the *sui generis* of his style and philosophy'; remarking that Bloch 'represents what physicists call "a singularity", an idiosyncratic twist in the rule-bound and predictable skein of natural forces'.[3] Walter Benjamin recognised this same quality after reading *Spirit of Utopia* and meeting Bloch in 1919: 'the author stands alone and philosophically stands up for his cause, while almost everything we read today of a philosophical nature written by our contemporaries is derivative and adulterated.'[4] This invests his work with a strength which is likely to command continuing attention.

Fundamental to the whole project is a deeply rooted utopianism. Adorno recognised the temperamental basis of this in his claim that Bloch 'is one of the very few philosophers who does not recoil in fear from the idea of a world without domination and hierarchy'.[5] Confronted with Bloch's achievements it is easy to forget the bold originality involved in placing utopianism at the heart of a social theory which claimed to be both serious and Marxist. By the beginning of the twentieth century 'utopian' had become a synonym for the impractical, and amongst the dominant scientism of Second International Marxism, 'utopian socialism' was deemed to be the hopelessly outdated competitor to rigorous scientific socialism.[6] In *Spirit of Utopia* (1918), Bloch developed a self-conscious defence of the utopian, and in his later work integrated this into an explicitly Marxist framework. In the process he elevated the concept of utopia to new levels of sophistication, and invested it with a theoretical respectability which it previously lacked.

The construction of a utopian Marxism was never going to be easy. The fiercest of Marx's own criticisms of utopianism centred on a fear that fanciful visions spun by well-meaning theoreticians might distract or mislead the revolutionary proletariat. Bloch was well aware of these strictures, and sought to stress the need for both sobriety and enthusiasm in the revolutionary moment. Unfortunately, Bloch's own particular brand of sobriety included a willingness to defend the USSR publicly, and to be less than forthright in his criticisms of the international Communist movement. Hence the apparent paradox that the author of some of the most sublime passages in humanist Marxism was also willing to pen vituperative defences of the Moscow Show Trials. It took his own residence in Stalinist East Germany to give him some inkling of the true costs of the Soviet way. Only in his final years was he able to integrate his subtle sociocultural analyses into a politics in which there was far greater congruence between ends and means.

Bloch's work contains analyses and speculations of great power and subtlety. His philosophical radicalism is both ambitious and challenging; in the cultural sphere, he has produced insightful and fruitful work on both high and popular culture; the profundity of his religious thought is attested to by a number of modern theologians; his analysis of the Fascist co-option and distortion of human fears and aspirations is compelling; he has few peers among the theoreticians of twentieth-century humanist Marxism; the exploration of the natural law tradition is both a serious contribution to scholarship and a telling critique of deficiencies in Marxist theory and practice; his achievements in the field of utopianism have long been recognised; while his work on nature generates a highly original ecological perspective. He thus provides the academy with a storehouse of provocative distinctions and hypotheses, and political radicalism with both vision and a defence of the visionary.

In his obituary of Bloch, George Steiner evokes the extraordinary fascination of the man and his work:

> his style was that of a prose poet. It modulates brilliantly between the apocalyptic and the everyday, the lyric and the polemic. It sings and stabs. It can be utterly luminous (the early morning was Bloch's hour as it had been Nietzsche's) but it can also be portentously opaque. But above all, it comprises and enacts a range of experience immensely beyond that of customary philosophic and political debate.[7]

NOTES

INTRODUCTION

1 G. Steiner, *Language and Silence: Essays 1958–1966*, London, Faber, 1967, p. 113.
2 J. K. Dickinson, 'Ernst Bloch's "the Principle of Hope": a review of and comment on the English translation', *Babel*, 1990, vol. 36, no. 1, p. 8.
3 R. Aronson, 'Review of *The Principle of Hope*', *History and Theory*, 1991, vol. 30, no. 2, p. 223.
4 D. Kaufmann, 'Thanks for the memory: Bloch, Benjamin and the philosophy of history', *The Yale Journal of Criticism*, 1993, vol. 6, no. 1, p. 143.

1 LIFE AND CONCEPTS

1 A short family tree can be found in *Bloch-Almanach*, 1983, vol. 3, p. 11. The best English account of Bloch's life can be found in W. Hudson, *The Marxist Philosophy of Ernst Bloch*, London, Macmillan, 1982, Chapter 1; the best biography is P. Zudeick, *Der Hintern des Teufels*, Moos and Baden-Baden, Elster, 1985; a useful short biography is S. Markun, *Ernst Bloch*, Reinbek bei Hamburg, Rowohlt, 1977.
2 K. Bloch, *Aus meinem Leben*, Pfullingen, Neske, 1981, p. 45.
3 The *Spuren* extract is quoted in T. Phelan, 'Ernst Bloch's "Golden Twenties": *Erbschaft dieser Zeit* and the problem of cultural history', in K. Bullivant (ed.), *Culture and Society in the Weimar Republic*, Manchester, Manchester University Press, 1977, pp. 111–112; E. Bloch, *The Principle of Hope*, trans. N. and S. Plaice and P. Knight, Oxford, Basil Blackwell, 1986, p. 23.
4 R. Traub and H. Wieser (eds), *Gespräche mit Ernst Bloch*, Frankfurt, Suhrkamp, 1975, p. 28.
5 Markun, *Ernst Bloch*, p. 16.
6 E. Bloch, *Heritage of Our Times*, trans. N. and S. Plaice, Oxford, Polity, 1991, p. 192.

7 M. Löwy, 'Interview with Ernst Bloch', *New German Critique*, 1976, vol. 9, p. 40.

8 Bloch, *Heritage of Our Times*, p.192.

9 Traub and Wieser, *Gespräche mit Ernst Bloch*, pp. 28–30.

10 P. Honigsheim, *On Max Weber*, New York, The Free Press, 1968, pp. 28–29; also p. 66.

11 Quoted in A. Rabinbach, 'Between enlightenment and apocalypse: Benjamin, Bloch and modern German Jewish messianism', *New German Critique*, 1985, no. 34, p. 103. Rabinbach is a good source for Bloch's views in this period.

12 G. Lukács, *Selected Correspondence*, trans. J. Marcus and Z. Tar, New York, Columbia University Press, 1986, p. 110.

13 Ibid., p. 146.

14 Löwy, 'Interview', p. 36.

15 G. Lukács, *Record of a Life: An Autobiographical Sketch*, London, Verso, 1983, p. 38.

16 M. Weber, *Max Weber: A Biography*, trans. H. Zohn, New York, Wiley, 1975, pp. 468–469.

17 Ibid., p. 466.

18 Quoted in E. Fekete and E. Karádi (eds), *György Lukács: His Life in Pictures and Documents*, Budapest, Corvina Kiadó, 1981, p. 58. Karl Jaspers attributes this remark to the philosopher Emil Lask. J. Marcus, *Georg Lukács and Thomas Mann: A Study in the Sociology of Literature*, Amherst, University of Massachusetts Press, 1987, p. 144.

19 From an unpublished manuscript of over 600 pages, cited by Marcus, *Georg Lukács and Thomas Mann*, p. 144.

20 Marcus, *Georg Lukács and Thomas Mann*, p. 144.

21 Ibid., p. 198.

22 Ibid., p. 132.

23 Quoted in M. Gluck, *George Lukács and his Generation 1900–1918*, Cambridge, Mass, Harvard University Press, 1985, p. 160.

24 K. Bloch, *Aus meinem Leben*, p. 46.

25 Löwy, 'Interview', p. 38.

26 Quoted in A. Kadarkay, *Georg Lukács: Life, Thought, and Politics*, Oxford, Basil Blackwell, 1991, p. 53.

27 Marcus, *Georg Lukács and Thomas Mann*, p. 144.

28 Quoted in Rabinbach, 'Between enlightenment and apocalypse: Benjamin, Bloch and modern German Jewish messianism', p. 110; see also F. Fehér, 'The last phase of romantic anti-capitalism: Lukács' response to the war', *New German Critique*, 1977, no. 10, p. 150.

29 Traub and Wieser, *Gespräche*, p. 301.

30 K. Bloch, *Aus meinem Leben*, pp. 45–46.

31 A Münster (ed.), *Tagträume vom aufrechten Gang Sechs Interviews mit Ernst Bloch*, Frankfurt, Suhrkamp, 1977, p. 36; see also Traub and Wieser, *Gespräche*, p. 300.

32 P. Heyworth, *Otto Klemperer: His Life and Times, Volume 1, 1885–1933*, Cambridge, Cambridge University Press, 1983, p. 111.

33 Testimony of Walter Benjamin recorded in G. Scholem, *Walter Benjamin: The Story of a Friendship*, London, Faber, 1982, p. 79.
34 Quoted in R. Wiggerhaus, *The Frankfurt School: Its History, Theories and Political Significance*, Oxford, Polity, 1994, p. 67.
35 H. Marcuse, 'The realm of freedom and the realm of necessity: a reconsideration', *Praxis*, 1969, no. 1, p. 20.
36 Cited in P. F. Zimdars-Swartz, *Apocalyptic Insight and Apocalyptic Experience: The Structure and Significance of Ernst Bloch's Theory of Knowledge*, unpublished Ph.D. thesis, Claremont Graduate School, 1978, p. 82.
37 E. Bloch, 'A jubilee for renegades', *New German Critique*, 1975, no. 4.
38 J. R. Bloch, 'How can we understand the bends in the upright gait?', *New German Critique*, 1988, no. 45, p. 25.
39 Ibid., pp. 10–11.
40 L. Feuchtwanger, *Moscow 1937*, London, Gollancz, 1937, p. 153.
41 Quoted in D. Pike, *Lukács and Brecht*, Chapel Hill, University of North Carolina Press, 1985, p. 292.
42 E. Bloch, 'Recollections of Walter Benjamin', in G. Smith (ed.), *On Walter Benjamin: Critical Essays and Recollections*, Cambridge, Mass, MIT Press, 1988, p. 339.
43 W. Benjamin, *Briefe*, vol. 1, Frankfurt, Suhrkamp, 1966, p. 353, p. 362; Scholem, *Walter Benjamin*, p. 177; G. Scholem (ed.), *The Correspondence of Walter Benjamin and Gershom Scholem 1932–1940*, trans. G. Smith and A. Lefevre, New York, Schocken, 1989, p. 160, p. 170.
44 J. R. Bloch, 'How can we understand the bends in the upright gait?', p. 34.
45 R. Taylor, *Kurt Weill: Composer in a Divided World*, London, Simon & Schuster, 1991, p. 75, pp. 79–80, p. 125; P. Heyworth (ed.), *Conversations with Klemperer*, London, Gollancz, 1973, p. 65.
46 T. Mann, *Diaries 1918–1939*, trans. R. and C. Winston, London, André Deutsch, 1983, p. 186.
47 B. Brecht, *Briefe*, Frankfurt, Suhrkamp, 1981, pp. 255–257.
48 Heyworth, *Otto Klemperer*, p. 266.
49 E. Bloch, 'Disrupted language, disrupted culture', *Direction*, December 1939, p. 16.
50 Ibid., p. 17.
51 Ibid., p. 36.
52 K. Bloch, *Aus meinem Leben*, p. 136.
53 L. Lowenthal, *An Unmastered Past*, Berkeley, University of California Press, 1987, p. 66.
54 E. Bloch, *Briefe 1903–1975*, vol. 2, Frankfurt, Suhrkamp, 1985, p. 530.
55 Wiggerhaus, *The Frankfurt School*, p. 190.
56 K. Bloch, *Aus meinem Leben*, p. 136.
57 Münster, *Tagträume*, pp. 70–71.
58 K. Bloch, *Aus meinem Leben*, p. 175.
59 Quoted in P. M. Lützeler, *Hermann Broch: A Biography*, London, Quartet, 1987, p. 229.
60 K. Bloch, *Aus meinem Leben*, p. 154.

61 V. Caysa, P. Caysa, K-D. Eichler and E. Uhl, *'Hoffnung kann enttäuscht werden'* – *Ernst Bloch in Leipzig/dokumentiert und kommentiert*,
Frankfurt, Anton Hain, 1992.

62 Lukács, *Record of a Life*, p. 126.

63 M. Landmann, 'Talking with Ernst Bloch: Korcula, 1968', *Telos*,
1975, no. 25, p. 177.

64 E. Bloch, *Briefe 1903–1975*, vol. 1, p. 193.

65 Caysa *et al.*, *'Hoffnung kann enttäuscht werden'*, p. 24.

66 Zudeick, *Der Hintern des Teufels*, p. 186.

67 Landmann, 'Talking with Ernst Bloch', p. 177.

68 R. Bahro, *From Red to Green*, trans. G. Fagan and R. Hurst, London,
Verso, 1984, p. 14.

69 J. Rühle, 'The philosopher of hope: Ernst Bloch', in L. Labedz (ed.),
Revisionism: Essays on the History of Marxist Ideas, London, George
Allen & Unwin, 1962, pp. 175–176.

70 Quoted in E. Bahr, 'The literature of hope: Ernst Bloch's philosophy
and its impact on the literature of the German Democratic Republic', in H. Birnbaum and T. Eekman (eds), *Fiction and Drama in
Eastern and South-Eastern Europe*, Columbus, Slavica, 1980, p. 12.

71 Ibid., p. 11. See also G. L. Baker, '(Anti-)utopian elements in Uwe
Johnson's *Jahrestage*: traces of Ernst Bloch', *Germanic Review*, 1993,
vol. 63, no. 1, pp. 32–45.

72 R. Römer, 'Erinnerungen an Ernst Bloch', *Bloch-Almanach*, 1990, vol.
10, p. 142.

73 J. Habermas, *Autonomy and Solidarity*, London, Verso, 1986, p. 37.

74 Landmann, 'Talking with Ernst Bloch', pp. 167–168.

75 Quoted in M. Buhr, 'Seven comments on Ernst Bloch's philosophy',
Studies in Soviet Thought, 1987, vol. 33, p. 339.

76 J. Jahn, 'Ernst Bloch und der Aufbau-Verlag: Eine Dokumentation',
Bloch-Almanach, 1993, vol. 13, pp. 103–168.

77 J. R. Bloch, 'How can we understand the bends in the upright
gait?', pp. 25–26.

78 Ibid., p. 26.

79 Landmann, 'Talking with Ernst Bloch', p. 177.

80 Rühle, 'The philosopher of hope', p. 177.

81 Ibid.

82 Landmann, 'Talking with Ernst Bloch', p. 177.

83 J. R. Bloch, 'How can we understand the bends in the upright
gait?', p. 32.

84 Bahro, *From Red to Green*, p. 18.

85 Landmann, 'Talking with Ernst Bloch', p. 177.

86 Rühle, 'The philosopher of hope', p. 178.

87 This has been translated as M. Buhr, 'A critique of Ernst Bloch's
philosophy of hope', *Philosophy Today*, 1970, vol. 14, no. 4, p. 269.

88 Landmann, pp. 177–178.

89 Zudeick, *Der Hintern des Teufels*, pp. 246–250.

90 J. Moltmann, *History and the Triune God: Contributions to Trinitarian
Theology*, London, SCM Press, 1991, p. 144, p. 145.

91 Landmann, 'Talking with Ernst Bloch', p. 165.

92 Zudeick, *Der Hintern des Teufels*, p. 314.
93 Hudson, *The Marxist Philosophy of Ernst Bloch*, Chapter 3.
94 Ibid.; see also C. Harper, *Dialectic in the Philosophy of Ernst Bloch*, unpublished Ph.D. thesis, The Queen's University of Belfast, 1993, pp. 92–102, and J. Habermas, 'Ernst Bloch: a Marxist Schelling', in *Philosophical-Political Profiles*, trans. F. G. Lawrence, Cambridge, Mass, MIT Press, 1983, pp. 63–79.
95 Bloch, *The Principle of Hope*, p. 860, p. 859.
96 Quoted in Harper, *Dialectic in the Philosophy of Ernst Bloch*, p. 92.
97 Hudson, *The Marxist Philosophy of Ernst Bloch*, pp. 71–72; Münster, *Tagträume*, p. 28; W. Hudson, 'Two interviews with Ernst Bloch', *Bloch-Almanach*, 1989, vol. 9, p. 119.
98 Hudson, *The Marxist Philosophy of Ernst Bloch*, pp. 21–30.
99 F. Jameson, *Marxism and Form: Twentieth-Century Dialectical Theories of Literature*, Princeton, Princeton University Press, 1971, pp. 158–159.
100 Bloch, *The Principle of Hope*, p. 1371.
101 E. Bloch, 'Man as possibility', *Cross Currents*, 1968, vol. xviii, p. 281.
102 Ibid.
103 E. Bloch, *A Philosophy of the Future*, trans. J. Cumming, New York, Herder & Herder, 1970, p. 112.
104 Bloch, *The Principle of Hope*, p. 235.
105 Bloch, *A Philosophy of the Future*, p. 110.
106 E. Bloch, 'Dialectics and hope', *New German Critique*, 1976, no. 9, p. 8.
107 Cited in Harvey Cox's Foreword to E. Bloch, *Man On His Own: Essays in the Philosophy of Religion*, trans. E. B. Ashton, New York, Herder & Herder, 1970, p. 9.
108 Bloch, *The Principle of Hope*, p. 289.
109 Ibid., p. 148.
110 Bloch, *A Philosophy of the Future*, p. 3.
111 Ibid., p. 1.
112 The English translation of *The Principle of Hope* renders 'absconditus' as 'vanished'; 'hidden' follows J.K. Dickinson in 'Ernst Bloch's "the Principle of Hope": a review of and comment on the English translation', *Babel*, 1990, vol. 36, no. 1, p. 13, p. 30.
113 E. Bloch, *Atheism and Christianity*, trans. J. T. Swann, New York, Herder & Herder, 1972, p. 211.
114 Bloch, 'Dialectics and hope', p. 4.
115 Bloch, *The Principle of Hope*, p. 7.
116 Ibid., p. 116.
117 Ibid., p. 124.
118 E. Bloch, 'On the present in literature', in *The Utopian Function of Art and Literature*, trans. J. Zipes and F. Mecklenberg, Cambridge, Mass, MIT Press, 1988, p. 208.
119 Quoted in D. Drew, 'Introduction' to E. Bloch, *Essays on the Philosophy of Music*, trans. P. Palmer, Cambridge, Cambridge University Press, 1985, p. xi.
120 Bloch, *The Principle of Hope*, p. 293.

121 Ibid., p. 298.
122 Ibid., p. 292.
123 Fredric Jameson uses 'ontological anticipation' in *Marxism and Form*, 1971, p. 150; N. and S. Plaice and P. Knight use 'pre-appearance' in their translation of *The Principle of Hope*, as does Wayne Hudson in *The Marxist Philosophy of Ernst Bloch*, p. 173; 'anticipatory illumination' is preferred by Jack Zipes in his Introduction to and translation of (with Mecklenberg) Bloch, *The Utopian Function of Art and Literature*.
124 Landmann, 'Talking with Ernst Bloch: Korcula, 1968', p. 178.
125 Ibid., pp. 178–179.
126 E. Bloch, *On Karl Marx*, trans. J. Maxwell, New York, Herder & Herder, 1971, p. 108.
127 Bloch, *The Principle of Hope*, p. 146.
128 Ibid., p. 1368.
129 Bloch, *Heritage of Our Times*, p. 97.
130 Bloch, *On Karl Marx*, p. 168.
131 Bloch, *Atheism and Christianity*, p. 251.
132 Quoted in J. R. Bloch, 'How can we understand the bends in the upright gait?', p. 10.
133 E. Bloch, *Natural Law and Human Dignity*, trans. D.J. Schmidt, Cambridge, Mass, MIT Press, 1986, p. 208.
134 Bloch, *The Principle of Hope*, p. 1376.
135 Ibid., p. 1375.
136 Bloch, *Atheism and Christianity*, p. 206.
137 Bloch, *A Philosophy of the Future*, p. 136.
138 Bloch, *The Principle of Hope*, p. 690.
139 Bloch, *A Philosophy of the Future*, p. 131.
140 Ibid., pp. 132–133.
141 Ibid., p. 133.
142 Bloch, *The Principle of Hope*, p. 1278.
143 J. Zipes, 'Notes on the translation and acknowledgments', in Bloch, *The Utopian Function of Art and Literature*, p. ix.
144 Dickinson, 'Ernst Bloch's "the Principle of Hope" ', p. 30.
145 Ibid., p. 15.
146 R. Aronson, 'Review of *The Principle of Hope*', *History and Theory*, 1991, vol. 30, no. 2, pp. 224–230.
147 J. R. Bloch, 'How can we understand the bends in the upright gait?', p. 15.
148 Aronson, 'Review of *The Principle of Hope*', p. 231.
149 J. R. Bloch, 'How can we understand the bends in the upright gait?', p. 15.
150 Ibid., pp. 15–16.

2 CULTURE

1 E. Bloch, 'Ideas as transformed material in human minds, or problems of an ideological superstructure (cultural heritage)', in *The*

Utopian Function of Art and Literature, trans. J. Zipes and F. Mecklenberg, Cambridge, Mass, MIT Press, 1988, p. 30.

2 Ibid.
3 Ibid., p. 32.
4 Ibid., pp. 33–34.
5 Ibid., p. 34.
6 Ibid., p. 33.
7 Ibid., p. 36
8 Ibid., p. 37.
9 Ibid., p. 38.
10 Ibid.
11 Ibid., p. 40.
12 Ibid., p. 42.
13 Ibid., p. 45.
14 Ibid., p. 47.
15 Ibid., pp. 47–48.
16 Ibid., p. 51.
17 Ibid., p. 54.
18 Ibid., p. 55.
19 Ibid.
20 T. Phelan, 'Ernst Bloch's "Golden Twenties": *Erbschaft dieser Zeit* and the problem of cultural history', in K. Bullivant (ed.), *Culture and Society in the Weimar Republic,* Manchester, Manchester University Press, 1977, p. 100.
21 E. Bloch, *Heritage of Our Times,* trans. N. and S. Plaice, Oxford, Polity, 1991, p. 5.
22 Phelan, 'Ernst Bloch's "Golden Twenties" ', p. 102.
23 J. R. Bloch, 'How can we understand the bends in the upright gait?', *New German Critique,* 1988, no. 45, pp. 23–24.
24 T. W. Adorno, 'Ernst Bloch's *Spuren*', in *Notes to Literature,* vol. 1, trans. S. Weber Nicholsen, New York, Columbia University Press, 1991, p. 207.
25 Quoted in J. M. Jones, *Hope among the Remnants of Babel: Ernst Bloch's Utopia of Heimat and the Uncompleted Edifice of Enlightenment,* unpublished Ph.D. thesis, Emory University, 1993, pp. 39–40.
26 A section of the second edition of *Spirit of Utopia* (1923) is translated in E. Bloch, *Essays on the Philosophy of Music,* trans. P. Palmer, Cambridge, Cambridge University Press, 1985, p. 120.
27 Ibid.
28 E. Bloch, *The Principle of Hope,* trans. N. and S. Plaice and P. Knight, Oxford, Blackwell, 1986, p. 1058.
29 Ibid., p. 1060.
30 Ibid.
31 Ibid., p. 1061.
32 Ibid., p. 1063.
33 Ibid.
34 Ibid.
35 Ibid.
36 Bloch, *Essays on the Philosophy of Music,* p. 9.

37 Ibid., p. 7.
38 Bloch, *The Principle of Hope*, p. 1067.
39 Ibid., p. 1068.
40 Ibid., p. 1069.
41 Ibid., p. 1101.
42 Ibid., p. 1097.
43 Ibid., p. 1070.
44 F. Jameson, *Marxism and Form: Twentieth-Century Dialectical Theories of Literature*, Princeton, Princeton University Press, 1971, p. 145.
45 E. Bloch, 'Marxism and poetry', in *The Utopian Function of Art and Literature*, p. 161.
46 E. Bloch, 'Recollections of Walter Benjamin', in G. Smith (ed.), *On Walter Benjamin: Critical Essays and Recollections*, Cambridge, Mass, MIT Press, 1988, pp. 338–345.
47 R. Wiggerhaus, *The Frankfurt School: Its History, Theories and Political Significance*, trans. M. Robertson, Oxford, Polity, 1994, p. 190.
48 L. Weissberg, 'Philosophy and the fairy tale: Ernst Bloch as narrator', *New German Critique*, 1992, no. 55, p. 36.
49 Bloch, *The Principle of Hope*, p. 339.
50 Ibid., p. 340.
51 Ibid., p. 341.
52 Ibid., p. 352.
53 Ibid., p. 353.
54 Ibid., p. 366.
55 Ibid., p. 363.
56 Ibid., p. 367.
57 Ibid., p. 375.
58 Ibid., p. 382.
59 Ibid., p. 387.
60 Ibid., p. 394.
61 Ibid.
62 Ibid.
63 Ibid.
64 Ibid., p. 397.
65 Ibid., p. 398.
66 Ibid., p. 405.
67 Ibid., p. 408.
68 Ibid.
69 Ibid., p. 409.
70 Ibid., p. 410.
71 Ibid., p. 411.
72 Ibid., pp. 445–446.
73 J. Habermas, 'Between philosophy and science: Marxism as critique', in *Theory and Practice*, trans. J. Viertel, London, Heinemann, 1974, p. 241.
74 J. Habermas, 'Walter Benjamin: consciousness-raising or rescuing critique', in *Philosophical-Political Profiles*, trans. F. G. Lawrence, Cambridge, Mass, MIT, 1983, p. 136.

75 S. Radnóti, 'Lukács and Bloch', in A. Heller (ed.), *Lukács Revalued*, Oxford, Blackwell, 1983, p. 71.
76 Bloch, *Essays on the Philosophy of Music*, p. 85.
77 Radnóti, 'Lukács and Bloch', p. 71.
78 Bloch, *Heritage of Our Times*, pp. 242–245.
79 E. Bloch, 'Marxism and poetry', p. 157.
80 Bloch, *Heritage of Our Times*, p. 246.
81 Bloch, 'Marxism and poetry', p. 157.
82 Bloch, *Heritage of Our Times*, p. 250.
83 Ibid., p. 225.
84 Ibid., p. 208.
85 Ibid., p. 212.
86 Ibid., pp. 212–213.
87 Adorno, 'Ernst Bloch's *Spuren*', in *Notes to Literature*, vol. 1, pp. 210–211.
88 G. Lukács, 'Realism in the balance', in R. Taylor (ed.), *Aesthetics and Politics*, London, New Left Books, 1977, p. 54.
89 Ibid., p. 42.
90 Quoted in N. Tertulian, 'Lukács' ontology', in T. Rockmore (ed.), *Lukács Today: Essays in Marxist Philosophy*, Dordrecht, D. Reidel, 1988, p. 254.
91 E. Bloch, 'On the present in literature', in *The Utopian Function of Art and Literature*, p. 209.
92 Ibid., p. 211.
93 Ibid.
94 Ibid., p. 212.
95 Ibid.
96 Ibid.
97 Ibid., p. 214.
98 Ibid., p. 223
99 Ibid., pp. 221–222.
100 E. Bloch, 'A philosophical view of the detective novel' and 'A philosophical view of the novel of the artist', in *The Utopian Function of Art and Literature*, pp. 245–264, pp. 265–277.
101 Ibid., p. 269.
102 Ibid., p. 255.
103 Ibid., p. 250.
104 Ibid., p. 251.
105 Ibid., p. 254.
106 Ibid., p. 255.
107 Ibid.
108 Ibid.
109 Ibid., p. 256.
110 Ibid., p. 261.
111 Ibid., p. 263.
112 Ibid., p. 262.
113 Ibid., p. 276.
114 Bloch, *The Principle of Hope*, p. 412.
115 Ibid.

116 Ibid.
117 Ibid., p. 413
118 Ibid.
119 Ibid.
120 Ibid., p. 414.
121 Ibid., p. 416.
122 Ibid.
123 Ibid., p. 419.
124 Ibid., pp. 419–422.
125 Ibid., p. 422.
126 Ibid., p. 426.
127 Ibid.
128 Ibid.
129 Ibid., pp. 426–427.
130 Ibid., p. 427.
131 Ibid., p. 428.
132 Ibid., p. 430.
133 Adorno, 'Ernst Bloch's *Spuren*', in *Notes to Literature*, vol. 1, p. 207.
134 D. Drew, 'Introduction' to Bloch, *Essays on the Philosophy of Music*, p. xxvi.
135 Ibid.
136 Ibid.

3 RELIGION

1 Quoted in P. F. Zimdars-Swartz, *Apocalyptic Insight and Apocalyptic Experience: The Structure and Significance of Ernst Bloch's Theory of Knowledge*, unpublished Ph.D. thesis, Claremont Graduate School, 1978, p. 84.
2 Quoted in Ibid., p. 87.
3 A. Rabinbach, 'Between enlightenment and apocalypse: Benjamin, Bloch and modern Jewish messianism', *New German Critique*, 1985, no. 34, pp. 78–124; Z. Levy, 'Utopia and reality in the philosophy of Ernst Bloch', *Utopian Studies*, 1990, vol. 1, no. 2, pp. 3–12; M. Löwy, 'Jewish messianism and libertarian utopia in Central Europe (1900–1933)', *New German Critique*, 1980, no. 20, pp. 105– 115.
4 Quoted in J. K. Dickinson, 'Ernst Bloch's philosophical ethnicity', *Bloch-Almanach*, 1991, vol. 11, p. 21.
5 N. Finkelstein, 'The utopian function and the refunctioning of Marxism', *Diacritics*, 1989, vol. 19, no. 2, p. 60.
6 W. Hudson, 'Two interviews with Ernst Bloch', *Bloch-Almanach*, 1989, vol. 9, p. 120.
7 J. Moltmann, *History and the Triune God: Contributions to a Trinitarian Theology*, London, SCM Press, 1991, p. 147.
8 J. B. Metz, 'The responsibility of hope', *Philosophy Today*, 1966, vol. 10, no. 4, p. 286.
9 W. Pannenberg, 'The God of hope', *Cross Currents*, 1968, vol. xviii, pp. 286–287.

10 See T. Moylan, 'Bloch against Bloch: The theological reception of *Das Prinzip Hoffnung* and the liberation of the utopian function', *Utopian Studies*, 1990, vol. 1, no. 2, pp. 27–51.

11 Moltmann, *History and the Triune God*, p. 145.

12 Hudson, 'Two interviews with Ernst Bloch', p. 118.

13 E. Bloch, *Atheism in Christianity: The Religion of the Exodus and the Kingdom*, trans. J. T. Swann, New York, Herder & Herder, 1972, p. 268.

14 Ibid., p. 266.

15 E. Bloch, *The Principle of Hope*, trans. N. and S. Plaice and P. Knight, Oxford, Blackwell, 1986, p. 1284.

16 Ibid., p. 1201.

17 Ibid., p. 1191.

18 Ibid., p. 1193.

19 Bloch, *Atheism in Christianity*, pp. 21–22.

20 Ibid, p. 21

21 Ibid., p. 24.

22 Ibid., p. 38.

23 Bloch, *The Principle of Hope*, p. 1274.

24 E. Bloch, 'Man as possibility', *Cross Currents*, 1968, vol. xviii, pp. 282–283.

25 Bloch, *Atheism in Christianity*, p. 92.

26 Bloch, *The Principle of Hope*, p. 1234.

27 Bloch, *Atheism in Christianity*, p. 86.

28 Ibid.

29 Bloch, *The Principle of Hope*, p. 1268.

30 Bloch, *Atheism in Christianity*, p. 110.

31 Ibid., p. 122.

32 Ibid.

33 Ibid., p. 128.

34 Bloch, *The Principle of Hope*, p. 1263.

35 Ibid.

36 Bloch, *Atheism in Christianity*, p.146.

37 Ibid., p. 150.

38 Ibid., p. 151.

39 Ibid., p. 159.

40 Bloch, *The Principle of Hope*, p. 1265.

41 Ibid., p. 1271.

42 Bloch, *Atheism in Christianity*, pp. 176–177.

43 Ibid., p. 178.

44 Ibid., p. 182.

45 Ibid., pp. 182–183.

46 Bloch, *The Principle of Hope*, p. 509.

47 Bloch, *Atheism in Christianity*, p. 220.

48 Bloch, *The Principle of Hope*, p. 511.

49 E. Bloch, *Heritage of Our Times*, trans. N. and S. Plaice, Oxford, Polity, 1991, p. 118.

50 Ibid., p. 127.

51 K. Mannheim, *Ideology and Utopia*, London, Routledge & Kegan Paul, 1936, p. 191.
52 This work has not been translated into English. See A. James Reimer, 'Bloch's interpretation of Muenzer: history, theology, and social change', *Clio*, 1980, vol. 9, no. 2, pp. 253–267.
53 Bloch, *The Principle of Hope*, p. 1256.
54 Ibid., pp. 511–512.
55 Bloch, *Heritage of Our Times*, pp. 139–140.
56 Bloch, *Atheism in Christianity*, p. 206.
57 Ibid., p. 224–225.
58 Ibid., p. 213.
59 Ibid., p. 215.
60 Ibid., p. 221.
61 Ibid., p. 229.
62 Ibid., p. 236.
63 Ibid.
64 Ibid., p. 9.
65 Ibid., p. 239.
66 Bloch, *The Principle of Hope*, p. 1202.
67 Bloch, *Atheism in Christianity*, p. 266.
68 Ibid., p. 239.
69 Bloch, *Heritage of Our Times*, p. 372.
70 Bloch, *The Principle of Hope*, p. 1196.
71 E. Bloch, *Man On His Own: Essays in the Philosophy of Religion*, trans. E. B. Ashton, New York, Herder & Herder, 1970, p. 41.
72 E. Bloch, *Natural Law and Human Dignity*, trans. D. J. Schmidt, Cambridge, Mass, MIT, 1986, p. 277.
73 Bloch, *Atheism in Christianity*, pp. 241–242.
74 Ibid., p. 252.
75 Ibid., p. 253.
76 Ibid., p. 261.
77 Ibid.
78 Ibid., p. 265.
79 Bloch, *The Principle of Hope*, p. 1199.
80 Bloch, *Atheism in Christianity*, p. 265.
81 Bloch, *The Principle of Hope*, p. 1293.
82 T. H. West, *Ultimate Hope Without God: The Atheistic Eschatology of Ernst Bloch*, New York, Peter Lang, 1991, p. 256.
83 W. Zimmerli, *Man and his Hope in the Old Testament*, London, SCM Press, 1971, pp. 162–163.
84 R.H. Roberts, *Hope and its Hieroglyph: A Critical Decipherment of Ernst Bloch's Principle of Hope*, Atlanta, Scholars Press, 1990, pp. 179–180.
85 West, *Ultimate Hope Without God*, p. 202.
86 W. Hudson, *The Marxist Philosophy of Ernst Bloch*, London, Macmillan, 1982, p. 190.
87 J. M. Lochman, *Encountering Marx: Bonds and Barriers between Christians and Marxists*, Belfast, Christian Journals Limited, 1977, p. 97.

88 Quoted in J. Bentley, *Between Marx and Christ: The Dialogue in German-speaking Europe 1870–1970*, London, New Left Books, 1982, p. 94.
89 Pannenberg, 'The God of hope', p. 288.
90 Moylan, 'Bloch against Bloch', p. 42.
91 Quoted in J. Rühle, 'The philosopher of hope: Ernst Bloch', in L. Labedz (ed.), *Revisionism: Essays on the History of Marxist Ideas*, London, George Allen & Unwin, 1962, p. 174.
92 Quoted in West, *Ultimate Hope Without God*, p. 60.
93 L. Kolakowski, *Main Currents of Marxism: The Breakdown*, Oxford, Clarendon Press, 1978, pp. 438–439.
94 Hudson, *The Marxist Philosophy of Ernst Bloch*, p. 190.
95 F. Jameson, *Marxism and Form: Twentieth-Century Dialectical Theories of Literature*, Princeton, Princeton University Press, 1971, p. 117.

4 FASCISM AND MARXISM

1 E. Bloch, *Heritage of Our Times*, trans. N and S. Plaice, Oxford, Polity, 1991, p. 2.
2 T. Phelan, 'Ernst Bloch's "Golden Twenties": *Erbschaft dieser Zeit* and the problem of cultural history', in K. Bullivant (ed.), *Culture and Society in the Weimar Republic*, Manchester, Manchester University Press, 1977, p. 102.
3 Bloch, *Heritage of Our Times*, p. 1.
4 Ibid., p. 3.
5 Ibid., p. 41.
6 Ibid., p. 43.
7 Ibid., p. 44.
8 Ibid., p. 46.
9 Ibid., p. 53.
10 Ibid., p. 68.
11 Ibid., pp. 91–92.
12 Ibid., p. 97.
13 Ibid.
14 Ibid.
15 Ibid., p. 98.
16 Ibid., p. 99.
17 Ibid., p. 98.
18 Ibid., p. 100.
19 Ibid.
20 Ibid., p. 102.
21 Ibid.
22 Ibid.
23 Ibid., p. 103.
24 Ibid.
25 Ibid., p. 106.
26 Ibid., p. 107.
27 Ibid.

28 Ibid., p. 108.
29 Ibid.
30 Ibid.
31 Ibid.
32 Ibid., p. 109.
33 Ibid.
34 Ibid.
35 Ibid., p. 113.
36 Ibid., p. 114.
37 K. Theweleit, *Male Fantasies*, Oxford, Polity, 1987.
38 E. Bloch, *The Principle of Hope*, trans. N. and S. Plaice and P. Knight, Oxford, Blackwell, 1986, p. 595.
39 Bloch, *Heritage of Our Times*, p. 4.
40 Ibid.
41 A. Rabinbach, 'Unclaimed heritage: Ernst Bloch's *Heritage of Our Times* and the theory of Fascism', *New German Critique*, 1977, no. 11, p. 14.
42 G. Scholem and T. W. Adorno (eds), *The Correspondence of Walter Benjamin 1910–1940*, trans. M. R. and E. M. Jacobson, Chicago, The University of Chicago Press, 1994, p. 478.
43 E. Bloch, 'Karl Marx, death and the apocalypse', in *Man On His Own*, trans. E. B. Ashton, New York, Herder & Herder, 1970, p. 37.
44 G. Lukács, *History and Class Consciousness*, trans. R. Livingstone, London, Merlin, 1971, p. 193.
45 Bloch, *The Principle of Hope*, p. 125.
46 E. Bloch, 'The university, Marxism and philosophy', in *On Karl Marx*, trans. J. Maxwell, New York, Herder & Herder, 1971, p. 124.
47 E. Bloch, 'Marx and the dialectics of idealism', in *On Karl Marx*, p. 114.
48 Bloch, *The Principle of Hope*, p. 1358.
49 Ibid.
50 E. Bloch, 'Marx as a student', in *On Karl Marx*, 1971, p. 15.
51 Bloch, *The Principle of Hope*, p. 1358.
52 Ibid.
53 Bloch, 'The university, Marxism and philosophy', pp. 133–134.
54 E. Bloch, 'Marx and the dialectics of idealism', p. 107.
55 Ibid.
56 Ibid., pp. 107–108.
57 Ibid., p. 108.
58 Bloch, *The Principle of Hope*, p. 1363.
59 E. Bloch, 'Art and society', in *The Utopian Function of Art and Literature*, trans. J. Zipes and F. Mecklenberg, Cambridge, Mass, MIT Press, 1988, p. 51.
60 Bloch, *The Principle of Hope*, p. 1367.
61 Ibid., p. 1368.
62 Ibid.
63 Ibid., p. 1369.
64 Ibid., p. 1370.

65 E. Bloch, 'Upright carriage, concrete utopia', in *On Karl Marx*, p. 166.
66 Ibid.
67 Bloch, *Heritage of Our Times*, p. 113.
68 Ibid., p. 114.
69 Ibid., p. 115.
70 Ibid., p. 116.
71 O. Negt, 'Ernst Bloch – the German philosopher of the October Revolution', *New German Critique*, 1975, no. 4, p. 10.
72 See M. Löwy, 'Interview with Ernst Bloch', *New German Critique*, 1976, no. 9, p. 44; also J. R. Bloch, 'How can we understand the bends in the upright gait?', *New German Critique*, 1988, no. 45, p. 22; Bloch's political essays of this period can be found in M. Korol (ed.), *Kampf, nicht Krieg: Politische Schriften 1917–1919*, Frankfurt, Suhrkamp, 1985.
73 Quoted in J. M. Jones, *Hope among the Remnants of Babel: Ernst Bloch's Utopia of Heimat and the Uncompleted Edifice of Enlightenment*, unpublished Ph.D. thesis, Emory University, 1993, p. 107.
74 Bloch, 'Upright carriage, concrete utopia', p. 163.
75 Quoted in Negt, 'Ernst Bloch – the German philosopher of the October Revolution', p. 8.
76 E. Bloch, 'A jubilee for renegades', *New German Critique*, 1975, no. 4, p. 18.
77 Ibid.
78 Ibid., p. 24.
79 Bloch, *Heritage of Our Times*, p. 2.
80 The only English translation (see note 81) omits the reference to Stalin. For the German text see E. Bloch, *Philosophische Aufsätze zur objecktiven Phantasie*, Frankfurt, Suhrkamp, 1969, p. 291.
81 Bloch, 'The university, Marxism and philosophy', p. 139.
82 Ibid.
83 Bloch, *The Principle of Hope*, p. 532.
84 J. R. Bloch, 'How can we understand the bends in the upright gait?', p. 32.
85 Bloch, 'Upright carriage, concrete utopia', pp. 163–164.
86 Ibid., p. 164.
87 Ibid.
88 Ibid., p. 169.
89 Ibid., p. 171.
90 Ibid., p. 173.
91 W. Hudson, *The Marxist Philosophy of Ernst Bloch*, London, Macmillan, 1982, p. 66.
92 Martin Jay also has doubts over whether 'Bloch's syncretic system was entirely true to Marx'; *Marxism and Totality*, Oxford, Polity, 1984, p. 186.
93 J. R. Bloch, 'How can we understand the bends in the upright gait?', p. 26.
94 M. Landmann, 'Talking with Ernst Bloch: Korcula, 1968', *Telos*, 1975, no. 25, p. 166.

5 NATURAL LAW, UTOPIANISM AND NATURE

1 E. Bloch, 'Disrupted language, disrupted culture', *Direction*, December 1939, p. 36.
2 Bloch, 'A jubilee for renegades', p. 25.
3 E. Bloch, *Natural Law and Human Dignity*, trans. D. J. Schmidt, Cambridge, Mass, MIT, 1986, p. xxviii.
4 Ibid., pp. xxvii–xxix.
5 Ibid., p. xxix.
6 Ibid.
7 Ibid., p. xxx.
8 Ibid., p. 16.
9 Ibid., pp. 83–84.
10 Ibid., p. 119.
11 Ibid., p. 174.
12 Ibid., p. 177.
13 Ibid.
14 Ibid., pp. 177–178.
15 Ibid., p. 178.
16 Ibid., p. 184.
17 Ibid.
18 Ibid., p. 185.
19 Ibid., p. 203.
20 Ibid., p. 221.
21 Ibid., p. 224.
22 Ibid., p. 227.
23 Ibid., p. 228.
24 M. Landmann, 'Talking with Ernst Bloch: Korcula, 1968', *Telos*, 1975, no. 25, p. 171.
25 Bloch, *Natural Law and Human Dignity*, p. 184.
26 W. Hudson, *The Marxist Philosophy of Ernst Bloch*, London, Macmillan, 1982, p. 171.
27 Bloch, *Natural Law and Human Dignity*, p. 48.
28 Ibid., p. 65.
29 P. Osborne, 'The idea of socialist right', *Radical Philosophy*, 1987, no. 46, p. 36.
30 E. Bloch, *The Principle of Hope*, trans. N. and S. Plaice and P. Knight, Oxford, Blackwell, 1986, p. 624.
31 Ibid., p. 315.
32 E. Bloch, *A Philosophy of the Future*, trans. J. Cumming, New York, Herder & Herder, 1970, p. 91.
33 Ibid., pp. 86–87.
34 Ibid., p. 88.
35 Bloch, *The Principle of Hope*, p. 15.
36 Ibid., pp. 19–42.
37 Ibid., p. 457.
38 Ibid., pp. 634–639.
39 Ibid., pp. 654–657.
40 Ibid., pp. 720–721.

41 Ibid., pp. 797–798.
42 Ibid., p. 751.
43 Ibid., p. 750.
44 Ibid., pp. 838–885.
45 Ibid., p. 534.
46 Ibid., p. 581.
47 Ibid., p. 146.
48 Ibid.
49 Ibid., pp. 584–585.
50 Ibid., p. 612.
51 Ibid., p. 471.
52 Ibid., p. 745.
53 Ibid., p. 837.
54 Ibid., p. 885.
55 Ibid., p. 624.
56 Bloch, *A Philosophy of the Future*, p. 91.
57 T.W. Adorno, 'Ernst Bloch's *Spuren*', in *Notes to Literature*, Vol. 1, trans. S. W. Nicholsen, New York, Columbia University Press, 1991, p. 210.
58 Bloch, *The Principle of Hope*, p. 519.
59 Ibid., pp. 613–615.
60 Ibid., p. 595.
61 R. Levitas, *The Concept of Utopia*, Hemel Hempstead, Philip Allan, 1990, p. 105.
62 'Something's missing: a discussion between Ernst Bloch and Theodor W. Adorno on the contradictions of utopian longing', in E. Bloch, *The Utopian Function of Art and Literature*, trans. J. Zipes and F. Mecklenberg, Cambridge, Mass, MIT Press, 1988, p. 1.
63 Bloch, 'Art and society', in *The Utopian Function of Art and Literature*, p. 63.
64 Bloch, *The Principle of Hope*, p. 207.
65 Ibid., p. 665.
66 Ibid., p. 668.
67 Ibid.
68 Ibid., p. 669.
69 Ibid., p. 670.
70 Ibid., p. 671.
71 Ibid., p. 673.
72 Ibid., p. 674.
73 Bloch, *A Philosophy of the Future*, p. 134.
74 Ibid., p. 135.
75 Ibid., p. 136.
76 Ibid.
77 Ibid., p. 138.
78 A. Schmidt, *The Concept of Nature in Marx*, trans. B. Fowkes, London, New Left Books, 1971, p. 161.
79 Ibid., pp. 159–160.
80 J. Habermas, 'Ernst Bloch: a Marxist Schelling', in *Philosophical-*

Political Profiles, trans. F. G. Lawrence, Cambridge, Mass, MIT Press, 1983, p. 74.
81 Ibid., p. 72.
82 Ibid., p. 78.
83 Ibid., p. 73.
84 Ibid., p. 74.

CONCLUSION

1 E. Hobsbawm, 'The Principle of Hope' in *Revolutionaries: Contemporary Essays*, London, Weidenfeld & Nicolson, 1973, p. 141.
2 F. Jameson, *Marxism and Form: Twentieth-Century Dialectical Theories of Literature*, Princeton, Princeton University Press, 1971, pp. 121–122.
3 G. Steiner, 'Sojourns in the wondrous', *Times Literary Supplement*, 4 October 1985, p. 1087.
4 G. Scholem and T. W. Adorno (eds), *The Correspondence of Walter Benjamin 1910–1940*, trans. M. R. and E. M. Jacobson, Chicago, The University of Chicago Press, 1994, p. 148.
5 T. W. Adorno, 'Ernst Bloch's *Spuren*', in *Notes to Literature*, vol. 1, trans. S. Weber Nicholsen, New York, Columbia University Press, 1991, p. 214.
6 V. Geoghegan, *Utopianism and Marxism*, London, Methuen, 1987, Chapter 3.
7 G. Steiner, 'Obituary of Dr Ernst Bloch', *The Times*, 6 August 1977.

BIBLIOGRAPHY

WORKS BY BLOCH

English translations (in chronological order of publication)

'Disrupted language, disrupted culture', *Direction*, December 1939, trans. unknown, pp. 16–17, and p. 36.

'Man as possibility', *Cross Currents*, 1968, vol. xviii, trans. W.R. White, pp. 273–83.

A Philosophy of the Future, trans. J. Cumming, New York: Herder & Herder, 1970.

'Alienation, estrangement', *The Drama Review*, 1970, vol. 15, no. 1, trans. A. Halley and D. Suvin, pp. 120–125.

Man On His Own: Essays in the Philosophy of Religion, trans. E. B. Ashton, New York, Herder & Herder, 1970.

On Karl Marx, trans. J. Maxwell, New York, Herder & Herder, 1971.

Atheism in Christianity, trans. J. T. Swann, New York, Herder & Herder, 1972.

'Causality and finality as active, objectifying categories (categories of transmission)', *Telos*, 1974, no. 21, trans. G. Ellard, pp. 96–107.

'A jubilee for renegades', *New German Critique*, 1975, no. 4, trans. D. Bathrick and N. V. Shults, pp. 17–25.

'Dialectics and hope', *New German Critique*, 1976, no. 9, trans. M. Ritter, pp. 3–10.

'Formative education, engineering form, ornament', *Oppositions*, 1979, no. 17, trans. J.O. Newman and J.H. Smith, pp. 45–51.

'Theory-praxis in the long run', trans. W. Hudson, in R. Fitzgerald (ed.), *The Sources of Hope*, London, Pergamon, 1979, pp. 153–157.

'The dialectical method', *Man and World*, 1983, vol. 16, no. 4, trans. J. Lamb, pp. 281–313.

Essays on the Philosophy of Music, trans. P. Palmer, Cambridge, Cambridge University Press, 1985.

Natural Law and Human Dignity, trans. D. J. Schmidt, Cambridge, Mass, MIT, 1986.

The Principle of Hope, trans. N. and S. Plaice and P. Knight, Oxford, Blackwell, 1986.

'Recollections of Walter Benjamin', trans. M. W. Jennings, in G. Smith (ed.), *On Walter Benjamin: Critical Essays and Recollections*, Cambridge, Mass, MIT Press, 1988, pp. 338–345.

The Utopian Function of Art and Literature, trans. J. Zipes and F. Mecklenberg, Cambridge, Mass, MIT Press, 1988.

Heritage of Our Times, trans. N. and S. Plaice, Oxford, Polity, 1991.

German editions

Sixteen volumes of collected works were published by Suhrkamp Verlag in Bloch's lifetime; a posthumous volume, *Tendenz-Latenz-Utopie*, was later published. Publication dates are between 1959 and 1978:

1 *Spuren*
2 *Thomas Münzer als Theologe der Revolution*
3 *Geist der Utopie* (1923 edition)
4 *Erbschaft dieser Zeit*
5 *Das Prinzip Hoffnung*
6 *Naturrecht und menschliche Würde*
7 *Das Materialismusproblem – seine Geschichte und Substanz*
8 *Subjekt–Objekt – Erläuterungen zu Hegel*
9 *Literarische Aufsätze*
10 *Philosophische Aufsätze zur objektiven Phantasie*
11 *Politische Messungen – Pestzeit Vormärz*
12 *Zwischenwelten in der Philosophiegeschichte (Aus Leipziger Vorlesungen)*
13 *Tübinger Einleitung in die Philosophie*
14 *Atheismus im Christentum*
15 *Experimentum Mundi – Frage, Kategorien des Herausbringens, Praxis*
16 *Geist der Utopie* (1918 edition)
Posthumous volume – *Tendenz-Latenz-Utopie*

OTHER WORKS

Adorno, T. W. 'Ernst Bloch's *Spuren*', in *Notes to Literature*, Vol. 1, trans. S. W. Nicholsen, New York, Columbia University Press, 1991, pp. 200–215.

Aronson, R. 'Review of *The Principle of Hope*', *History and Theory*, 1991, vol. 30, no. 2, pp. 220–232.

Asperen, G. M. van. *Hope and History: A Critical Inquiry into the Philosophy of Ernst Bloch*, unpublished thesis, Rijksuniversiteit, Utrecht, 1973.

Bahr, E. 'The literature of hope: Ernst Bloch's philosophy and its impact on the literature of the German Democratic Republic', in H. Birnbaum and T. Eekman (eds), *Fiction and Drama in Eastern and South-Eastern Europe*, Columbus, Slavica, 1980, pp. 11–26.

Bahro, R. *From Red to Green*, trans. G. Fagan and R. Hurst, London, Verso, 1984.

Baker, G. L. '(Anti-)utopian elements in Uwe Johnson's *Jahrestage*: traces of Ernst Bloch', *Germanic Review*, 1993, vol. 63, no. 1, pp. 32–45.

Benjamin, W. *Briefe*, vol. 1, Frankfurt, Suhrkamp, 1966.

Bentley, J. *Between Marx and Christ: The Dialogue in German-speaking Europe 1870–1970*, London, New Left Books, 1982.

Bloch, J. R. 'How can we understand the bends in the upright gait?', *New German Critique*, 1988, no. 45, pp. 9–39.

Bloch, K. *Aus meinem Leben*, Pfullingen, Neske, 1981.

Brecht, B. *Briefe*, Frankfurt, Suhrkamp, 1981.

Breines, P. 'Bloch magic', *Continuum*, 1970, vol. 7, no. 4, pp. 619–624.

Buhr, M. 'A critique of Ernst Bloch's philosophy of hope', *Philosophy Today*, 1970, vol. 14, no. 4, pp. 259–279.

—— 'Seven comments on Ernst Bloch's philosophy', *Studies in Soviet Thought*, 1987, vol. 33, pp. 333–340.

Caysa, V., Caysa, P., Eichler, K-D. and Uhl, E. *'Hoffnung kann enttäuscht werden' – Ernst Bloch in Leipzig/dokumentiert und kommentiert*, Frankfurt, Anton Hain, 1992.

Cox, H. 'Foreword', in E. Bloch, *Man On His Own: Essays in the Philosophy of Religion*, trans. E. B. Ashton, New York, Herder & Herder, 1970, pp. 7–18.

Daniel, J. O. 'Warm thought: reassessing Bloch's aesthetics', *Utopian Studies*, 1990, vol. 1, no. 2, pp. 13–26.

Dickinson, J. K. 'Ernst Bloch's "the Principle of Hope": a review of and comment on the English translation', *Babel*, 1990, vol. 36, no. 1, pp. 7–31.

—— 'Ernst Bloch's philosophical ethnicity', *Bloch-Almanach*, 1991, vol. 11, pp. 11–39.

Drew, D. 'Introduction', in E. Bloch, *Essays on the Philosophy of Music*, trans. P. Palmer, Cambridge, Cambridge University Press, 1985, pp. xi–xlviii.

Ely, J. 'Ernst Bloch and the second contradiction in capitalism', *Capitalism, Nature, Socialism*, 1989, no. 2, pp. 93–107.

Fehér, F. 'The last phase of romantic anti-capitalism: Lukács' response to the war', *New German Critique*, 1977, no. 10, pp. 139–154.

Fekete, E. and Karádi, E. (eds), *György Lukács: His Life in Pictures and Documents*, Budapest, Corvina Kiadó, 1981.

Feuchtwanger, L. *Moscow 1937*, London, Gollancz, 1937.

Finkelstein, N. 'The utopian function and the refunctioning of Marxism', *Diacritics*, 1989, vol. 19, no. 2, pp. 54–65.

Geoghegan, V. *Utopianism and Marxism*, London, Methuen, 1987.

Gluck, M. *George Lukács and his Generation 1900–1918*, Cambridge, Mass, Harvard University Press, 1985.

Gross, D. 'Marxism and utopia: Ernst Bloch', in B. Grahl and P. Piccone (eds), *Towards a New Marxism*, St Louis, Telos Press, 1973, pp. 85–100.

Habermas, J. 'Between philosophy and science: Marxism as critique', in *Theory and Practice*, trans. J. Viertel, London, Heinemann, 1974, pp. 195–252.

—— 'Ernst Bloch: a Marxist Schelling', in *Philosophical-Political Profiles*, trans. F. G. Lawrence, Cambridge, Mass, MIT Press, 1983, pp. 63–79.

—— 'Walter Benjamin: consciousness-raising or rescuing critique', in *Philosophical-Political Profiles*, trans. F. G. Lawrence, Cambridge, Mass, MIT, 1983, pp. 131–165.

—— *Autonomy and Solidarity*, London, Verso, 1986.

Harper, C. M. 'Ernst Bloch: A bibliography of primary sources in English', *Bloch-Almanach*, 1992, vol. 12, pp. 167–180.

—— *Dialectic in the Philosophy of Ernst Bloch*, unpublished Ph.D. thesis, The Queen's University of Belfast, 1993.

Heyworth, P. *Otto Klemperer: His Life and Times, Volume 1, 1885–1933*, Cambridge, Cambridge University Press, 1983.

Hobsbawm, E. 'The Principle of Hope', in *Revolutionaries: Contemporary Essays*, London, Weidenfeld & Nicolson, 1973.

Honigsheim, P. *On Max Weber*, New York, The Free Press, 1968.

Howard, D. 'Marxism and concrete philosophy: Ernst Bloch', in *The Marxist Legacy*, London, Macmillan, 1977, pp. 66–78.

Hudson, W. *The Marxist Philosophy of Ernst Bloch*, London, Macmillan, 1982.

—— 'Two interviews with Ernst Bloch', *Bloch-Almanach*, 1989, vol. 9, pp. 115–121.

Jahn, J. 'Ernst Bloch und der Aufbau-Verlag: Eine Dokumentation', *Bloch-Almanach*, 1993, vol. 13, pp. 103–168.

Jameson, F. *Marxism and Form: Twentieth-Century Dialectical Theories of Literature*, Princeton, Princeton University Press, 1971.

Jay, M. *Marxism and Totality*, Oxford, Polity, 1984.

Jones, J. M. *Hope among the Remnants of Babel: Ernst Bloch's Utopia of Heimat and the Uncompleted Edifice of Enlightenment*, unpublished Ph.D. thesis, Emory University, 1993.

Kadarkay, A. *Georg Lukács: Life, Thought, and Politics*, Oxford, Blackwell, 1991.

Kaufmann, D. 'Thanks for the memory: Bloch, Benjamin and the philosophy of history', *The Yale Journal of Criticism*, 1993, vol. 6, no. 1, pp. 143–162.

Kearney, R. 'Ernst Bloch', in *Modern Movements in European Philosophy*, Manchester, Manchester University Press, 1986, pp. 190–202.

Kellner, D. and O'Hara, H. 'Utopia and Marxism in Ernst Bloch', *New German Critique*, 1976, no. 9, pp. 11–34.

Kolakowski, L. *Main Currents of Marxism: The Breakdown*, Oxford, Clarendon Press, 1978.

Landmann, M. 'Talking with Ernst Bloch: Korcula, 1968', *Telos*, 1975, no. 25, pp. 165–185.

Levitas, R. *The Concept of Utopia*, Hemel Hempstead: Philip Allan, 1990.

Levy, Z. 'Utopia and reality in the philosophy of Ernst Bloch', *Utopian Studies*, 1990, vol. 1, no. 2, pp. 3–12.

Lochman, J. M. *Encountering Marx: Bonds and Barriers between Christians and Marxists*, Belfast, Christian Journals Limited, 1977.

Lowenthal, L. *An Unmastered Past*, Berkeley, University of California Press, 1987.

Löwy, M. 'Interview with Ernst Bloch', *New German Critique*, 1976, no. 9, pp. 35–45.
—— 'Jewish messianism and libertarian utopia in Central Europe (1900–1933)', *New German Critique*, 1980, no. 20, pp. 105–115.
Lukács, G. *History and Class Consciousness*, trans. R. Livingstone, London, Merlin, 1971.
—— 'Realism in the balance', in R. Taylor (ed.), *Aesthetics and Politics*, London, New Left Books, 1977, pp. 28–59.
—— *Record of a Life: An Autobiographical Sketch*, London, Verso, 1983.
—— *Selected Correspondence*, trans. J. Marcus and Z. Tar, New York, Columbia University Press, 1986.
Lützeler, P. M. *Hermann Broch: A Biography*, London, Quartet, 1987.
Mann, T. *Diaries 1918–1939*, trans. R. and C. Winston, London, André Deutsch, 1983.
Mannheim, K. *Ideology and Utopia*, London, Routledge & Kegan Paul, 1936.
Marcus, J. *Georg Lukács and Thomas Mann: A Study in the Sociology of Literature*, Amherst, University of Massachusetts Press, 1987.
Marcuse, H. 'The realm of freedom and the realm of necessity: a reconsideration', *Praxis*, 1969, no. 1, pp. 20–25.
Markun, S. *Ernst Bloch*, Reinbek bei Hamburg, Rowohlt, 1977.
Metz, J. B. 'The responsibility of hope', *Philosophy Today*, 1966, vol. 10, no. 4, pp. 280–288.
Moltmann, J. *History and the Triune God: Contributions to a Trinitarian Theology*, London, SCM Press, 1991.
Moylan, T. 'Bloch against Bloch: The theological reception of *Das Prinzip Hoffnung* and the liberation of the utopian function', *Utopian Studies*, 1990, vol. 1, no. 2, pp. 27–51.
Münster, A. (ed.), *Tagträume vom aufrechten Gang Sechs Interviews mit Ernst Bloch*, Frankfurt, Suhrkamp, 1977.
Negt, O. 'Ernst Bloch – the German philosopher of the October Revolution', *New German Critique*, 1975, no. 4, pp. 3–16.
—— 'The non-synchronous heritage and the problem of propaganda', *New German Critique*, 1976, no. 9, pp. 46–70.
Osborne, P. 'The idea of socialist right', *Radical Philosophy*, 1987, no. 46, pp. 37–38.
Pannenberg, W. 'The God of hope', *Cross Currents*, 1968, vol. xviii, pp. 284–295.
Phelan, T. 'Ernst Bloch's "Golden Twenties": *Erbschaft dieser Zeit* and the problem of cultural history', in K. Bullivant (ed.), *Culture and Society in the Weimar Republic*, Manchester, Manchester University Press, 1977, pp. 94–121.
Piccone, P. 'Bloch's Marxism', *Continuum*, 1970, vol. 7, no. 4, pp. 627–631.
Pike, D. *Lukács and Brecht*, Chapel Hill, University of North Carolina Press, 1985.
Rabinbach, A. 'Unclaimed heritage: Ernst Bloch's *Heritage of Our Times* and the theory of Fascism', *New German Critique*, 1977, no. 11, pp. 5–21.

—— 'Between enlightenment and apocalypse: Benjamin, Bloch and modern German Jewish messianism', *New German Critique*, 1985, no. 34, pp. 78–124.

Radnóti, S. 'Lukács and Bloch', in A. Heller (ed.), *Lukács Revalued*, Oxford, Blackwell, 1983, pp. 63–74.

Reimer, A. J. 'Bloch's interpretation of Muenzer: history, theology, and social change', *Clio*, 1980, vol. 9, no. 2, pp. 253–267.

Roberts, R. H. *Hope and its Hieroglyph: A Critical Decipherment of Ernst Bloch's Principle of Hope*, Atlanta, Scholars Press, 1990.

Römer, R. 'Erinnerungen an Ernst Bloch', *Bloch-Almanach*, 1990, vol. 10, pp. 107–162.

Rühle, J. 'The philosopher of hope: Ernst Bloch', in L. Labedz (ed.), *Revisionism: Essays on the History of Marxist Ideas*, London, George Allen & Unwin, 1962, pp. 166–178.

Schmidt, A. *The Concept of Nature in Marx*, trans. B. Fowkes, London, New Left Books, 1971.

Schmidt, B. 'The political nature of epistemological categories: introduction to Bloch', *Telos*, 1974, no. 21, trans. G. Ellard, pp. 87–91.

Scholem, G. *Walter Benjamin: The Story of a Friendship*, London, Faber, 1982.

—— (ed.), *The Correspondence of Walter Benjamin and Gershom Scholem 1932–1940*, trans. G. Smith and A. Lefevre, New York, Schocken, 1989.

Scholem, G. and Adorno, T. W. (eds) *The Correspondence of Walter Benjamin 1910–1940*, trans. M. R. and E. M. Jacobson, Chicago, The University of Chicago Press, 1994.

Solomon, M. 'Marx and Bloch: reflections on utopia and art', *Telos*, 1972, no. 13, pp. 68–85.

Steiner, G. *Language and Silence: Essays 1958–1966*, London, Faber, 1967.

—— 'Obituary of Dr Ernst Bloch', *The Times*, 6 August 1977.

—— 'Sojourns in the wondrous', *Times Literary Supplement*, 4 October 1985, pp. 1087–1088.

Taylor, R. *Kurt Weill: Composer in a Divided World*, London, Simon & Schuster, 1991.

Theweleit, K. *Male Fantasies*, Oxford, Polity, 1987.

Traub, R. and Wieser, H. (eds), *Gespräche mit Ernst Bloch*, Frankfurt, Suhrkamp, 1975.

Weber, M. *Max Weber: A Biography*, trans. H. Zohn, New York, Wiley, 1975.

Weissberg, L. 'Philosophy and the fairy tale: Ernst Bloch as narrator', *New German Critique*, 1992, no. 55, pp. 21–44.

West, T. H. *Ultimate Hope Without God: The Atheistic Eschatology of Ernst Bloch*, New York, Peter Lang, 1991.

Wiggerhaus, R. *The Frankfurt School: Its History, Theories and Political Significance*, trans. M. Robertson, Oxford, Polity, 1994.

Zimdars-Swartz, P. F. *Apocalyptic Insight and Apocalyptic Experience: The Structure and Significance of Ernst Bloch's Theory of Knowledge*, unpublished Ph.D. thesis, Claremont Graduate School, 1978.

Zimmerli, W. *Man and his Hope in the Old Testament*, London, SCM Press, 1971.

Zipes, J. 'Introduction: toward a realization of anticipatory illumination', in E. Bloch, *The Utopian Function of Art and Literature*, Cambridge, Mass, MIT, 1988, pp. xi–xliii.

Zudeick, P. *Der Hintern des Teufels*, Moos and Baden-Baden, Elster, 1985.

INDEX

Picasso, Pablo 63
Pisano, Andrea, *Spes* (Hope) 56–7
Piscator, Erwin 20
Plato 56
Plessner, Helmut 12
Popper, Leo 12
popular culture: antique-
collecting 59–60; dance 60; film
60–1; jazz 5, 60; personal
display 57–8; popular literature
58–9; role of dreams 57–8, 61–2;
travel 59; and utopianism 55–7;
see also culture
popular literature: 'colportage'
58–9; fairy tales 57, 58–9;
magazines and best-sellers 58;
and utopianism 58–9
positive (state) law 137–8, 139–40,
141–3
possibility, as 'partial
conditionality' 31–2
*Prinzip Hoffnung, Das (The
Principle of Hope)* (Bloch) 2, 3,
7, 51; autobiographical
elements 10; on culture 57; on
music 53–4; on natural subject
41–2; on past and present 34,
144–5, 153–4, 160–1; on public
good 20, 22, 25; on religion
81–2, 83–4, 96; on rights 115, 127
process, Bloch's concept of 32–4
'process' philosophy 28–9
proletariat: development as
potentially revolutionary force
33; dictatorship of 128–9; and
Fascism 107–8, 114, 115; and
non-contemporaneity 123–4;
role in Bloch's socio-political
theory 122–3; women's role in
151–2
Prometheus 71–2

Rabinbach, Anson 116
Radnóti, Sándor 62–3
realism: 'critical' 68; and
Expressionism 63–5; and
literature 67–72; and
utopianism 144
reality: and 'darkness of the lived

moment' 36, 93–4; movement
of 32–4
recollection 76; as historicism 50
Reich, Wilhelm 105
religion 5–6; Bloch's influence on
theologians 81–2, 163; Bloch's
reading of Bible 83–90; the
second coming (*Parousia*) 89,
90; *see also* Bible; Christianity
Rickert, Heinrich 29
Ricoeur, Paul 55
Riedel, Manfred 52
Riemannian time 42, 156
rights, subjective and objective
141
Ritoók, Emma 13
Roberts, Richard 98–9
Römer, Ruth 22
Rosenberg, Alfred 50
Rousseau, Jean-Jacques 143; *Emile*
138; *The Social Contract* 138
Rubens, Peter Paul, 'Garden of
Love' 147
rule of law, Bloch's attitude to
142–3
Russia *see* USSR

Scheler, Max 29
Schelling, Friedrich, influence on
Bloch 28, 154, 159
Schmidt, Alfred, *The Concept of
Nature in Marx* 157–8
Schoenberg, Arnold 54, 63
scientism 129, 162
Simmel, Georg 11, 13, 15, 29
Slanksky trial (Czechoslovakia,
1952) 23
sobriety and revolution 122, 125
socialism: distinction between
subjective and objective right
141; liberal-federative 148; and
positive law 139–40; and
violations of legality 137–8; *see
also* Marxism
socialist realism 5, 47, 73, 77, 126
sociologism 123
Soviet Union *see* USSR
Stalin, Josef 128, 139; Khruschev's